MAN
MADE THE LAND

STUDIES IN HISTORICAL GEOGRAPHY

GENERAL EDITORS

Alan R. H. Baker, *University Lecturer in Geography and Fellow of Emmanuel College, Cambridge*, and J. B. Harley, *Montefiore Reader in Geography at the University of Exeter*

PUBLISHED

Alan R. H. Baker John D. Hamshere John Langton (editors)	*Geographical Interpretations of Historical Sources: Readings in Historical Geography* (1970)
Josiah Cox Russell	*Medieval Regions and Their Cities* (1972)
Alan R. H. Baker (editor) J. B. Harley (editors)	*Progress in Historical Geography* (1972) *Historical Geography* (1973)

IN PREPARATION

Australia: an Historical Geography	Michael Williams
Celts, Saxons and Vikings: Studies in Settlement Continuity	Glanville R. J. Jones
British Farming in the Great Depression: an Historical Geography	Peter J. Perry
Climate, Agriculture and Settlement: Studies in Geographical Change	M. L. Parry
English Market Towns before the Industrial Revolution	J. H. C. Patten
English Provincial Cities of the Nineteenth Century	David Ward
Finland, Daughter of the Sea	Michael Jones
Historical Geography: an Introduction	Alan R. H. Baker
Historical Geography of Rural Settlement in Britain	Brian K. Roberts
Historical Geography of Sugar Cultivation	J. H. Galloway
History through Maps	J. B. Hartley
A Social Geography of Britain in the Nineteenth Century	D. R. Mills
South America: an Historical Geography	D. J. Robinson
Southern Africa: an Historical Geography	A. J. Christopher
Tithe Surveys	Hugh C. Prince and Roger J. P. Kain

MAN MADE THE LAND

ESSAYS IN ENGLISH HISTORICAL GEOGRAPHY
A Series from the Geographical Magazine

CONTRIBUTORS

GORDON MANLEY   JOHN SHEAIL
GLANVILLE JONES   JAMES YELLING
H. C. DARBY   JOHN PATTEN
BRIAN ROBERTS   ROBERT I. HODGSON
ALAN R. H. BAKER   HUGH C. PRINCE
H. S. A. FOX   J. B. HARLEY
M. W. BERESFORD   J. T. COPPOCK
JOAN THIRSK   DAVID WARD

EDITORS
ALAN R. H. BAKER and J. B. HARLEY

ROWMAN AND LITTLEFIELD
Totowa, New Jersey

First published in the United States 1973
by Rowman and Littlefield, Totowa, New Jersey

© IPC Magazines Ltd 1973
Preface, Alan Baker and J. B. Harley

Library of Congress Cataloging in Publication Data

Baker, Alan R   H   comp.
Man made the land.

Includes bibliographies.
    1. Anthropo-geography—England—Addresses, essays,
lectures. 2. Land—England—Addresses, essays,
lectures. 3. England—Historical geography—Addresses,
essays, lectures. I. Harley, John Brian, joint comp.
II. Title.
GF551.B34   911'.42   73–5602
ISBN 0–87471–184–3

Printed in Great Britain

CONTENTS

PREFACE

STUDIES of the past are very relevant to the problems of the present and the prospects for the future. Historical studies can provide a basis for an understanding of how cultural and economic activities develop, flourish or decay, and such knowledge can be applied to the fashioning of the future. Even if the spatial patterns of the past may never be exactly repeated, the processes which produced them hold lessons for today. Just as the irreversible destruction of natural resources did not begin with the Industrial Revolution, so too the intrusion of man into the delicate balance of ecosystems can be traced to earlier phases of human settlement. The environmental crises of today are so largely a cumulative legacy from the past that it becomes almost a truism to state that their analysis is of limited validity without an historical perspective. A continuing use of historical geography lies in its contribution to our understanding of the present.

Geographical reconstructions of past conditions and changes also provide an intellectual end in themselves, in the same manner as historical studies in general have not sought to justify themselves solely in terms of modern 'relevance'. To this viewpoint can be added the equally familiar contention that few 'pure' studies in modern geography can afford to ignore the dimension of time completely because by so doing they would put themselves at risk: drawing data from the past to test a hypothesis framed with modern materials may improve its analytical potential as well as its predictive qualities. A static analysis of the present is open to the same criticisms – that it ignores process and the dynamics of the situation – as may be levelled at 'cross-sectional' studies of the past.

In any case no academic sleight of hand is ever likely to make the past disappear. Even if our towns and countrysides were not so obviously built-up from layers of past ages, there are forces at work in society which counterbalance the tendency for constant change and replacement. Laws, customs, public opinion, a deep seated desire for 'roots', organised pressure groups, all lend weight to the preservation of the visible past. Here is another role for the historical geographer – helping to formulate objective criteria for the selective preservation of past features.

How in fact do planners and politicians perceive the nature and value of the past? It is easy to romanticise the sculpturing of the English landscape by the hand of man – the creation of an intricate and beautiful scene, the fashioning of fields, farms and factories, the modelling of roads, rivers and railways, the making of market towns and metropoli. It is equally possible to traduce the process as one involving the destruction of nature's endowment, the disturbance of an ecosystem, the pollution of the environment. The truth – and therefore the proper basis for future action about the past – lies somewhere between these two extremes, between the beauty of a landscape garden and the ugliness of an industrial wasteland, between the majesty of a motorway and the bareness of cultivated fields stripped of their hedges. Historical geographers who have made studies of these features advise on their preservation on grounds of age, rarity, aesthetics or scientific interest. But historical geography can also take a broad view of man's activities through time and synthetic studies of the whole assemblage of historic features within a landscape may turn out to be equally useful in planning the past. As competing claims intensify for habitable space, the past can hardly be evaluated as a series of disconnected fragments and the overall management of the historic environment, in the light of a sound knowledge of its characteristics, becomes increasingly important. Whichever way we look at it, then, historical studies are likely to retain an important place in both the pure and applied aspects of geography.

These remarks should not be taken as special pleading for the essays which follow. They do not require it, nor were they written to a brief subscribing to these particular views of the uses of historical geography. On the other hand, such beliefs help to give justification to their publication in book form.

6

The fact that no general survey of the historical geography of England has appeared for over a decade is an additional justification, for the essays help to chart some of the essential themes in the history of man's modification of the English environment.

Each chapter first appeared as an article in the *Geographical Magazine* between February 1970 and May 1971. The contributors acknowledge the enthusiasm of the staff of the magazine in helping to conceive the series, as well as their skill in editing and designing the original articles. In producing the present book minor modifications have been made to this material: some titles and subheadings have been altered and Professor Manley's account of the changing climate now sets the scene for the other contributions; a few deletions and additions have been made to the text; some illustrations have been omitted and a number of new ones – mainly maps of features relating to the country as a whole – have been added; as a guide to further reading for the interested student every author has appended a select bibliography to his essay.

The general intention of the series was to trace chronologically some important themes in the historical geography of England from the period of earliest settlement through to Victorian times, but there was no overall methodological framework and no attempt to be comprehensive in topical coverage. Each essay was written independently of the others, to a particular rather than a general brief. In a modest way the book illustrates the value of interdisciplinary approaches to the past because the contributors include a climatologist and two economic historians as well as historical geographers. Because these essays were written independently, the editors have not attempted to excise the contradictory views which were expressed in different places. Indeed one of the corporate features of these essays is their emphasis on controversies and debates, on what is uncertain as much as on what is more certain. A striking difference of opinion is to be seen, for example, in the essays of Glanville Jones and H. C. Darby, with the former arguing in favour of the continuity of settlements from the prehistoric into Saxon times, and the latter maintaining that 'as far as there ever is a new beginning in history, the coming of the Anglo-Saxons, in the fifth and sixth centuries, was such a beginning.' Within other essays there is also much that is conjectural – for example, about the functioning of field systems, the origin of village forms, the mechanisms of medieval markets, the growth of commercial agriculture, and spread and impact of industry. Some essays explore research topics but others attempt a broad coverage of a period. All say something about the role of man in changing the English landscape. This collection of essays is not, then, offered as the last word on any of these subjects. Rather it provides points of entry into some of the many intriguing problems in the historical geography of England.

Cambridge and Exeter   Alan R. H. Baker
May 1972   J. B. Harley

GENERAL BIBLIOGRAPHY

In this and subsequent bibliographies, place of publication is given only if outside London.

Baker, A. R. H. 'Today's Studies of Yesterday's Geographies' *Geographical Magazine*, 43 (1970–71), 452–3

Baker, A. R. H., Butlin, R. A., Phillips, A. D. M. and Prince, H. C. 'The Future of the Past' *Area* 4 (1969), 46–51

Darby, H. C. *An Historical Geography of England before A.D. 1800* (Cambridge, 1936)

Darby, H. C. 'The Changing English Landscape' *Geographical Journal*, 117 (1951), 377–98

Darby, H. C. 'Historical Geography from the Coming of the Anglo-Saxons to the Industrial Revolution' in Watson, J. W. and Sissons, J. B. (eds) *The British Isles. A Systematic Geography* (1964), 198–220

Emery, F. V. *Wales* (1969)

Evans, E. E. 'Prehistoric Geography' in Watson and Sissons, *The British Isles*, 152–97

Hoskins, W. G. *The Making of the English Landscape* (1955)

Lawton, R. 'Historical Geography: the Industrial Revolution' in Watson and Sissons, *The British Isles*, 221–44

Mitchell, J. B. *Historical Geography* (1954)

Pollard, S. and Crossley, D. W. *The Wealth of Britain 1085–1966* (1968)

ACKNOWLEDGEMENTS

THE editors would like to thank the contributors for their patience and co-operation during the rather protracted transition from article to book. They would also like to acknowledge John Lavis of the *Geographical Magazine* who suggested the series. Some of the maps were prepared in the drawing office of the Department of Geography, University of Exeter, and the editors would like to thank Mr. Rodney Fry, Miss Pat Gregory and Mr Clive Thomas for their careful work.

Pictures appear by courtesy of:
Addys, 95; Aerofilms, 26, 68, 255; Warden and Fellows, All Souls College, Oxford, 66, 71; Ashmolean Museum, 23; Barnaby's Picture Library, 2, 13; Lord Barnard, 56; Bath City Council, 119; Professor Beresford, 110; Bristol Archives Office, 166; Trustees of the British Museum, 40, 41, 63, 77, 81, 83, 104, 120, 122, 141, 142, 150, 152, 169, 170, 171, 172, 173, 222; Col R. H. Carr-Ellison, TD, ADC, 193; J. Allan Cash, 197; Chapman, Chambers and Sharpe, *The Beginnings of Industrial Britain*, 118; Colour Library International, 79; *Country Life*, 249; Crosby Lockwood Staples Ltd, 155, 156, 160, 161, 162, 163; Ministry of Defence, Crown Copyright, 158; Diocesan Registry, Durham, 50; Dept of Palaeography and Diplomatic, University of Durham, 194; Durham County Record Office, 43 (D/Bo/A945), 190 (D/XP, 15, 16, copy plan of Lanchester Fell); Museum of English Rural Life, 133, 202, 239, 240; Express Dairy, 238; Folger Shakespeare Library, 159; *Geographical Magazine*, 3,

5, 19, 20, 44, 48, 49, 51, 54, 61, 62, 86, 87, 93, 100, 103, 136, 182, 183, 184, 185, 186, 224, 228, 230; Frank Graham, 85; Guildhall Library, 121; Sir Richard Hamilton, Bt, 113; Hunting Surveys, 105; Ironbridge Gorge Museum Trust, 223, 225; David Jones, 117; A. F. Kersting, 200, 234; Donald Kidman, 11; Lambeth Palace Library, 78; Museum of Leathercraft, 124; Leeds City Library, 252, 256, 257, 259; London Museum, 168, 250; Manchester Corporation Waterworks, 10; Manchester Public Library, 253; Mansell Collection, 126, 132, 134, 201, 205; National Dairy Council, 237; National Monuments Record, 227; Norfolk and Norwich Record Office, 167; Ordnance Survey, 55, 84; Peterborough Museum, 245; Picturepoint, 138, 139; Popperfoto, 8; Ministry of Public Building and Works, 108; Public Record Office, 33, 34, 102, 125, 143; *Radio Times* Hulton Picture Library, 7, 196, 242, 244; Raymonds News Agency, 89; Royal Meteorological Society, 9; Dr St Joseph, 12, 14, 15, 16, 18, 22, 30, 35, 42, 46, 67, 71, 75, 90, 91, 94, 96, 97, 98, 115, 116, 127, 128, 129, 135; Marquis of Salisbury, 140; Science Museum, 229, 231 (Crown Copyright); Tate Gallery, 207; County Borough of Teeside, 52, 53; Rex Wailes, 157; National Museum of Wales, 217; Waterways Museum, 216; Tom Weir, 1; Lord Willoughby de Broke, 112; Gordon Winter, 241, 248; Wisbeach and Fenland Museum, 243; Adam Woolfit, 69; Worcestershire County Record Office, the Bishop of Worcester, F. H. Sargeant, Diosesan Archivist, 153 (008.7 BA 358/66 39/1579).

1 CLIMATE IN BRITAIN OVER 10,000 YEARS

by GORDON MANLEY

IN north-west Europe, apart from some relics in the more remote mountains, the ice of the last glaciation disappeared about 10,000 years ago. Since then the climatic fluctuations have largely been established from studies of changes in the prevailing vegetation cover. Improvement to a 'Climatic Optimum' some-time in the fourth millenium BC is shown by the spread of such trees as the lime into Scotland and by evidence that in the Cairngorms trees were growing to about 300 metres above their present limit. At that time the summers inland in Britain were probably about 2°C. warmer than the average today, and winters were milder, probably by at least 1°C.

In understanding the effects of climatic change, it is important to note that such figures do not lie outside our own experience. Taking June-August as summer, and December-February as winter, the averages in the West Midlands today are 15.6°C and 4.0°C; and for the year 9.6°C. In the Optimum these probably lay close to 18°C, 6°C and 11°C. In 1949 they were 16.5°C

1 The changing climate of north-west Europe is revealed by studies of the former vegetation cover. In the Cairngorms the treeline was once far above its present level.

2   *The Forest of Bowland, on the borders of Lancashire.*
Great contrast in vegetation is often apparent in England.
This area of open, wet moorland begins within 20 km of
the lush varied growth along the sheltered Kent estuary.

and 5.6°C, with 10.6°C for the year; in 1826, the warmest summer on record, 17.6°C was attained; in 1869, the mildest winter, 6.8°C. In other words the range of climate we have experienced over the last 5,000 years lies scarcely beyond the possibilities of individual years today; ie it lies within the capacity of the present atmospheric circulation. Hence the reasons for past variations, both of temperature and rainfall, can fairly be sought within the period for which we have instrumental observations.

While the range of variation in Britain may appear quite small, it has lain across values of temperature, of consequent evaporation, and of rainfall that have often proved very critical. Witness the quite extraordinary change in the vegetation, in what will thrive and what will fail, that accompanies a walk of 16 kilometres, a climb of only 300 metres, a fall of a mere 2°C, a doubling of the rainfall, between the shores of Morecambe Bay and the Lake District or Bowland fells. It is therefore understandable that slight swings between groups of

years that have been predominantly cloudy, rainy and cool (such as 1954) and other groups favoured by more persistent anticyclones in summer, exemplified by years such as 1947 or 1955, would after a time be reflected in the character of the vegetation.

The character of the pollen shows that at intervals there were swings from relatively warm and dry spells to wetter, cooler and more cloudy spells. For at least half a century, perhaps more, cool unsettled weather would predominate in the majority of years. Evaporation loss fell, and the character of the prevailing forest vegetation appreciably changed. Perhaps the most effective decline, with a fall in the average summer temperature to values much like those of today, was the onset of generally wetter conditions around 550 BC. Among other things, dated remains of wooden trackways in Somerset bogs support these events. Cooler and wetter groups of years around 100 BC, AD 400 and towards AD 1300 are also well supported.

3   Sheltered slopes beside the Kent estuary.

Further corroboration comes from studies of the past extent of the mountain glaciers in the Alps and Scandinavia; it is evident that they advanced, as they have done within the past three centuries, when the summer climate became cooler and more cloudy.

FLUCTUATIONS IN HISTORIC TIMES

Throughout the past ten thousand years minor climatic oscillations of varying length have occurred, some more effective than others. Britain shares in the climatic fluctuations that affect her continental neighbours. Nevertheless the incidence of more or less favourable years has not been uniform, and no clearly defined periodicity appears from inspection. This can be shown by the occurrence of severe winters. Many people recall how few severe winters were experienced in the early decades of this century; between 1895 and 1940 there

were only two that would reasonably qualify, 1917 and 1929. Then came the bitter winters of 1940, 1941 and 1942, 1947 and 1963. Moreover, in each of the winters of 1945, 1951 and 1956 there was one exceptionally cold month, by the standards of the earlier part of this century. February 1956, for example, was the fifth coldest in more than 200 years.

A table listing severe and hard winters in England since the mid-seventeenth century is based on the criterion that the overall mean temperature in the Midlands for the three months December to February should fall below 2.3°C. Years in which some earlier mildness was offset by an exceptionally cold March have been added. This critical temperature may not seem low, but in England it is quite sufficient to ensure that snow will both fall and lie considerably more than usual, and quite probably there will be a sufficient spell

TABLE OF HARD OR SEVERE
WINTER'S SINCE 1650
(severe winters in bold type)

1656 (?), **58, 60**	1800, 02, 08
1663, 65	**1814,** 16
1677, 78, 79	1820, **23**
1681, **84**	**1830, 38**
1691, 92, **95,** 97, **98**	**1841,** 45, 47
1709	**1855**
1716	1860
1729	1871, **79**
1740, 46	1880, **81,** 86
1755	**1891, 95**
1766	**1917**
1776	1929
1780, **84, 85, 89**	**1940,** 42, 47
1795, 99	**1963**

4 *The annual average number of mornings with snow cover, 1931–60. Isopleths at 5, 10, 15, 20, 30, 50, and 100 days. At 1500 feet the upland averages can be generalised, broadly, as 20 Dartmoor, 30 SE Wales, 40–45 NE Wales-Derbyshire-West Riding, 50 to 55 Durham-Cheviots, 80 Eastern Highlands; there is a decrease as we move westward. At 4000 feet persistence averages about 200 to 220 days. Drawn by the author from* Meteorological Office Monthly Weather Reports, *with additional data.*

of hard frost for the smaller lakes and rivers to freeze. Moreover on the uplands at 200 metres, the average will lie very close to the freezing point. In the Scottish Borders, the Pennines and the north Welsh border country, and even in upland Devonshire the presence of snow and the effects of frost will be conspicuous for all countryfolk. Places like Peebles and Buxton, the suburbs of Halifax and Sheffield, upland Denbighshire and perhaps Dartmoor will figure in the news. In the past notes were often entered in local annals such as church registers, for example the Youlgreave entry from Derbyshire recording the very deep and lasting snowfall in 1615, and that at Marske in north Yorkshire on the extraordinary snowfall of 20–21 January, 1972.

There is considerable evidence for the amplitude and dating of significant climatic fluctuations within historical time. The periods of increased wetness about AD 400 and again towards the end of the thirteenth century are shown by the Scandinavian pollen records. From eastern Sweden there are also indications of the effect of a series of wetter and cooler seasons around 1450 and again towards 1570. Still further away, Sirén's careful work on the growth-rings of trees in northern Lapland, which can be shown to respond closely to the summer temperature, indicates marked declines setting in for a decade or two after 1235, and after 1585. The increased drift of Arctic sea-ice towards the coasts of Iceland in the later thirteenth century is well documented; then, after a diminution, a much greater increase set in after 1590. After 1890 the drift of ice diminished, but since 1960 an increase has caused the Icelanders to become anxious, with good reason. Each of these episodes appears to have been reflected in reports of unfavourable weather in Britain; late and cold springs, or cool wet summers, or the early onset of autumn. Sometimes all three occurred in the same year following a severe winter as well, as in 1695, 1784 and 1879.

THREE CENTURIES OF INSTRUMENTAL MEASUREMENTS IN ENGLAND

For the last 300 years it has been possible to assemble more exact and detailed evidence from daily instrumental and eye observations; indeed details of the wind and weather in the London area can now be provided for every day since November 1668. But the maintenance of a network of strictly comparable observations is by no means easy; in Britain officially standardised

records go back, at best, little more than a hundred years. The beginnings of official meteorology can be sought around 1840 when the rapid growth of towns excited interest in public health, sanitation and water supply. Not only temperature and pressure, but also upland rainfall data began to be needed, especially in the Pennines. Sheffield has a rainfall record for its Redmires reservoir since 1836; Bolton began a record in 1843; while Manchester's renowned water undertaking began to supply the city from Longdendale in 1847. By 1860 countrywide rainfall data began to be collected by G. J. Symons' British Rainfall Organisation in which amateur and professional co-operated. As a result of Symons' efforts we can take pride in the most comprehensive set of rainfall statistics in the world.

Here and there classical-style observatory buildings of that vigorous era remain; Durham, Bidston, Glasgow, Stonyhurst, Falmouth, Aberdeen and Armagh are examples. But even after 1840, methods and techniques of measurement of temperature and rainfall were not agreed; instruments and the manner of their exposure were imperfect. The range of variation of the mean temperature for any given month or year is quite small, but to be of value the air temperatures must have been read at a standard height and at regular hours and have been unaffected by reflected sunshine from adjacent walls, or by location in a courtyard or on a roof.

But long before the dawn of officially-maintained observations there were the amateurs, beginning from the first introduction of the sealed Florentine thermometer into England by Sir Robert Southwell in 1659. Dr Wilkins advocated in 1663 at the newly-founded Royal Society the keeping of 'a history of the weather, so that we should know its changes in future'. Robert Hooke was commissioned to construct a thermometer 'to serve as a standard', and to devise a scheme for daily instrumental and eye observations.

John Locke's manuscript of daily readings at Oxford during 1666–67 is our earliest record; and from 1671 an almost continuous sequence of daily instrumental observations for London can be assembled. The gaps are gradually being filled by the reduction of other early English observations. Abroad, we have monthly mean temperatures for Utrecht since 1706, Berlin 1719, Leningrad 1743, Basle 1755, Stockholm 1756, and Paris 1757. Edinburgh's record begins in 1731 but is not continuous until 1764. Berlin has a short series beginning in 1691; and at Paris a brief record exists for

5 *Meteorological observations have been kept at Durham University since 1843 when the observatory was built.*

1658–60, probably the earliest north of the Alps. For rainfall, Paris provides measurements from 1688, Holland has a continuous run from 1715, and England from 1727. Perhaps the most remarkably persistent of the early English amateurs was Thomas Barker, brother-in-law of Gilbert White and squire of Lyndon in Rutland; where he kept his daily record from 1736 to 1798.

Before the beginning of instrumental measurement we have to rely on descriptive journals of daily weather such as those for Zurich in 1546–76, Elsinore in 1582–97, and Kassel in 1621–49. There are several accounts from Britain, but generally for much shorter periods. From these, the wind directions can be usefully extracted. The various reductions from these scattered, primitively maintained records in Western Europe agree to a remarkable extent. Not only do fluctuations at Basle reflect the behaviour of the nearby Alpine glaciers; the overall trends are closely paralleled by those at Utrecht or London.

Barometer readings were maintained, but the imperfection of early instruments makes it hard to bring readings, uncorrected for temperature and in units such as Paris lines, to modern standards. H. H. Lamb's researches in the Meteorological Office have, however, enabled the construction of maps showing the average distribution of pressure for the North Atlantic region since 1760, and, with the aid of wind directions, the estimation of probabilities before that date.

OTHER EVIDENCE OF CLIMATIC CHANGE

There is a marked association between periods of ice advance in the western Alps and periods of falling spring and summer temperature in England. It seems safe to say that Alpine glaciers are unlikely to advance unless the mean spring temperature in England for at least a decade falls below 8.2°C. Since 1950 our spring temperatures have tended to fall, but they have only just come to that figure. Many are inclined to think that widespread advance of the ice, after many years, may again be imminent.

Dating of glacier advances before 1600 is much more difficult, because the advances that culminated soon after 1600, or in some cases around 1820 or 1850, obscured any earlier evidence, as they appear to have

10 Early official records are available for Pennine catchment areas like Longdendale which has supplied water to the Manchester area since 1847.

CLIMATIC TENDENCIES IN BRITAIN
Approximate dates:

1000 onward	Prevailing impression; springs and summers slightly warmer than at present.
1090–1100	Slight recession; more disturbed and rainy, at least one severe winter.
1170–1200	Probably a minor optimum: mild winters, probably forward springs, quite warm summers and autumns.
1305–1325	Recession: generally rainy, some severe winters, 1314–17 wet, very bad harvests.
1430–1445	Recession: severe winters in 1430s, many reports of cool, wet, disturbed summers; distress 1438; limited improvement till after 1460.
1500–1526	Inclined to improvement: 1517–25 generally favourable.
1555–1574	Appreciable recession: distress 1556; 1568 drier, later years cooler.
1585–1610	Appreciable recession: prevailingly cooler, tardy springs, some rainy summers; severe winters 1595 and 1601, very severe 1608.
1620–1650	Variable, but few reports of drought or heat (1636); prevailingly wet 1620s (notably 1621, 1629) and unsettled 1640s with some late springs; severe winters, 1621, 1635, 1649.
1650s	Often dry and favourable in summer, cold in winter; 1658 severe. (H. H. Lamb thinks much of seventeenth century drier than now, but cooler).
1690s	Remarkable predominance of cool weather 1692–1702, late springs, cool summers, cold in winter, notably 1695 and 1698, severe distress in Scotland.
1726–1739	Notably forward springs, warm, dry summers, warm autumns; good harvests. (Earlier, 1714 and 1717–19, good dry

	summers.)
1740–1748	Generally dry summers, frequent east or north winds; historic severe winter 1740.
1759–1783	Prevailing warm summers: frosty winters in 1770s; 1763–71 wetter, with much cold weather in spring.
1799–1820	More east or north winds: tendency for extremes, numerous cool unfavourable seasons, either spring or summer or both, with cold or severe winters; 1799, 1812 and 1816 much distress; hot in 1808, 1818.
1836–1845	Inclined to cold with wet summers and poor harvests in several years.
1846–1871	Often dry and favourable especially 1846–47, 1854–59, 1864–71; but 1848 very wet and 1860 cold and wet.
1872–1880	Generally rainy; 1879 extremely bad.
1881–1895	Generally drier, but four severe winters and much coolness in spring.
1896–1939	Period of increasingly westerly weather; increasing rainfall in 1920s; only two severe winters. Warmer springs caused the Ben Nevis snowbed to disappear in 1933 for the first time since long before 1840. (Since then it has completely melted in nine summers.)
1940 onward	Climate inclined again to dryness and wider extremes: 1940s, cold in winter, warm in spring and summer; since 1950 a tendency for summers to become cooler (1959 excepted) and for rainfall to increase, springs also show signs of cooling. (Notable return of ice to Iceland coasts in recent years.) Autumns still relatively mild.

Whether irregular climatic oscillations are a property of the atmosphere and the energy it receives, or how far they owe something to volcanic dust, or to events in the ocean, is not yet known. There is no clear evidence of periodicity, or of relationships with such phenomena as sunspots. Some have been disposed to see hints of periodicities of 23, 55, 80 to 90, and 200 years; and if the details can be pieced together over a wider area for a longer period some kind of pattern may yet be discerned.

All manner of details have been brought into the effort to interpret events before 1600; for example, in Baden, sometime in the earlier Middle Ages, the vine was being cultivated about 200 metres above its present limit, in agreement with contemporary efforts by Englishmen as far north as Lincolnshire. But what might be achieved even in Yorkshire by a band of enthusiastic young monks endeavouring to ripen their grapes in their walled garden remains open to discussion.

From the course of climatic fluctuations in the past, interpreted with the aid of our growing knowledge of meteorology, a start is being made in the investigation of what the future may hold. In the populous Britain of today, the signs of recession from what appears to be a peak of warmth about 1950 must be considered very seriously. The economic load, if our climate becomes cooler, will be quite considerable; crops, transport and welfare will all be appreciably affected.

Under medieval conditions, with a yield of corn per acre thought to average little more than a tenth of what we now obtain, with weeks of anxiety or grinding toil to get in a late and poor harvest in a wet autumn after a cold late spring, a series of three or four bad harvests caused considerable distress. For six or seven to occur in succession would lead to widespread misery, conspicuous decline in energy and enterprise, perhaps even in the birth-rate or at least in the survival-rate of children among the poorer countryfolk. The great famine of 1315 came just about one generation before the Black Death, and two generations before the Peasants' Revolt of 1381.

Statistics of prices, especially of corn, at a number of markets in England and southern Scotland have been assembled and much used by economic historians, notably Beveridge in a celebrated paper in 1921; they reflect the vicissitudes of the harvest yield. They should not, however, be regarded as a very close index of the immediate summer weather; it has been demonstrated that the yield of crops, especially those sown in autumn, can be affected by a number of meteorological factors. Moreover, under medieval conditions prices might differ considerably from one market to another; the difficulty of working heavy soils in certain seasons and proximity to navigable rivers might play a part. We know also how greatly the impression of the weather in any given season can vary between one part of Britain and another, even between such counties as Lancashire and Kent. Nevertheless the nature of the variations is well demonstrated by Dr Hoskins's diagram, and the incidence of 'groups of dear years' becomes evident.

The improvement of shipping and the efficiency of sea-borne trade, together with faster inland water and road transport, gradually ensured that distress

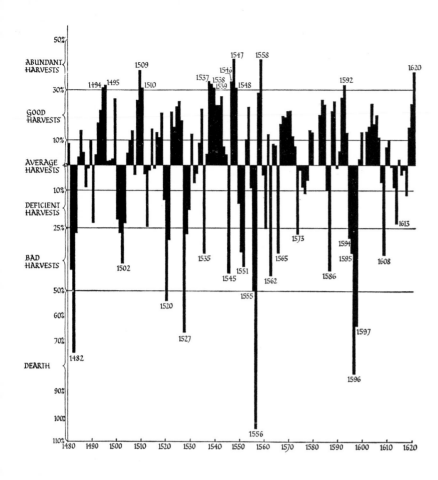

11 *The quality of English harvests, 1480–1620. The percentage figures in the left-hand margin represent the deviation of the annual average price from the thirty-one year moving average for that year (after Hoskins).*

would be less immediately felt; but economic effects would still be present.

It must not be assumed that these small but significant climatic swings would govern the course of history, although they might influence it. The 1590s and the 1690s saw much distress in Sweden and Scotland, but in England the sense of increased security that followed the defeat of the Armada and, a century later, the relief when the Toleration Act was passed did much to mitigate the feeling of depression that might otherwise have prevailed. The comely eighteenth-century mansions of Norfolk, the cheerful growing industry of a sunny little Manchester, the lively invention, the elegant craftsmanship, and even the beginnings of the August seaside holiday, tell something of the tale of those splendid corn harvests of the 1730s when we could even export; and Walpole could let sleeping dogs lie. The age indeed when England began to accumulate the capital for the formidable developments that were to follow.

FURTHER READING

Ahlmann, H. W. 'Glaciers and Climate' Bowman Lecture, *American Geographical Society* (New York, 1953)

Brandon, P. F. 'Late-Medieval Weather in Sussex and its Agricultural Significance', *Transactions of the Institute of British Geographers*, 54 (1971), 1–17

Ladurie, E. le Roy *Histoire du climat depuis l'an mil* (Paris, 1967)

Ladurie, E. le Roy *Times of Feast. Times of Famine: a History of Climate since the year 1000* (New York, 1971; London 1972) see also *Geogr Mag* March 1973.

Lamb, H. H. *The Changing Climate* (1966)

Lamb, H. H. *The English Climate* (1964)

Manley, G. *Climate and the British Scene* (4th imp, 1970)

Manley, G. 'Early Meteorological Observations', *Endeavour*, 21 (1962) 43–50

Manley, G. 'The mean temperature of Central England, 1698–1952' *QFRoyMetS*, 78 (1953), 242–61

2 THE EARLIEST SETTLERS IN BRITAIN

by GLANVILLE JONES

EVERY narrative is the better for a dramatic beginning. Hence the appeal of the traditional interpretation which held that the rural landscape of the Lowland Zone of England began in all essentials with the Anglo-Saxon colonisation in the middle decades of the fifth century AD. Thus it was argued that in lowland areas denuded of their Romano-British inhabitants, if indeed they had been inhabited at all, a new beginning was made with co-operative communities of Anglo-Saxon freemen housed in large nucleated villages. In not dissimilar vein, it was claimed that the Highland Zone was a pastoral retreat, inhabited by Celtic 'cowboys' in their long surviving wild west, until the scattered farms and hamlets appropriate for an ingrained pastoral tradition

were established during the Middle Ages. In the east and west alike the impress of prehistoric man was deemed to be slight and confined in the main to the light-soiled uplands. But, over recent decades, these traditional tenets have been found wanting. Increasingly it has been appreciated that the rural economy of Britain as recorded in 1066 has roots which strike very deep into prehistoric antiquity and at all stages of our

12 At the Neolithic camp of Windmill Hill, Wiltshire, which was made c 2960 BC, concentric ditches with their causeways of undisturbed soil enclosed an area of about eight hectares. The smaller mounds are Bronze Age barrows.

13 *At Stonehenge command over substantial resources is implied by the use of stones brought over considerable distances, some possibly from as far as Pembrokeshire. Successive rebuildings from c 1800 to 1400 BC suggest a continuity of this authority.*

14 *The Thornborough Circles, York-shire, are henge monuments dating from the beginning of the Bronze Age. An even earlier sacred use of this lowland site on gravel is indicated by a Neolithic cursus, or long avenue of two parallel ditches, in part underlying the central henge.*

prehistory there is evidence to suggest that the lowlands and the uplands were occupied, if not simultaneously, at least in alternate halves of the year.

Our first farmers were Neolithic immigrants who came from Europe in the fourth millennium BC. Equipped with stone hoes they tilled, probably by hand, light soils carrying a thin woodland cover, but there is growing evidence to suggest that in open country they also ploughed small fields. We know tantalisingly little of their homesteads but the remains of their causewayed camps are most spectacular. These are enclosures of up to eight hectares which served as rallying points where numerous tribes foregathered periodically for trade, ceremonial and the sorting of cattle. Such was the purpose of the site on Windmill Hill, an exposed chalk summit at about 190 metres, and apparently used principally from spring to autumn.

But it cannot be too strongly emphasised that cause-wayed camps were also sited on lowland riversides and that the camp established on gravel at Staines in the Thames valley appears to have been one of the most densely occupied in Britain.

Similarly, in the late Neolithic period when the construction of the Stonehenge temple was initiated on a low chalk plateau, other henges were being established at still lower elevations, as for example near Thornborough in Yorkshire. The so-called Celtic fields, whose rectangular form presupposes cross-ploughing by means of an ard, or light plough, became a widespread feature of our chalk uplands in subsequent periods, and notably during the Roman occupation. Yet even by the early part of the second millennium BC, there were furrows indicative of cross-ploughing on the coastal lowlands at Gwithian in Cornwall.

SUMMER HOMES AND REFUGES IN THE UPLANDS

The hill-forts of the Iron Age betray a similar tendency. Some in the lowlands yield evidence suggesting permanent occupation over long periods, and seem to have served as administrative centres for the rulers of tribal areas. Others, principally in the uplands, were occupied during the summer months of upland pasturage and for much longer when danger threatened.

This latter appears to have been the function of the large settlement of 150 huts sited within the hill-fort of Tre'r Ceiri in North Wales. The hill-fort was probably started before the Roman invasion but excavation of sixty-nine of the huts yielded finds within the range AD 150–400. Below the hill-fort are a number of enclosed homesteads on or near well-drained loams, the brown earths named, from local type sites, as the Penrhyn and Arvon Series. These homesteads, which are interpreted as single farms, have been attributed to the same period as the hill-fort, and notably to the second and third centuries AD. Since they occupy the same well-drained loams as the farmsteads of the

15 Rectangular Celtic fields on Fyfield Down, Wiltshire, of the kind produced by cross ploughing with an ard.

nineteenth century, it is probable that these enclosed homesteads were originally more numerous but have been concealed by later settlement. This is especially true of the main nucleation at Llanaelhaearn, immediately below the hill-fort. There was almost certainly a settlement of some importance here from the fifth to the seventh centuries AD when early Christian inscribed stones were set up near the present church. These considerations, and the fact that no corn-grinding querns were discovered in excavations in the hill-fort, justify the suggestion that Tre'r Ceiri served as the summer abode and refuge of the lowland community represented by the enclosed homesteads.

Although it has long been recognised that there was some prehistoric settlement in the lowlands, evidence in the form of surface remains has survived far more frequently in the uplands. In recent decades, however, aerial photography has revealed abundant traces of

25

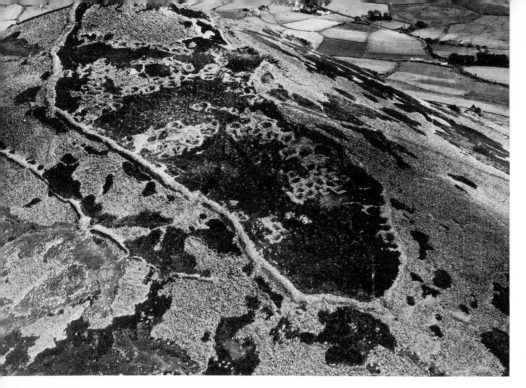

16　Enclosed by a strong stone wall, the hill-fort of Tre'r Ceiri, Caernarvonshire, crowns an exposed summit over 450 metres high.

17　The setting of Tre'r Ceiri. The hill-fort was probably a refuge for lowland homesteads in the adjoining district. The main permanent settlement was probably on the site of the present hamlet of Llanaelhaearn.

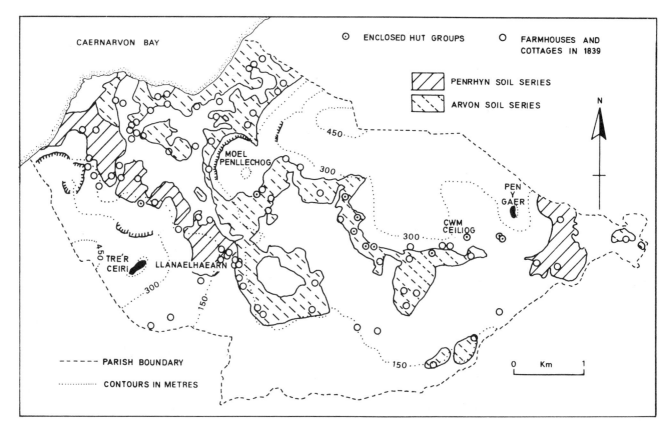

CAERNARVON BAY

⊙ ENCLOSED HUT GROUPS ○ FARMHOUSES AND COTTAGES IN 1839

▨ PENRHYN SOIL SERIES
▨ ARVON SOIL SERIES

N

MOEL PENLLECHOG

450
300

PEN Y GAER

CWM CEILIOG

300

TRE'R CEIRI
450
LLANAELHAEARN
300
150

150

0　Km　1

- - - - PARISH BOUNDARY
.... CONTOURS IN METRES

lowland settlement in the form of crop-markings of enclosures and ceremonial structures on the gravel deposits of major valleys like the Thames, the Warwickshire Avon, and the Trent. After a careful survey, the Royal Commission on Historical Monuments has suggested that many of these gravel terraces which proved attractive to Anglo-Saxon colonists had earlier been occupied from the Neolithic to the Roman period. Providing sites easily cleared of light vegetation and reasonably well-drained at least on the upper terraces, these valleys seem to have been continuously inhabited. Accordingly, there must have existed some form of early territorial organisation capable of ensuring the cohesion of upland and lowland settlements and permitting the mobilisation of sufficient labour forces for the construction of, for example, causewayed camps, ceremonial temples and major hill-forts. Since the traditions of the Iron Age were perpetuated in early British society, some pointers to such an organisation may be sought in the earliest historical records of Welsh society.

ORGANISATION BY MULTIPLE ESTATES

The Welsh Laws of the twelfth and thirteenth centuries, together with near-contemporary surveys, record the existence of ancient multiple estates. Organised around the lord's court, each estate consisted of a number of hamlets, sometimes far-flung, as well as scattered farms. These were inhabited by bondmen and freemen who, in return for their lands, paid rents in kind and performed various services. The services of the bondmen were communal hamlet obligations and included the cultivation of the lord's demesne lands, the construction of his court, and the building of distant encampments. A similar social structure is recorded in 1183 for the multiple estates or *shires* of County Durham. Here the tenants owed similar obligations, some of which bore identical names of British (proto-Welsh) origin.

Such parallels indicate that this organisation common to Wales and Durham was already in being before the early seventh century AD when the Anglo-Saxons succeeded in severing the North from Wales.

18 A narrow Neolithic cursus is revealed by parallel crop marks on gravel in the Thames valley at North Stoke, Oxfordshire. The circles were used for burials in the Bronze Age.

Hamsterley Castles, in County Durham, a massive stone-built fort exhibiting parallels with a Welsh fort of c AD 700, is attributed to the pre- English period and, like the medieval hunting lodges of the Bishop of Durham, was probably erected by the obligatory labour of the bondmen of Aucklandshire.

Many multiple estates either survived until, or were reconstituted by, the Middle Ages in various parts of England and Wales. A characteristic feature of these estates is that their headquarter settlements or courts usually lie on lowland near important prehistoric sites like Yeavering Bell in Northumberland, Cissbury hill-fort in Sussex, and even Stonehenge. They sometimes adjoin Romano-British settlements as at Hovingham in Yorkshire. At Dinorben in North Wales the small township which contained the medieval court of a multiple estate also included an Iron Age hill-fort within whose ramparts a large round hut housed an opulent household during the fourth century AD. Such similarities suggest that it was an organisation by multiple estates, akin to that of medieval Wales and Durham, which made possible the erection of our major prehistoric structures. It also made possible their reconstruction in the protohistoric period, in the way that between AD 450 and 600 the Iron Age ramparts of South Cadbury were capped with some 1,100 metres of timber-reinforced stone-walling. The same organisation appears to have provided a territorial framework into which subsequent rural settlement was dovetailed.

19 & 20 Concealed in deep woodland above upper Weardale, and defended by drystone walls, the Castles at Hamsterley were probably a British fortification built after the Romans had left.

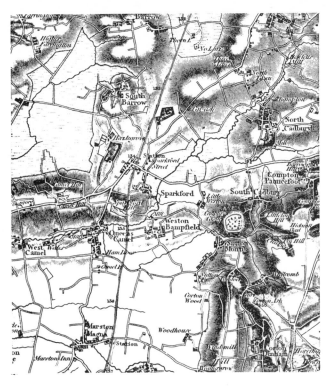

21 *Cadbury Castle, in south-east Somerset, was occupied in the Neolithic, Late Bronze and Early Iron Ages. Subsequently it was re-fortified in the Post-Roman and in the Late-Saxon periods.*

There are indications that English villages were an outgrowth of existing British hamlets. Some exceptions help to justify this point of view. Mrs Sylvia Hallam could demonstrate the existence of numerous Romano-British hamlets in the Lincolnshire Fens largely because this area was inundated in the post-Roman period and was therefore not available for continuous later settlement which would have destroyed evidence of the earlier inhabitants. Maxey, on the Welland gravels, provides another exception in that the centre of settlement shifted eastwards during the Dark Ages to reveal, around the Norman church, traces of an important Romano-British settlement, a village or at least the centre of an estate occupied over a considerable period.

22 *Crop marks indicate Romano-British settlement to the east of Maxey church in the Welland Valley, Northamptonshire.*

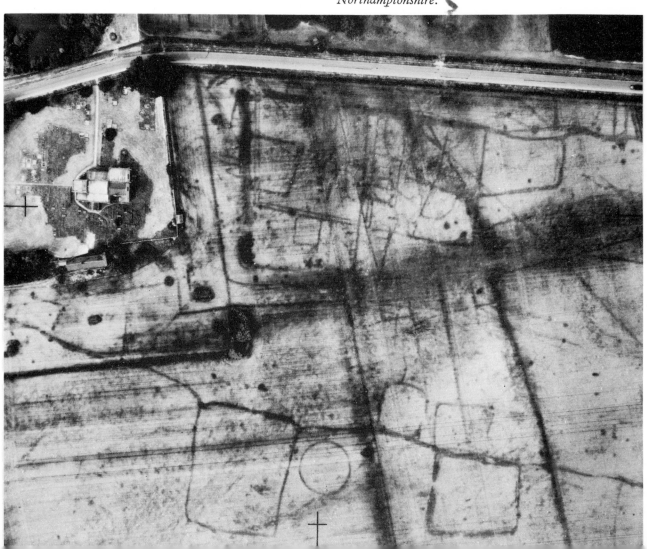

23 *The rectangular enclosure of the modest Romano-British villa on limestone at about 125 metres near Ditchley, Oxfordshire. The granary in the bottom right of the enclosure has been calculated to reflect an estate of about 400 hectares.*

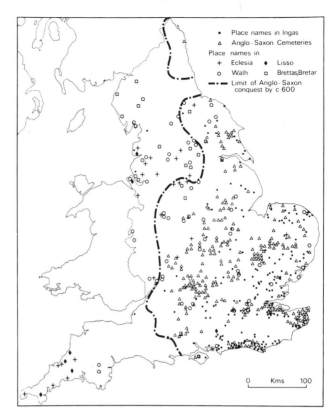

24 *Some place-name evidence of surviving British settlement in relation to the zone of earlier Anglo-Saxon settlement (after Cameron, Jackson and Smith).*

Acceptance of the multiple estate as the organisational framework would help to resolve many puzzling features of our early settlement history. Such an organisation would have provided the large labour force necessary for the cultivation of the landed estates centred on Romano-British villas. Surplus bath accommodation at some villas like Stroud in Hampshire and Castle Dikes in Yorkshire was perhaps for the use of such estate workers. Romano-British villas were in the main sited on the richer intermediate loams, and from two of them there is evidence in the form of asymmetrical ploughshares to suggest that the mould-board plough, suitable for even heavier soils, was used. It is reasonable to suppose therefore that much villa land came under Anglo-Saxon cultivation. Sometimes no doubt part of a later village might come to overlie a villa but, hitherto at least, it has not been possible to prove that there was any continuity *in situ* between the two types of settlement. The failure of villa names to survive tends to confirm the archaeological evidence that the villa buildings were abandoned during the fifth century, if not earlier. Yet the paradox implied by the probable abandonment of the buildings but the retention of the lands could be resolved if we were to assume that the villa owners were displaced or exterminated and their estates, but not their villa buildings, taken over by aristocratic Anglo-Saxon leaders who allotted parts of these estates to their own free followers.

In addition the new lords could have retained the villa slaves and tenants in their out-settlements to serve as an organised labour force. Significantly, the early English place-names ending in *-ingas*, when compounded with a personal name, are interpreted as meaning the dependants and followers of the named person, as in Hastings. These names point to an Anglo-Saxon settlement organised by estates shortly after the earliest phase of pagan immigration.

DIAGNOSTIC PLACE-NAMES

Abundant English place-names testify to the impress of Anglo-Saxon settlers, but their predecessors were certainly not completely exterminated. Thus, the presence of Welsh cultivators in some parts of Wessex is confirmed by the Laws of King Ine (AD 688–695), one of which states that the food-rent from an estate of ten hides of land should include, among other items, ten ambers of Welsh ale as compared with thirty of clear ale. There are place-names which indicate the survival of British settlements alike in the zone of

31

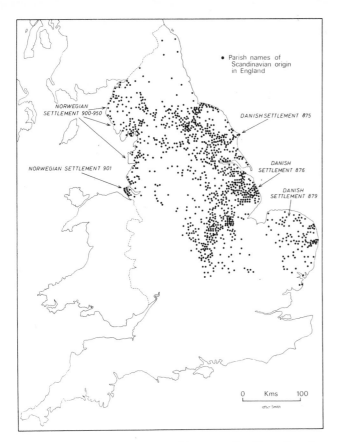

NORWEGIAN SETTLEMENT 900-950

DANISH SETTLEMENT 875

NORWEGIAN SETTLEMENT 901

DANISH SETTLEMENT 876

DANISH SETTLEMENT 879

0   Kms   100

after Smith

25 Some place-name evidence of Scandinavian settlement (after Smith).

earliest English settlement and further west. Place-names containing the British *eclesia*, a church, as in Eccles (Kent) and Eccleston (Cheshire), imply the existence of British population centres with organised worship. Those containing the British *lisso*, meaning a court, as in Liss (Hampshire) and Treales (Lancashire), hint at the perpetuation of former multiple estates. There are also Old English names which denote the recognition by Anglo-Saxons of British settlements. Such are names in *walh*, meaning a Welshman or serf, as in the hamlet of Wales (Yorkshire) and in a number of settlements named Walton, though by no means all those so designated. Similarly, the Old English *Brettas* had the meaning Britons, as in Bretton (Yorkshire). These diagnostic place-names are found not only in the areas settled by the Anglo-Saxons but also in those settled from the ninth century by Scandinavians, Irish-Norsemen in the north-west and Danes in the

26 Former common field on the seaward flank of the ancient Welsh hamlets of Llan-non and Llansanffraid, Cardiganshire.

east. Thus, for example, Birkby near Leeds, originally Bretby, derived from the Old Norse *Bretar* and *by*, indicates a settlement of the Britons.

Sometimes singly, sometimes in combination, place-names indicative of British settlement were often used to designate the hamlets of multiple estates. For one such estate in Yorkshire there is written evidence of the early eighth century to indicate that the name *walh* was applied to that component hamlet of the estate, now Walton Head, which had best retained its British character. Although the Anglo-Saxons and the Scandinavians pioneered many new settlements in England, the latter in particular by infilling, they also settled in or alongside the best sited of the British hamlets. These accordingly acquired new English or Scandinavian names. As they grew into villages so their links with the parent estates were progressively reduced. Thus, on the richest lands, the multiple estate often disappeared. In the north and west, however, such estates and their component hamlets survived.

In medieval Wales the ideal bond hamlet was deemed in law to contain only nine houses. These were closely grouped so that the corn-drying kiln and public bath house – both probably a Romano-British inheritance – were placed at a distance so as to minimise fire hazards in the hamlet. Using the common plough the hamlet community cultivated, year in year out, a permanent infield with arable strips so small that they could easily have been dovetailed into pre-existing Celtic fields. The common herd of the community grazed on extensive common pastures, parts of which were

subject to temporary outfield cultivation. Where conditions for cultivation were favourable, extensive common fields sometimes developed from the infield and outfields, as at Llan-non and Llansanffraid on the west coast of Wales.

In parts of England also some British hamlets survived – Birkby (Bretby), for example, which still retains its characteristic small marginal green resembling that of some Romano-British hamlets. At Walton Head the hamlet has virtually disappeared but a reminder of the ancient communal organisation is still provided by a small marginal green. Save on elevated or unpropitious sites such as these, most hamlets in England had developed into villages by the Middle Ages. The history of East Witton, a village in the Pennine dales which once had three common fields, illustrates this point. The original settlement was a hamlet straggling from the ancient church of St Ella (Helen) north-west towards a once extensive marginal green near Scane Sike. In 1086 there were only thirteen houses in the township but a map of 1627 shows not only the straggling hamlet, now of seventeen houses, but also a well-defined street green with twenty-two houses on the northern side and twenty-five on the southern. Professor Beresford has suggested that the monks of Jervaulx Abbey, who had acquired control of the township by the late thirteenth century, were responsible for the development of the new village on the edges of a street green designed to provide a setting for the Monday market and Michaelmas fair first held here in 1307. It is equally important to stress that these developments of 'central place' functions took place within the framework of a multiple estate which was certainly in being when the Old English *middel* (middle) was applied to a *ham* (homestead) sited between the headquarters at East Witton and its appendant hamlet at West Witton. Since the homestead was presumably of some importance, the suffix in the name Middleham could well imply a recollection even in the Old English period of the Romano-British villa near the centre of the estate. The dedication to Helen, mother of the Emperor Constantine, hints also at the presence in East Witton of a settlement in Romano-British times, a hint reinforced by the existence on an adjacent valleyside ledge of the hill-fort at Braithwaite Banks. In East Witton, as in many other areas, it was probably an age-old multiple estate organisation which facilitated the establishment of the hill-fort, the villa and the developed village form.

27 *The hamlet of Birkby, near Leeds. There was formerly a small marginal green on the site of the field bisected by the road running north-westwards from the hamlet.*

28 *At the site of the ancient British hamlet of Walton Head, Yorkshire, a reminder of the former communal organisation is provided by a small marginal green which survives only in the form of very wide verges along the road to the north-west.*

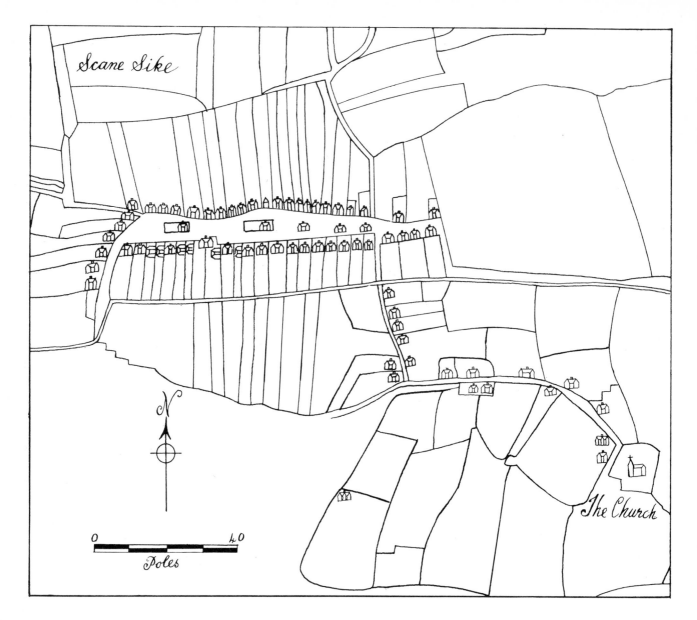

Scane Sike

N

0   40

Poles

The Church

29 & 30   *The 1627 map of East Witton in Wensleydale shows that the ancient church and original nucleus of settlement were distant from the site of the present church at the east end of the street green. The village green was established in 1307 as part of the ancient multiple estate organisation of East Witton and district.*

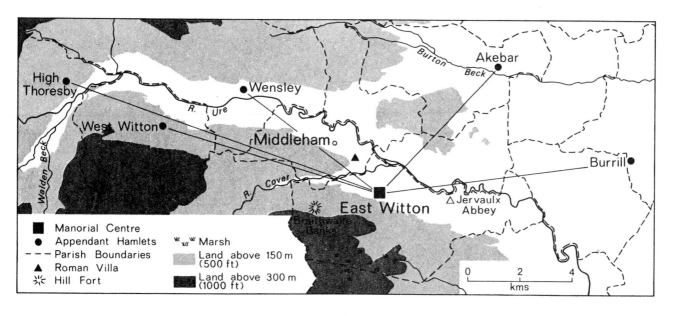

31 The component hamlets of the East Witton multiple estate in 1086, as recorded in Domesday Book.

32 The tall 'rood stone', an Early Bronze Age monolith of religious significance, adjoining the church of Rudston in the Yorkshire Wolds, provided the name of the village. Rudston re-emerged as a prosperous settlement before 1066.

CONTINUITY OF SETTLEMENT

The origins and growth of rural settlement in England and Wales are best explained in terms of a continuity, not of site necessarily, but almost certainly of organisational setting. Even so, there are some sites where the roots of settlement manifestly strike deep. At Rudston, a settlement on one of the few permanent streams in the Yorkshire Wolds, three Neolithic ceremonial avenues converge on a point some 350 metres north-east of the present village, and immediately adjoining the church there is a huge standing stone apparently brought here over a distance of sixteen kilometres in the Early Bronze Age. Moreover, evidence of Iron Age settlement has been found beneath a Roman villa sited on the western outskirts of the village. The very name of the village, which means 'rood stone', indicates that the monolith was in evidence when the Anglo-Saxons gave an English name to this already ancient settlement. That our villages bear English names is no proof of an exclusively English, and thus relatively late, origin.

FURTHER READING

Addyman, P. V. 'A Dark-Age Settlement at Maxey, Northants', *Medieval Archaeology*, 8 (1965), 20–73

Alcock, L. 'Excavations at South Cadbury Castle: 1969, A Summary Report', *The Antiquaries Journal*, 50 (1970), 15–25

Beresford, M. W. and St Joseph, J. K. S. *Medieval England: An Aerial Survey* (Cambridge, 1958)

Bowen, H. C. and Fowler, P. J. 'Romano-British rural settlements in Dorset and Wiltshire', *Rural Settlement in Roman Britain* (ed Thomas, A. C.), 1966, 43–67

Cameron, K. 'Eccles in English Place-Names' *Christianity in Britain, 300–700* (eds Barley, M. W. and Hanson, R. P. C.), (Leicester, 1968), 87–92

Dodgson, J. M. 'The Significance of the English Place-Names in -*ingas*, -*inga*- in South-East England', *Medieval Archaeology*, 10 (1967), 1–28

Dymond, D. P. 'Ritual Monuments at Rudston, E. Yorkshire, England', *Proceedings of the Prehistoric Society*, 32 (1966), 86–95

Finberg, H. P. R. *Roman and Saxon Withington*, Leicester, 1965

Fowler, P. J. and Evans, J. G. 'Plough-marks, Lynchets and Early Fields', *Antiquity*, 41 (1967), 289–301

Fowler, P. J. and Thomas, A. C. 'Arable Fields of the pre-Norman period at Gwithian', *Cornish Archaeology*, I (1962), 61–84

Frere, S. S. *Britannia* (1967)

Hallam, S. J. 'Villages in Roman Britain: Some Evidence', *The Antiquaries Journal*, 44 (1964), 19–32

Hodgkin, J. E. 'The Castles Camp, Hamsterley, Co. Durham', *Architectural and Archaeological Society, Durham and Northumberland*, 7 (1934–6), 92–8

Hogg, A. H. A. 'Garn Boduan and Tre'r Ceiri, excavations at two Caernarvonshire Hill-forts', *Archaeological Journal*, 117 (1960), 1–39

Jackson, K. H. *Language and History in Early Britain* (Edinburgh, 1953)

Jones, G. R. J. 'Settlement Patterns in Anglo-Saxon England', *Antiquity*, 35 (1961), 221–32

Jones, G. R. J. 'The Tribal System in Wales: a Re-assessment in the light of Settlement Studies', *Welsh History Review*, I (1961), 111–32

Jones, G. R. J. 'Basic Patterns of Settlement Distribution in Northern England', *Advancement of Science*, 71 (1961), 192–200

Jones, G. R. J. 'Early Settlement in Arfon: the Setting of Tre'r Ceiri', *Caernarvonshire Historical Society Transactions*, 24 (1963), 1–20

Jones, G. R. J. 'The Multiple Estate as a Model Framework for Tracing Early Stages in the Evolution of Rural Settlement' in *L'habitat et les paysages ruraux d'Europe* (ed Dussart, F.), Liège, 1971, 251–67

Keiller, A. *Windmill Hill and Avebury* (Oxford), 1965

Ordnance Survey Professional Papers, 13, *Field Archaeology*, 1963

Phillips, C. W. (ed) *The Fenland in Roman times*, The Royal Geographical Society (1970)

Ralegh Radford, C. A. 'The Roman Villa at Ditchley, Oxon.', *Oxoniensia*, I (1936), 24–69

Rees, W. 'Survivals of Ancient Celtic Custom in Medieval England' *Angles and Britons* (O'Donnell Lectures, Cardiff, 1963), 148–68

Royal Commission on Historical Monuments, *A Matter of Time: An Archaeological Survey* (1960)

Smith, A. H. *English Place-Name Elements* (1956)

Stenton, F. M. 'Early English History, 1895–1920', *Transactions Royal Historical Society*, 28 (1946), 7–19

Taylor, C. C. *The Making of the English Landscape: Dorset* (1970)

Thomas, N. 'The Thornborough Circles near Ripon, North Riding', *Yorkshire Archaeological Journal*, 38 (1955), 425–45

3 DOMESDAY BOOK: THE FIRST LAND UTILISATION SURVEY

by H. C. DARBY

As FAR as there ever is a new beginning in history, the coming of the Anglo-Saxons, in the fifth and sixth centuries was such a beginning. They were followed in the eighth and ninth centuries by Scandinavians – Danes in the east and Norse by way of the western seas. Both groups of invaders covered Roman Britain with their villages, and so began a new chapter in the evolution of the geography of England. No later migration was greatly to modify the Anglo-Scandinavian settlement; the Norman Conquest in 1066 was the work of a small power-group, and did not involve a mass movement of people in search of new homes. Twenty years after their coming the Normans instituted the inquiry that resulted in the Domesday Book. With hindsight, we can say that it came at a fortunate moment for us because it enables us to inspect the economic and social foundations of English geography after the great age of migration was over.

We speak of the Domesday Book, but it is really two volumes. The smaller volume covers Norfolk, Suffolk and Essex; the larger volume, in somewhat less detail, covers the rest of England with the exception of

33   The first ever survey of England's land resources was recorded in Domesday Book soon after the Norman Conquest. Domesday Book is in two volumes. The larger volume is shown open at part of the description of Cambridgeshire. The top half of the right hand column describes the holdings of the Count of Mortain (Terra Comitis Moritoniensis).

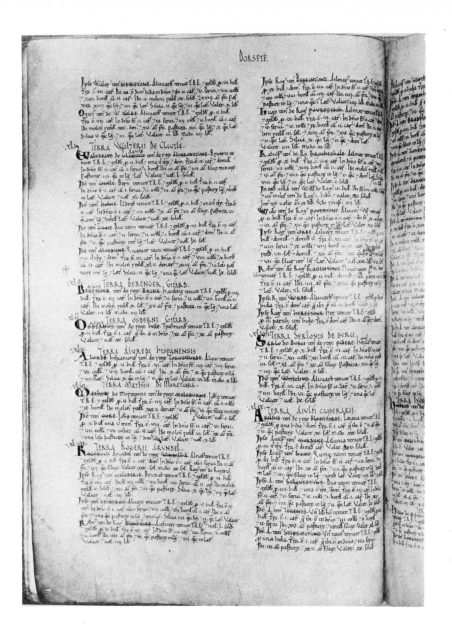

34 *Domesday Book, open at the entry for Powerstock in Dorset (right hand column, folio 82b).*

the four northern counties. The word 'Domesday' does not occur in the Book itself, and there are varying opinions about how it got this name. The Treasurer of England, writing in 1179, said: 'This book is called by the natives Domesday – that is, metaphorically speaking, the day of judgement'. So thorough was the inquiry that its result may well have seemed comparable to the Book by which one day all will be judged (*Revelations XX*, 12).

Domesday Book is far from being a straightforward document. The exact method of its making is the subject of controversy, and many of its entries bristle with difficulties of interpretation. Even so, it is probably the most remarkable statistical document in the history of Europe. Its information is arranged under the heading of each county. Within each county it is then set out under the names of the principal landholders, beginning with the king himself and going on to the great ecclesiastical lords, and then the lay lords. The holding of each lord in each village is described. If, say, three lords held land in a village, the three sets of information must be put together in order to obtain a picture of the village as a whole. The account of Powerstock, north-east of Bridport in Dorset, is fairly representative. It was entirely held by Roger Arundel – who had sublet it – and so is described in a single entry on folio 82b:

35 *At the village of Ingarsby in Leicestershire the two holdings in 1086 had thirty-one recorded inhabitants, which may imply a population of about 150. The village passed entirely into the possession of Leicester Abbey during the fourteenth and fifteenth centuries but was abandoned in 1469 when it was enclosed and converted into pasture. A series of banks and ditches is all that remains today.*

Hugh holds Powerstock of Roger. Ailmar held it in the time of King Edward, and it paid geld for 6 hides. There is land for 6 plough-teams. In demesne are 2½ plough-teams and 5 slaves, and 5 villeins and 9 bordars with 2½ plough-teams. There, 2 mills render 3s; and 13 acres of meadow; and 15 furlongs of pasture in length and 2 in breadth. Wood 11 furlongs long and 2½ furlongs broad. It was worth £4; now £6.

The variety of detail in such entries as this falls into two categories. In the first phase there are those items that recur in almost every entry: hides (or carucates in the Danish districts), meaning units of taxation; plough-lands; plough-teams; population; and annual values for 1066 and 1086, and sometimes for an intermediate date. The second group comprise such items as mills, meadow, pasture, woodland and also, where relevant, salt-pans, fisheries, vineyards, marsh and waste. Faced with this array of information, we must be selective in order to attempt a brief general account of England in 1086. The most revealing items are perhaps those relating to population, to arable, to waste, to woodland and also to towns.

DOMESDAY POPULATION
The details of Domesday population cover a whole series of categories ranging from freemen to slaves. Between these extremes come villeins, bordars, cottars

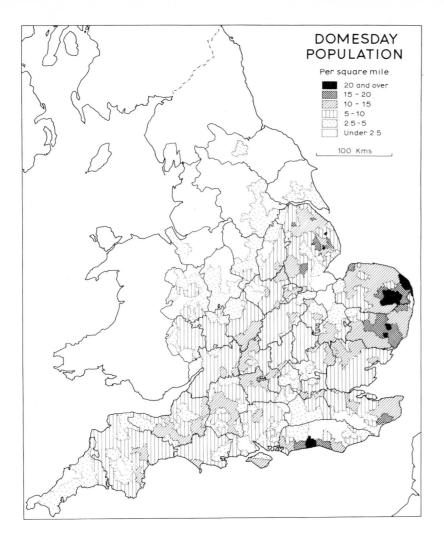

DOMESDAY POPULATION

Per square mile

- 20 and over
- 15 - 20
- 10 - 15
- 5 - 10
- 2·5 - 5
- Under 2·5

100 Kms

36 *Domesday Population.*

and many other groups. The total number of people entered amounts to about 250,000. This recorded population is usually taken to refer to heads of households, and, in order to obtain the actual population, we must multiply it by some factor according to our ideas of the size of a medieval family; the factor usually used is five. The total that results, however, is subject to many doubts. Thus the information about towns is very fragmentary, and there are a number of other possible omissions. Taking these doubts into consideration, it may be fair to say that the total population of England, excluding the four northern counties, amounted to between 1½ and 1¾ millions in 1086. Merely to be able to make such an estimate for such a remote date is in itself an indication of the value of Domesday Book as a source of information.

Whatever the factor used to convert recorded into

actual population, the value of the statistics for making comparisons between one district and another remains unaffected. East Anglia stands out as the most densely populated area often with over 15 people recorded per square mile, and sometimes with over 20; concentrations along the coastlands of Sussex and Kent are also notable. Generally speaking, the density of population decreases towards the west and north. Nowhere in the Midlands is a density of over 15 reached and northwards the figure falls to 5 and under. The variations in density of population reflected to a large extent the fertility of the land. Upland areas were inherently infertile, so were the light soils of the lowlands before the days of improved farming.

DOMESDAY ARABLE

Entry after entry states (a) the amount of land for

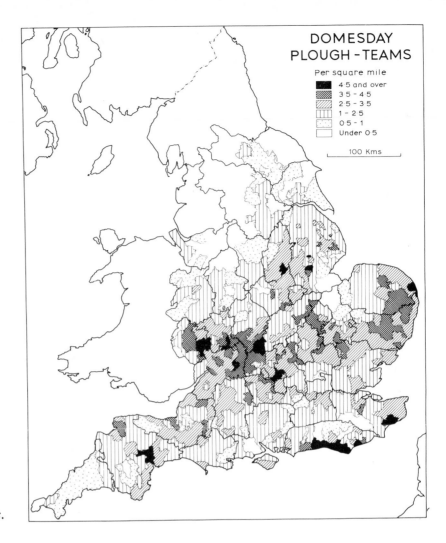

37   *Domesday Plough-teams.*

which there was teams (*terra carucis*): (b) the number of plough-teams (*carucae*) actually at work, both on the demesne and on the land of the peasants. The first statement sounds very straightforward, but its implications are far from clear and have provoked considerable discussion. The second statement also sounds straightforward and may well be so. It is reasonable to suppose that we are being given an idea of the land actually cultivated. Although the teams at work in the field may have varied in size on different soils, a comparison of parallel Domesday entries shows that eight oxen made a team just as twelve inches make a foot. It is true that this has been challenged, particularly for the south-western counties for which a variable Domesday team has been postulated, but the balance of evidence seems to be in favour of a standard eight-ox team.

On the map, variations in the distribution of plough-teams reflect, to a great extent, the fertility of the land. The areas with the most arable, those with, say, over $3\frac{1}{2}$ teams per square mile included the coastal plain of Sussex, the eastern part of East Anglia, and districts in the Midlands and elsewhere where, in the context of the time, soils were favourable – districts such as the 'red lands' of north Oxfordshire and the Vale of Evesham. Conversely, districts with less than a team per square mile included the Weald, the New Forest, the Dorset and Surrey heathlands, the Fenland and the Breckland. To these must be added much of the northern counties of Domesday England. Natural conditions do not explain all these low density areas; those of the north, in particular, were lacking in teams, as in population, because they had been deliberately devasted.

DOMESDAY WASTE

The term waste found in many Domesday entries seems to imply not the natural waste of mountain, heath and marsh, but land that had gone out of cultivation, mainly it seems as a result of deliberate devastation, but also perhaps because of some local vicissitude that is lost to us. To a large extent such deliberate wasting by armies and raiders was the reason for the low densities in the west and particularly in the north. Some of the wasted villages in Herefordshire, Shropshire and Cheshire were, we may suppose, the result of Welsh raiders. But many were due to the crushing of rebellion by the king's armies during the years 1068–70. Much of the waste of those years was still evident in 1086. The account of Cheshire is unusual in that we have details of waste not only for 1066, before the Conquest, and for 1086, the year of the inquiry, but also for the date when the existing owner received the estate, about 1070. Out of a total of 264 there were 52 villages waste or partly waste in 1066, presumably as a result of Welsh raiding; by about 1070 the figure had become 162; and by 1086 some 58 villages still lay waste. What we hear of in 1086 is a countryside on its way to recovery.

It was to the north that William took the most terrible revenge, and left the countryside in a condition in which it could give him no trouble again. The entry under the year 1069 in the Anglo-Saxon Chronicle is brief, and it merely says of Yorkshire that the king 'laid waste all the shire'. Yorkshire suffered most, but we are told in one early account that the harrying also extended over Derbyshire, Cheshire, Shropshire and Staffordshire, nor did Nottinghamshire escape. The general statements of the chronicles are borne out vividly when the Domesday entries are plotted on a map. Seventeen years or so had not been enough to obliterate the effects of the harrying. Entry after entry for these northern villages reads *Wasta est*. As well as villages specifically described as waste, there were others without population, and most of these, too, we must suppose were the result of William's campaigns. The emptiness of much of the population map then becomes very understandable.

DOMESDAY WOODLAND

One of the outstanding facts about the landscape of eleventh-century England was its wooded aspect. The Anglo-Saxons and Scandinavians, it is true, had pierced the woodland and broken it everywhere with

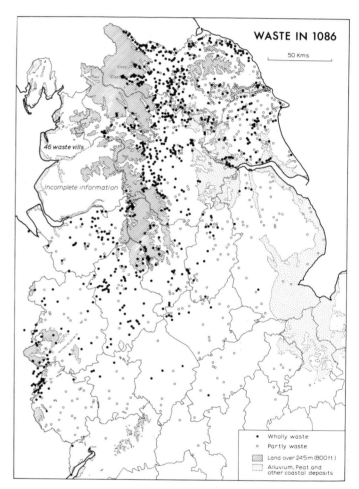

38   *Waste in 1086.*

their 'dens' and 'leys' and 'skogrs' as seen in such place-names as Somerden in Kent, Henley in Oxfordshire, and Litherskew in the North Riding. Even so, almost every page of Domesday Book shows that a great deal still remained. One of the questions put by the Domesday commissioners was 'How much wood?'. Broadly speaking, the answers fell into one of five categories. Sometimes, they said that there was enough wood to support a given number of swine, for the swine fed upon acorns and beechmast. A variant of this was a statement not of total swine but of the number returned as rent from a wood. A third type of answer gave the length and breadth of a wood in terms of leagues, furlongs and perches, but whether the information referred to mean diameters or to extreme diameters or to some other notion, we cannot say. A fourth type of entry stated the size of the wood in terms of acres, but we do not know what area was implied by such an 'acre'. The fifth category of answers was a miscellaneous one that included a number of variants and idiosyncrasies occasionally encountered in the text. Normally, each county was characterised by one main type of entry with a few other entries of a different style.

The difficulty presented by this array of information can be simply stated. It is impossible satisfactorily to equate swine, acres and linear dimensions and so reduce them to a common denominator. Any map of Domesday woodland covering a number of counties must therefore suffer from this restriction, and we cannot be sure that the visual impression as between one set of symbols and another is correct. There are other difficulties such as the fact that some woods were unrecorded. Despite these limitations, much can be gained from such a map. With all its problems, it leaves us in no doubt about the wooded aspect of large tracts of England in 1086. One surprising feature on the map is the absence of wood from the Weald. This arises from the fact that much of the wood of the Weald was entered under the names of surrounding

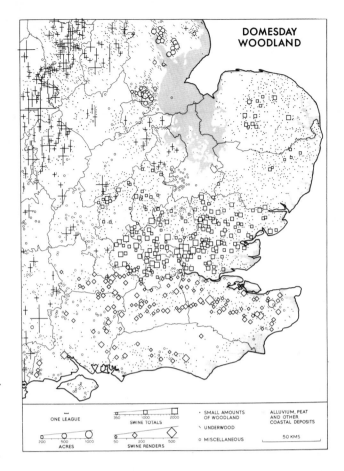

40 The feeding of swine on acorns or beechmast was a feature of the Domesday woodlands. Illustrations from an eleventh-century British Museum manuscript depict conditions more or less contemporary with the making of the Domesday inquest.

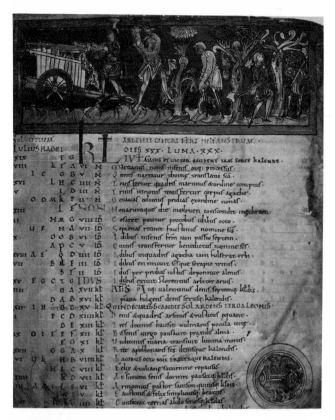

41 *Clearing of woodland is one of the great themes in the history of the English countryside. Wood was being cut and loaded into a rough cart with sides made of planks. A yoke of animals stands to draw the cart. From an eleventh-century manuscript in the British Museum.*

42 *Wallingford, by the Thames in Berkshire, was a Domesday borough. In 1066 the king held 276 of the 500 holdings, but by 1086 eight of them had been destroyed to make room for a castle. Its grass-covered mound can be seen to the north-east of the modern town.*

villages. It must therefore be 'spread out' so to speak, by eye. But we may well suspect the existence of unrecorded wood.

Domesday Book tells us practically nothing about the process of clearing. The fuller information of the Little Domesday Book for Norfolk, Suffolk, and Essex enables us to know that wood was being cut down in at least 109 villages out of 1811. The circumstantial evidence about Wealden 'denes' in swine pastures in the folios for Kent also indicate clearing; so do the references to cartloads of wood that fed the Droitwich salt industry in Worcestershire. Iron works must have consumed more wood but we are told nothing of this. It is certain that clearings for cultivation were already known as 'assarts', a word derived from the French *essarter*, meaning to grub up or clear land of bushes and trees. Hereford is the only county for which the Domesday entries mention them, but there is every reason to believe that what was happening in Herefordshire was also happening in other counties.

DOMESDAY TOWNS
Whatever the difficulties of interpretation, the Domesday information for rural England is very systematically presented and is remarkable for the economic and geographical evidence it provides. When we turn from the countryside to the towns, all is different. The information is so incomplete and so unsystematic that it is often impossible to form any clear idea of the size of a town or of the economic and other activities that sustained it. Altogether some 112 places seem to have been boroughs. By far the largest must have been London. The customs of the port of London about the year 1000 show active trade with the Channel ports of the continent. Later in Edward the Confessor's reign (1042–66) it had over 20 moneyers who minted coins; York came next with over 10; and Lincoln and Winchester had at least 9 each. It is therefore particularly unfortunate that Domesday Book contains no account of London; the 126th folio, where it should have come, is blank, and all is contained in a few incidental references.

There are likewise only incidental references to Winchester, the city to which the results of the inquiry were brought, and in which Domesday Book was at first kept. Of the other boroughs, we may conjecture, from the fragmentary evidence, that the following had at least 4000 inhabitants each: York, Lincoln, Norwich, and probably also Thetford in Norfolk. As for the rest, they were a varied lot. Some were substantial, in the context of the time, with well over 2000 inhabitants, for example Canterbury, Bury St Edmunds, Stamford and Wallingford; some were very small and poor such as the south-western boroughs of Bodmin, Frome and Milverton. The Anglo-Saxon word borough or 'burgh' signified a fortified centre, and the test of burghal status was neither size nor general prosperity.

The immediate effect of the Norman Conquest on many boroughs was the destruction of houses for the building of castles, like those at Cambridge, Gloucester, Shrewsbury, Wallingford and York. We also hear of houses destroyed by fire at Exeter, Norwich and Lincoln; and at other boroughs there were wasted or unoccupied houses for which no reason is given. Out of 112 Domesday boroughs, waste, due to one cause or another, is recorded for as many as 33. But as well as these temporary set-backs, there were long-term tendencies of a different character at work.

Long before the coming of the Normans, a force had begun to operate which was ultimately to give the English borough its most lasting characteristic – that of a trading centre. Many Domesday entries reveal the continued expansion of commerce. One indication is the establishment of new boroughs alongside the old at Norwich, Northampton and Nottingham; groups of French burgesses had settled at Hereford, Shrewsbury, Southampton and Wallingford. Around the castle at Tutbury in Staffordshire, there were forty-two men who devoted themselves entirely to trade. Such hints as these point forward to the new age that the Norman Conquest had inaugurated.

FURTHER READING
Darby, H. C. *The Domesday Geography of Eastern England* (Cambridge, 3rd ed, 1971)

Darby, H. C. and Terrett, I. B. (eds) *The Domesday Geography of Midland England* (Cambridge, 2nd ed, 1971)

Darby, H. C. and Campbell, Eila M. J. (eds) *The Domesday Geography of South-East England* (Cambridge, 1962)

Darby, H. C. and Maxwell, I. S. (eds) *The Domesday Geography of Northern England* (Cambridge, 1962)

Darby, H. C. and Welldon Finn, R. (eds) *The Domesday Geography of South-West England* (Cambridge, 1967)

Welldon Finn, R. *An Introduction to Domesday Book* (1963)

4 PLANNED VILLAGES FROM MEDIEVAL ENGLAND

by BRIAN ROBERTS

ENGLAND is a land of villages. It has been estimated that there are 13,000 in the country, and most of us have an idealised picture of them – an 'ivy-mantled tower' of a church, overlooking a cricket-ground village green, surrounded by comfortably conforming cottages built at least two centuries ago. In this rural scene haywain and thatch have more place than motor-cars and concrete, the tractor is seen as a concession to necessity, and change is regarded as positively harmful. However, our 'rude forefathers' held no such impractical attitudes and the appearance of the village is the product of many centuries of change, the product of a multitude of adjustments reflecting changing relationships between man and land, and man and man.

The evidence of Domesday Book points to nearly one thousand years of continuous existence for many settlements, and by means of Anglo-Saxon land charters or archaeology it is often possible to add two, three or even five centuries to this life span. Time has given villages a diversity and a fortuitousness; time has mellowed church, dwellings, lanes and fields, welding them into one coherent personality, whether in the folds of the good red lands of Devon and Somerset, the open vales of the Midlands, or the harsher dales of the North. Yet there is no simple chronological sequence of village forms, no inevitable progression of village plans from simple to complex, from irregular to regular; rather are we dealing with several parallel and interlocking developments.

The forces which have created our villages involve factors as diverse as the fortunes of war, the presence or absence of lordly power, the availability or absence of good arable land or extensive grazings, and the farming skills and inheritance practices of the inhabitants, together with their pride in cornfields or in cattle. Such factors combine to give to each village a unique history and plan. The villages are concentrated within the lowlands of Britain and, through the medium of building materials, they reflect the character of the underlying geology – the limestone villages of the Cotswolds, the timber and brick of the Midlands, and the cob and thatch of Devon which are in their present forms largely the product of the centuries after 1600.

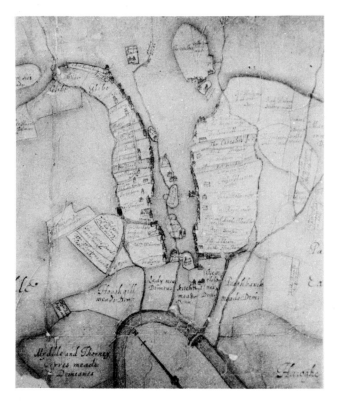

43 Early maps often provide the first documentary evidence of village plans. In the village of Eggleston, Teesdale, in 1612 the green was merely an extension of the open fell. Some encroachment had already occurred. Today the southern half of the village lies within the extended grounds of the Hall.

46

LINEAR, GREEN AND AGGLOMERATED VILLAGES

There are three basic types of village plan, found widely scattered throughout the country. The most obvious plan-type is the street village, where the farms and cottages have responded to a physical or cultural control, such as a levee or a road, and are strung out in a line. A second category is best described as a green village, a plan-type in which a large open space, usually grassy, is dominant. In some, the homesteads are marshalled in an orderly way around the edges of the open space, while in others they form a disorded tangle, with the majority actually sitting on the green. These settlements are widely scattered throughout the Lowland Zone of Britain. The third category of village, which may be described as agglomerated, comprises an apparently formless tangle of lanes, house plots or tofts, and homesteads, often with no clear nucleus, possibly resulting from the accretion of later dwellings to a smaller settlement. Many villages, of course, are composite, and their structural complexity may reflect growth phases. In all cases there is still too little known of the subtle relationships between village form and site. The presence of the medieval church within the village framework frequently hints that the streets, lanes and toft-boundaries of the existing plan antedate the present buildings, but by how long? Detailed work being undertaken in County Durham to examine such problems may help to reveal how much the various village forms of today owe to the past.

The northern marcher county of Durham was excluded from Domesday Book and our first clear

44   The large rectangular green of Heighington. Situated between the Norman church and an old conduit-head, the former school building is now used as a village hall.

45   The render of cornage, a form of pasture rent levied on horned cattle, possibly of Celtic origin, has been used to identify the oldest generation of villages in Durham. Colonisation of the Pennine foothills during the period after 1200 mainly took the form of single farm units. Occasionally small clusters of farms were established.

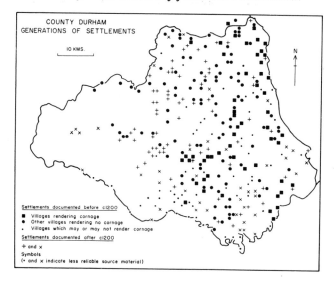

picture of the county is provided by the Boldon Book, the great survey of Bishop Hugh de Pudsey compiled in 1183. By this date villages were concentrated on the better lands of the south and east of the county, but settlement was actively pushing westwards into the wooded, deer-haunted spurs of the Pennines. In Durham, as elsewhere, the pace of village foundation was slowing sharply by 1200, and subsequent development took the form of the foundation of single farms or at the most hamlets. Durham is remarkable for its high proportion of villages arranged around a tidy, rectangular green, and it is tempting to view these as defensive arrangements within a zone constantly exposed to the danger of Scottish raids. This may well have been a factor in deciding the siting and layout of some Durham villages, but village plans of this type are too widespread outside the county for this explanation of their function to be adopted universally.

TWO-ROW SETTLEMENTS

In the Durham green villages, the basic form is a two-row settlement, that is, a village made up of two rows of homesteads backed by their tofts, with the houses facing each other across an open space. This space may comprise no more than a street, but is more usually a roughly rectangular open green where homesteads fronting directly upon it have the right to graze commonable beasts. In some cases the building line

has been 'closed', where the cottages and farms form a continuous frontage; in others it is 'open', and considerable spaces may exist between the buildings. These patterns broadly reflect differing administrative policies on the part of the two former major landowners within the county of Durham, the bishop and the Cathedral Priory.

The evolution of village plans is most easily studied through maps, and the Durham two-row villages can be securely documented in this way in the eighteenth century, or more rarely in the seventeenth century. Except in the few cases where a cataclysmic change has occurred, as a result of mining activity for example, the earlier village only differs from that of the present in minor details, such as buildings which have been added to or completely reconstructed. The problem for the historical geographer is to project these plans back into the period before the first maps, and in this respect it is important that many Durham villages possess a definite orientation, running either east-west or north-south. Byers Green, for example, has a unique entry in an extensive survey of the Bishopric lands compiled on the order of Bishop Hatfield and completed in about 1381. The homesteads of this village are explicitly described

46 Wheldrake in Yorkshire, a two-row village, possessing a regular plan which has tentatively been traced back to the eleventh century.

as lying on the west side and the east side, making it very probable that the medieval form is closely reflected in the present plan. In the records of the Cathedral Priory there are references to numerous villages using the descriptive terms *Eastrawe* and *Westrawe* or *Northrawe* and *Southrawe*, and in every known case these correspond to the present orientation of the village. This correspondence is too consistent to be coincidental. Although these references occur in documents of the early fifteenth century, they clearly relate to a situation prevailing during the thirteenth century, and indeed the terminology found in the account of one schedule of rents can be associated with the late twelfth and early thirteenth centuries. This evidence allows us to conclude that at least some of the two-row villages originated before 1200. Some, but not all, for in 1183 Byers Green was merely an assart, or forest clearing, and the village must therefore be of late twelfth- or early thirteenth-century foundation.

It is noticeable that nearly all the villages which may be documented in this way are very regular in form, with clear-cut, straight or gently curving building lines and a regular pattern of tofts. There is another group of two-row villages in which the building lines are less regular, hence the street or green varies very much in width, and usually straggles out of one or both ends of

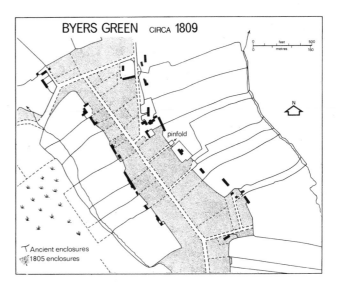

47 *The green at Byers Green was enclosed in 1805 and subsequently filled in with terraced rows. Modern redevelopment is exhuming the former green.*

48 *Staindrop, a large village arranged around a green, has its houses grouped tightly together with a closed building line. By the tenth century, it was already the focus for a large estate, and in 1378 acquired market rights.*

the village in the form of a driftway or cattle track leading out to the rough grazings. In this form we perhaps see a clue to the origin of the green, an area of common pasture, safely enclosed by homesteads and having many uses for a cattle-proud northern peasantry.

A particularly distinctive feature of these irregular two-row villages is their asymetrical form with the tofts on one side being highly attenuated. Such long-tofts are clearly former infield strips, representing the intensively tilled lands which once formed the only permanently cultivated field of the village. Wherever these features occur the settlement in 1183 tends to be but poorly developed. It may be that the village was newly founded and indeed this form is commonest in the late-colonised western portions of the county. Significantly, Byers Green shows traces of such tofts on the east side. Moreover, closely allied to this form is a group of one-row settlements, and thus, although there is no definite evidence, it is reasonable to postulate a sequence of development, the one-row form becoming a two-row village with the addition of further homesteads as population increased. One-row survivals are scattered throughout the county.

MULTIPLE-ROW SETTLEMENTS

A further distinctive category of Durham villages may be termed multiple-row. This may comprise either a very large two-row form, with some irregularities in layout as at Staindrop, sometimes possessing a headrow as documented in the fifteenth century at West Auckland, or a village arranged around what Professor Thorpe has termed a broad green, an open space which is polygonal in form rather than elongated. At Aycliffe, Billingham and Wolviston this type can be documented in the early thirteenth century. At Wolviston certain

49 The 'townish' village of West Auckland, Co Durham. The green extends over nearly five hectares, far beyond the more recent encroachments shown in the centre of the photograph.

lanes or *kevyles* radiating from the core were already built-up at that time. Such developed villages undoubtedly owe their size and complexity to the fact that they possessed an enhanced function, either acting as service centres for the surrounding estates and a focus for the Halmote – the hall-*moot*, or court, held in the Bishop's hall – or in some cases actually possessing market rights.

From our first clear pictures of the Durham vills, derived from Boldon Book, it is noticeable that many have a regular tenemental structure – all of the farms are the same size and occupied by farmers of approximately the same status. Thus Boldon itself had twenty-two bondmen or servile tenants, each with a farm two bovates in extent, while Middridge possessed fifteen bondmen also having two bovates each. A bovate, or oxgang, was a measure of land between twelve and sixteen acres, and farms assessed in this way almost certainly originated before the end of the twelfth century, if not very much earlier. It was a fiscal tenement or taxable farm unit which was used in the Middle Ages throughout the whole of northern England. In the south the virgate, or yardland, of about thirty acres served the same purpose. Both measures derive from the centuries before the Norman conquest. Eight bovates were generally considered to make one carucate, roughly the amount of land worked by a team of eight oxen throughout one year, and each bovate was supposed to contribute one ox to such a team – an eminently practical way of assessing land in a peasant society.

Carlton provides an excellent example of the regularity concealed within some of the village entries in Boldon Book. In this vill twenty-three farmers held forty-six bovates – two bovates per farm; one Gerobod

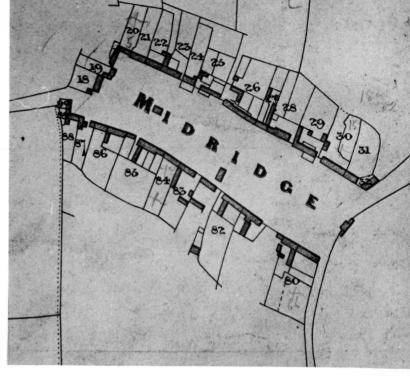

50 *The tithe map, about 1840, of the regular two-row village of Middridge shows a characteristically straight building line, with the houses backed by short tofts.*

held another four bovates; a further three persons, including a miller, held six bovates between them; and William son of Orm held one carucate. This totalled fifty-six bovates or seven carucates, plus William's carucate, making a grand total of eight carucates. This arrangement clearly has an artificial regularity and although Boldon Book gives us no picture of village plans, it is logical to seek a relationship between these regular fiscal and tenemental arrangements and the regular village plans. The holdings represented by the eight carucates of 1183 can be traced in 1381 and did indeed survive until the early seventeenth century. Although direct proof is not available, there are good

51 *Middridge. Photographed today, it shows suprisingly little change from the days of the tithe map, although the south row has been opened up and the green has been further appropriated. The orientation of the village can be seen: south or sun-side tofts get the sunlight, while the north or shadow-side house-plots lie in the shadow of the buildings.*

51

52 *Carlton, a regular two-row village. The contrast with Cowpen Bewley, which has the same basic plan, reflects the differing administrative policies pursued by the two former landowners.*

53 *Cowpen Bewley, a regular two-row village.*

grounds for arguing that the basic plan of Carlton, based upon two rows flanking a green, was already present by 1183. Middridge affords a further example of such continuity. In the strips and furlongs of the townfields of Middridge in 1183, fifteen bondmen held thirty bovates and various officials held a further seven bovates, each bovate being fifteen acres. In 1638 some thirty-seven bovates of townfield land were enclosed at Middridge, each bovate being fifteen acres. The bond tenements seem, therefore, to have preserved their essential identity for nearly 500 years without further additions, no doubt because the tenants of this vill were very much under the control of the Bishops' officers, and largely engaged in working their lord's great demesne farm at Middridge Grange. Indeed, within this demesne to this day is a group of fields known as 'Old Towns Middridge' which were docu-

mented as early as the fifteenth century. There is a strong presumption in this case that the present village represents the re-founding of one, or perhaps more, earlier vills and that this had already occurred by 1183.

Such a circumstance would have offered an opportunity to create a new, more regular, form; and in seeking an explanation for such a drastic step, it is worth recalling Symeon of Durham's statement concerning northern England following the harrying by the Norman armies between 1068–70: 'there was no village inhabited between York and Durham'. This is perhaps an overstatement, but Domesday Book bears ample witness to the extent of wasting in Yorkshire. This, however, is not the whole story and the links between village plans and the fiscal and tenemental arrangements are likely to have been exceedingly complex.

54 Cockfield. The irregular building lines and long tofts are distinguishing features of twelfth- and thirteenth-century colonisation in the Pennine foothills.

VILLAGES REGULATED BY SUN-DIVISION

Work is currently being done in Sweden and Denmark to trace the origin of certain very regular field systems, including an arrangement known as *solskifte* or sun-division. The characteristic elements of sun-division were as follows: the village was laid out and the toft widths were made proportional to the assessment figures of the farm holdings attached to each toft; in English terms a one bovate farm would rate a toft x rods wide along the street, a two bovate farm a toft $2x$ rods wide and so on, the precise length of x varying from village to village. The tofts were often placed in two rows, facing each other across a street or green, and were considered to be arranged in a clockwise direction around the village. This is significant because in the northern hemisphere the course of the sun through the sky is clockwise, and a common belief in folklore is that the lucky way to make a circular motion is clockwise – hence sun-division. The order of the tofts around the village was followed for the strips in the arable fields, so that everywhere a man's strips lay between those of his neighbours in the village. According to the orientation of the furlong, the sequence of strips was counted out with reference to the apparent course of the sun across the sky, so that the holdings in the first part of each furlong were said to lie 'next to the sun' and holdings lying in the northern and western part of each furlong were considered to lie 'towards the shadow'. Furthermore, these field strips were, ideally, measured with the same land-rod as was used to lay out the village tofts. The village was thus *regulated*, although the concept was of course adapted to local circumstances.

Dr S. Göransson has demonstrated convincingly that

55   *The aerial view of Iveston shows a similar pattern of development to Cockfield.*

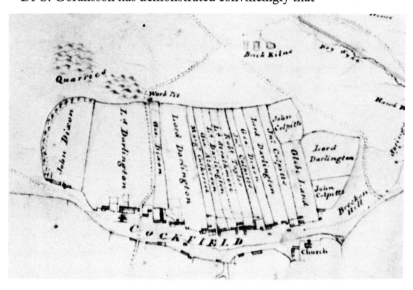

56   *The nineteenth-century estate map of Cockfield. Note the similarity to the aerial view of Iveston.*

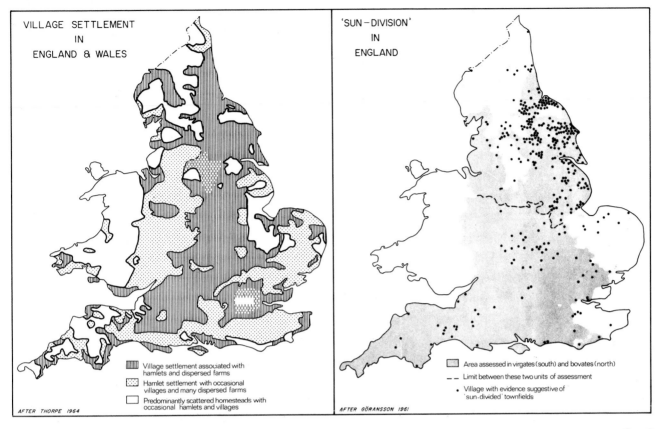

VILLAGE SETTLEMENT
IN
ENGLAND & WALES

▦ Village settlement associated with
hamlets and dispersed farms

░ Hamlet settlement with occasional
villages and many dispersed farms

☐ Predominantly scattered homesteads with
occasional hamlets and villages

AFTER THORPE 1964

'SUN–DIVISION'
IN
ENGLAND

▨ Area assessed in virgates (south) and bovates (north)

– – Limit between these two units of assessment

• Village with evidence suggestive of
'sun-divided' townfields

AFTER GÖRANSSON 1951

57 & 58

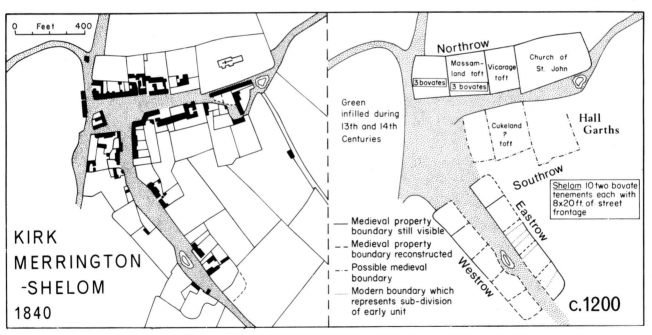

0 Feet 400

KIRK
MERRINGTON
-SHELOM
1840

Green
infilled during
13th and 14th
Centuries

—— Medieval property
boundary still visible

– – Medieval property
boundary reconstructed

–·– Possible medieval
boundary

······ Modern boundary which
represents sub-division
of early unit

Northrow

Massam-
land toft Vicarage
toft Church of
St. John

3 bovates 3 bovates

Cukeland
? toft Hall
Garths

Southrow

Shelom 10 two bovate
tenements each with
8x20 ft. of street
frontage

Eastrow

Westrow

c.1200

*59 Kirk Merrington – Shelom. A reconstruction of the
double village in about 1200 is shown beside a plan taken
from the tithe map of about 1836. Kirk Merrington itself
is orientated east to west; the second nucleus, Shelom,
is orientated approximately north to south.*

55

terms indicative of sun-division are found in medieval sources from all over England, and most frequently from the north-east. He is of the opinion that sun-division was appearing in Scandinavia by the eleventh century and that the arrangement originated in England, being transmitted at a time of close cultural contact between the two areas. Its origin lies in the obscure organisational developments of the Dark Ages.

Sun-division was present in County Durham. At Hulam we read of a grant of twelve acres in twelve furlongs, that is to say 'one acre lying towards the sun in each furlong, with a toft eight rods in breadth and seven and a half rods in length'. The plan of this village, however, tells us little, for desertion has occured, and the latest phase of occupation involved at most three farms, although those do in fact overlie earlier, fainter patterns.

At Kirk Merrington, where a thirteenth-century charter tells of a bovate 'lying towards the sun', it has proved possible to use a very detailed early thirteenth-century rent-schedule to reconstruct the plan in about 1200. This settlement was formerly a double village, with tofts laid out in the proportion of four twenty-foot rods of frontage for each bovate of farmland. Kirk Merrington, orientated east to west along the crest of the ridge on which stands the church of St John, comprised a hallgarth or demesne farm and a vicarage, together with three further major freehold tofts rated at three bovates each. Nearby *Shelom* was a village of eight servile farms and two free farms, each rated at two bovates, making a total of twenty bovates. This second nucleus, the name probably meaning 'at the huts', lay at right-angles to Kirk Merrington, running approximately north to south, and occupied a slight hollow in

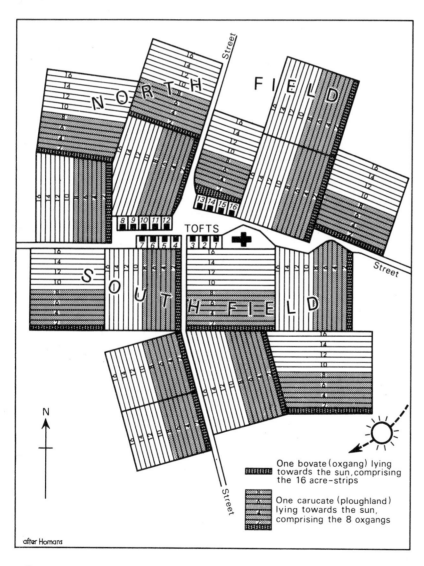

60 *An idealised layout of a sun-divided village: in practice, the arrangement of houses, tofts and fields would have been adapted to suit local circumstances.*

56

61 *Kirk Merrington. The orientation is revealed by sunlight. The original plan of the north row is preserved amid the properties on the right.*

62 *Shelom. Terraced housing retains the fossil building lines. In the foreground grass covers the former pond. The steep bank is named Bakehouse Hill and must record the site of a communal bakehouse.*

the dip-slope of the escarpment. The westernmost toft of the north row of Kirk Merrington is short of the correct width for a toft linked to a three-bovate farm. This deficiency is explained by the fact that if this toft had been of full width it would have encroached on the ancient trackway up the escarpment. It has not proved possible to identify the early boundaries along the south row of Kirk Merrington, and the plan of *Shelom* is undoubtedly much reconstructed, but there is sound documentary evidence for such proportionate divisions of tofts and farmlands. Kirk Merrington-*Shelom* was a regulated vill.

It appears probable that only archaeology can penetrate the darkness before the late twelfth century. Nevertheless, the study of village plans can produce useful results. In Yorkshire, Dr June Sheppard has convincingly traced the two-row village of Wheldrake back to the twelfth, if not to the eleventh century. The deserted village of Wharram Percy, at present being subjected to long-term excavation, reminds us of the compositeness of village plans. Recent work in this settlement has revealed fifteenth-century toft boundaries overlying earlier houses, a warning that caution must be used when assuming the persistence of property boundaries. Nevertheless, in villages, as in towns, there are circumstances which do preserve ancient divisions.

This work, which raises questions concerning village plans from Durham to Cornwall and from Cumberland to Kent, cannot yet be placed within a national context. How widespread are the indications of such deliberate ordering and careful delimitation? What relationship do planned forms have to other plan-types, and indeed at what point of disorder can one justifiably cease to apply the word 'planned'? In these regular plan-types we are seeing evidence for exceedingly formalised relationships, and the answers to the questions raised will only appear when the plans found between the Tyne and the Tees can be compared with studies of other regions. The need for these is pressing, for throughout the village lands of England the flight from the cities and the taking over of rural landscapes by townsfolk is destroying age-old patterns which are, at best, only partially recorded on maps. Former open building lines are being infilled and wholesale redevelopment is taking place. It may eventually be possible to assess the way in which variations in terrain and economy, cultural context and manorial control, or the unique accidents of history have affected village plans. However, at the moment, with Maitland we can only look forward to the time when 'instead of a few

photographed village maps, there will be many' and 'the history of land measures and field systems will have been elaborated'.

FURTHER READING

Allerston, P. 'English Village Development', *Transactions of the Institute of British Geographers*, 51 (1970), 95–109

Baker, A. R. H. 'The Geography of Rural Settlements', *Trends in Geography*, ed R. U. Cooke and J. H. Johnson (1969), 123–132

Beresford, M. W. and St Joseph, J. K. S. *Medieval England: An Aerial Survey* (1958)

Chisholm, M. *Rural Settlement and Land Use* (1964)

Darby, H. C. 'The Economic Geography of England, AD 1000–1250', *Historical Geography of England Before 1800* ed Darby, H. C. (reprint, 1951), 165–229

Göransson, S. 'Field and Village on the Island of Oland: A Study of the Genetic Compound of an East Swedish Rural Landscape', *Geografiska Annaler*, vol 40 (1958), 101–158

Göransson, S. 'Regular Open-field Pattern in England and Scandinavian Solskifte', *Geografiska Annaler*, vol 43 (1961), 80–104

Homans, G. C. *English Villagers of the Thirteenth Century* (1960), 83–106

Maitland, F. W. *Domesday Book and Beyond* (reprint 1960), especially Essay III, Chapter 1

Roberts, B. K. 'Rural Settlement' in Dewdney, J. C. (ed) *Durham County and City with Teeside*, British Association for the Advancement of Science (Durham, 1970), 233–250

Roberts, B. K. 'The Study of Village Plans', *The Local Historian*, 9, no 15 (1971), 233–241

Sharp, T. *The Anatomy of the Village* (1946)

Sheppard, J. A. 'Pre-Enclosure Field and Settlement Patterns in an English Township', *Geografiska Annaler*, 48 (1966), 59–77

Smith, C. T. *An Historical Geography of Western Europe before 1800* (1957), especially Chapters 4 and 5

Thorpe, H. 'The Green Villages of County Durham', *Transactions of the Institute of British Geographers*, vol 15 (1951), 150–180

Thorpe, H. 'Rural Settlement', *The British Isles*, ed Wreford Watson J. and Sissons, J. B. (1964), 358–379

Yates, E. M. 'A Study of Settlement Patterns' *Field Studies*, 1, no 3 (1961), 65–84

5 FIELD SYSTEMS IN MEDIEVAL ENGLAND

by ALAN R. H. BAKER

HISTORICAL geographers and economic historians alike have for generations been grappling with the problem of the origins and workings of the various agricultural systems in medieval England and the last few years have witnessed the re-opening of the debate about the form, function and formation of medieval field patterns and agrarian systems. Few visible remnants of medieval common-field farming survive in England today. Farming in unenclosed strips is still to be seen in a few localities such as Braunton in Devon and Laxton in Nottinghamshire, but the mere fact that open-field farming has survived in these areas suggests that they should be regarded as curious anomalies, as atypical cultural relicts rather than as master keys to the darker recesses of English medieval agriculture. Old maps and documents are a surer guide to the past than is the present landscape. Nonetheless, the Laxtons of England – and more especially those of the continent of Europe – arouse our curiosity, awaken our desire to know how these open fields were born, lived and, in most English cases, died.

TWO ORTHODOX MODELS

More than fifty years ago, H. L. Gray in his book *English Field Systems* (1915) provided a well-documented analysis of each of the systems which he identified in different parts of the country. Later C. S. and C. S. Orwin in their book *The Open Fields* (1938) produced a detailed study of the operation of the open-field system. These two books have provided

63 a, b and c   The delicate artistry of illuminated manuscripts often yields contemporary evidence of medieval life. The Luttrell Psalter from the mid-fourteenth century has several farming scenes: the harrow, which seems to have altered little since then, is followed by a boy who scares away birds with a sling and stones; uprooting thistles was a tiresome task, tackled from a respectful distance; harvesting was the busiest time of the year – sheaves were kept small to ease drying and handling.

the orthodox models of English medieval field systems which have, until recently, been widely accepted. Briefly, the open-field system was a method of co-operative farming under which the arable land of a village was divided into two or three fields, with the holdings of individual farmers consisting of unenclosed parcels scattered, more or less equally, throughout them. Under the two-field system, one field was under crop and the other lay fallow each year; under the three-field system, two of the fields were cropped and the third lay fallow in rotation. All villagers with land in the common fields had grazing rights over the fallow, pasturing rights over the commons, and a share in the available meadow land. With this arrangement a considerable degree of communal control of cultivation and pasturing was clearly necessary.

This was the theoretical arrangement. In practice, there were important deviations from the norm. The principal result of H. L. Gray's work, in fact, was a demonstration of the regional variety of medieval field arrangements. Claiming that the two- and three-field system was most widespread and characteristic in central England (he termed it the Midland System), Gray distinguished separate systems in East Anglia, the Lower Thames Basin and Kent, as well as the Celtic system in the west. These differences Gray ascribed primarily to the settlement of the areas by different peoples. He regarded the open-field system as a method of husbandry imported to England from the continent by Anglo-Saxons. The evolution of this system in Germany, however, is now considered to have been a prolonged process. The earliest evidence of a mature common-field system dates from the thirteenth century and many common fields came into existence in the sixteenth century and later. It is now argued by many German scholars that the first complete common-field system in Germany developed during a period of rising population, sometime between the tenth and thirteenth centuries. It can therefore no longer be claimed that in the fifth and sixth centuries Anglo-Saxons brought with them to England a ready-made and matured two- or three-field system.

Having labelled the Midland system Anglo-Saxon, Gray called the field systems of the west Celtic, and the Kentish system Roman. The East Anglian system he thought similar in origin to the Kentish but modified by the Danes and, having exhausted the supply of invading races who could be held responsible for the enigmatic open fields of the Lower Thames Basin, he

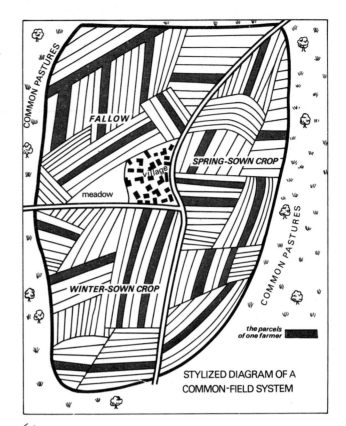

STYLIZED DIAGRAM OF A COMMON-FIELD SYSTEM

the parcels of one farmer

64
65

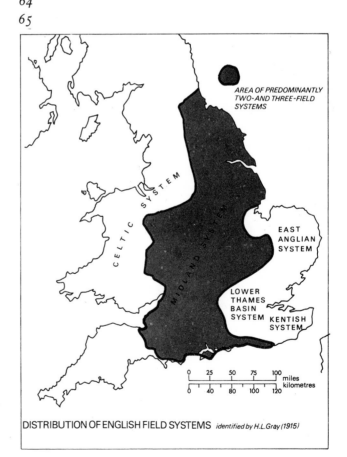

DISTRIBUTION OF ENGLISH FIELD SYSTEMS *identified by H.L.Gray (1915)*

66 *A map drawn in 1593 of part of an estate held by All Souls College, Oxford, in the parish of Weston Pinkney, Nottinghamshire, shows the village and its adjacent furlongs with their constituent narrow parcels of land.*

67 *Weston Pinkney. An aerial photograph of approximately the same area as on the All Souls map shows that the alignment of many parcels has been preserved in fossilised ridge-and-furrow.*

concluded that the system there was a hybrid of the Midland and Kentish systems. Gray's ethnic explanations of the origins of regional differences in field systems have never been widely accepted, although his elucidation of the workings of these regional systems has stood up well in the light of later research.

Gray's work was based on a careful examination of documents for places widely distributed throughout the British Isles. The second orthodox model, on the other hand, was established by C. S. and C. S. Orwin from a study of a single township: Laxton in Nottinghamshire. On this parochial study they erected a theoretical edifice of presumed universal significance. The Orwins thought themselves into the situation of those first farmers faced with the problem of clearing wood and scrub for cultivation of crops and grazing of livestock. The open-field system, they suggested, was a sensible method of insuring against hunger and famine, a product of the practical co-operation of pioneer peasant farmers. Parcels were long because no ploughman wanted to turn his plough more often than necessary, drawn as it was by a slow and cumbrous team of oxen; each parcel was narrow because the team could plough no more in a day's work; the animals, men and equipment needed to make a viable plough team were beyond the resources of individual peasants and so families had to join together; and having co-operated in this way, they naturally apportioned the units of ploughed land equally among themselves. A day's work of the plough was allotted to each contributor to the team and in this way each peasant received a share of good and bad lands, with his parcels scattered throughout the fields of the village.

In the first edition of their book, the Orwins included a map showing what they considered to be the distribution of the open-field system in England. There was not much evidence for it in Cheshire, Lancashire,

68 At Laxton in Nottinghamshire, some land is still preserved in open fields, whereby a man's holdings were scattered in unenclosed strips throughout the arable land of his village. The land closest to the village has numerous small enclosures but beyond that lie relicts of the once more extensive common fields.

69 *Laxton. Each year the boundaries of the common grass and arable are inspected and then freshly marked out by members of the Manor Court, which can also fine any transgressors of the system.*

Cumberland, Westmorland, Northumberland, the North Riding of Yorkshire, the fens of East Anglia, Kent, Devon or Cornwall, but in all other English counties the evidence was thought to be abundant. Further research led the Orwins subsequently to believe that no English county was without some examples of common fields. In consequence, no distribution map was included in the second edition of their book, published in 1954.

ONE UNORTHODOX MODEL

These old-established orthodoxies have constantly been examined in detail in particular places and at particular times, resulting in their minor modification but not in their radical revision. Only recently have they been critically re-examined on a broad front by Dr Joan Thirsk who has published a controversial alternative model. Investigations by Dr Thirsk in Lincolnshire and by myself in Kent have provided evidence of arable fields divided into unenclosed parcels which were not necessarily subject to common rules of cultivation and grazing. Furthermore, a number of studies have demonstrated that the strip-like shape of the parcels could have not a single but

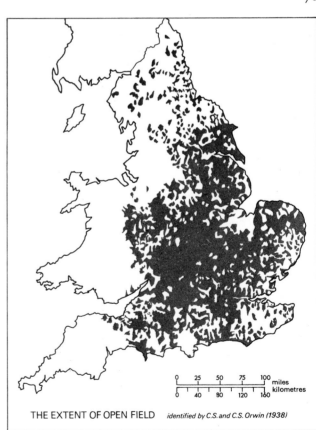

THE EXTENT OF OPEN FIELD   *identified by C.S. and C.S. Orwin (1938)*

71 *The open fields of Padbury, near Buckingham, survived until 1796 when large fields with parallel hedges were established by parliamentary enclosure. Within these fields, the pattern of ridge-and-furrow preserves that of parcels and furlongs recorded on the map of the parish drawn in 1591. Had there been no map, the antiquity of the ridge-and-furrow could have been deduced from the way in which even today the ploughing ridges follow the pre-enclosure strips and stubbornly ignore the hedges.*

72 *Map of the parish of Padbury, drawn in 1591 by Thomas Clerke of Stamford.*

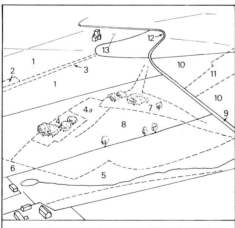

1 Whadden waye furlonge. 2 'Tho. Spratley'. 3 Whadden waye. 4 No detail given on 1591 map. 4a Block of strips, unnamed in 1591. 5 Cockmore Myers. 6 Cockemore small waye. 7 'Tho. Harris'. 8 Stighegate furlonge. 9 Stighegate waye. 10 Great whitelandes. 11 Great bamrache. 12 St Katherines waye. 13 Churchyard furlonge.

Key to Figure 71

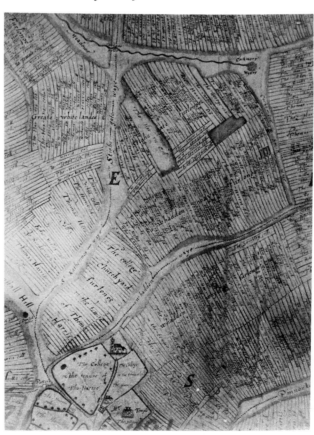

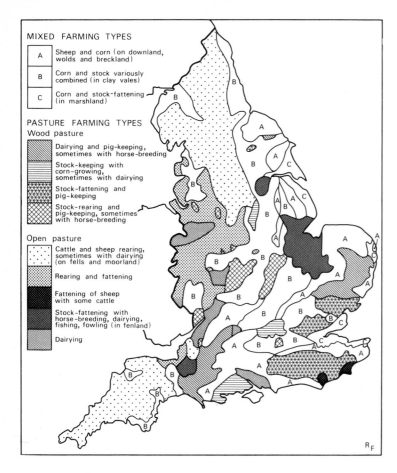

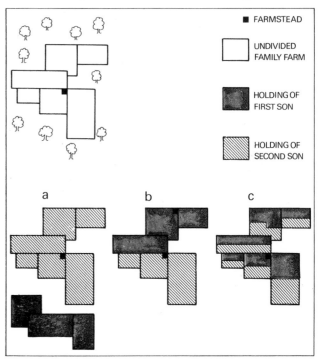

74 *Growth of population encouraged secondary colonisation, the carving out of agricultural land from the waste and (a) the building of a farmstead a short distance away from the 'mother' settlement. In areas where there was little space for such new expansion, partible inheritance could have very different results; it could lead to (b) the fragmentation of farms into smaller holdings or to (c) the subdivision of fields among co-heirs, producing a pattern of unenclosed parcels in intermixed ownership.*

multiple origins. Sometimes, as in Kent, it was the result of the division of land among sons in accordance with the rules of partible inheritance, for although farms were sometimes divided for this purpose into two, three or more blocks of land, the alternative, and in view of soil differences over short distances on occasion the only fair method, was to divide each field into parcels. Sometimes the strips resulted from the parcelling of the lord's land among tenants, when manorial lords abandoned direct farming and turned to leasing their properties. Sometimes the strips were a product of communally organised colonisation of waste land, followed by the partition of the cleared land among those who had done the work of clearing.

It is now necessary, therefore, to distinguish between 'open fields', or fields composed of strips which are not definitely known to have been cultivated or grazed in common, and 'common fields', the fields of strips over which common rules of cultivation and grazing are known to have operated.

Dr Thirsk argues that any new map of the field systems of England must differentiate between areas in which the classic common-field system prevailed, and those characterised by more loosely-organised, sometimes open-field, sometimes common-field systems. Our information is not yet sufficiently detailed for such a map to be constructed, although Dr Thirsk has provided a tentative map of farming regions in England in the sixteenth century, and a verbal generalisation of the distribution of field systems.

The classic common-field system represented an intensive system of farming for corn that was characteristic of all well-populated villages in plains and valleys in all parts of the kingdom. In pastoral areas, arable fields were a subsidiary element in a farming system based on the growing of grass. Those which were parcelled into strips were sometimes subject to common rules of cultivation and grazing, but sometimes not. Pasture farming was practised over much of the highland half of England and in all forests and fens in the lowlands.

The distinction between open-field systems and

66

73 *Farming regions in England: identified by J. Thirsk (1967). For medieval farmers the physical environment – altitude, slope of land, soils, drainage and climate – became less favourable as they moved from lowland to highland England. Farming was less intensive away from the sheep and corn husbandry areas of East Anglia and south-east England, and in the west crop yields were often lower and there was more emphasis on extensive pastoral farming. This farming pattern may also have been influenced by the way in which innovation in agriculture spread in medieval England. Change and development began in East Anglia and the south east: increasing distance from these centres decreasing the intensity of farming. The pattern of agriculture was also a reflection of the distribution of population. Recorded in the Poll Tax of 1377, the area of highest population density lay between Leicestershire and the east coast. Lowest density was in the far west.*

76 *On Catherton Common, Salop, the pattern of settlement is that of the 'squatter'. A single farmer settled on uncleared land and gradually established a series of hedged fields. Such piecemeal reclamation is indicated by the irregular shape of the fields, some of which are now returning to woodland or scrub.*

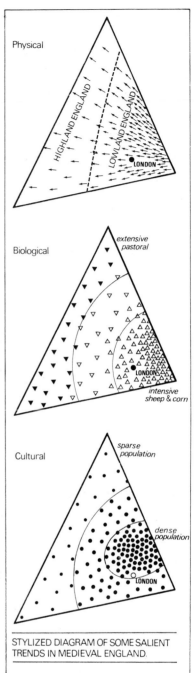

STYLIZED DIAGRAM OF SOME SALIENT TRENDS IN MEDIEVAL ENGLAND.

67

common-field systems was clearly spatial but Dr Thirsk further suggests that it might have been temporal, with an open-field system being, as it were, an immature common-field system. Until recently it has been generally believed that the common-field system was in full operation long before historical records began. Dr Thirsk now suggests, following German scholars, that the system developed slowly in response to the changing needs of the community and did not reach maturity in England before the mid-thirteenth century. Dr Thirsk places much importance on an example from twelfth-century Yorkshire where consolidated farms were newly carved out of the waste but became subsequently divided into many parcels and strips of land in succeeding generations and emerged two hundred years later as villages with a common-field system. In this example one can observe fields being divided up among heirs. If this is a typical example of the way settlement proceeded in virgin territory, then it is not, in Dr Thirsk's view, difficult to see why the common-field system emerged in the end. When the land became divided into hundreds of parcels, and when this process was accompanied by a rise in total population, acute problems arose of providing access to the many small pieces of land, of ensuring water for stock, and of enabling stubble to be eaten by livestock without damage to the crops of neighbours. Inescapably they called for some agreement and co-operation.

The new model advanced by Dr Thirsk has not yet been widely accepted and, indeed, has been hotly disputed in some quarters. Nevertheless, her arguments have raised the debate about English field systems to a new level and her ideas can only validly be accepted or rejected when they have been thoroughly tested. Many economic historians and historical geographers are now searching new evidence or re-examining old evidence to see how far the facts match the theory.

At the same time, it is clear that studies of field systems have often in the past lacked precision – the terminology employed has often been ambiguous, the relationships investigated have been inadequately described, let alone explained. A field system is clearly a product of a combination of three sets of factors: physical inputs such as relief, drainage, climate and soils; biological inputs such as the crops cultivated and livestock reared, and the abundance and quality of pastures; and cultural inputs such as the level of agricultural technology, the laws and customs of inheritance, and the density of population. It may be that we shall only be able to solve some of the problems which still surround the study of English medieval field systems by applying some of the concepts and methods of systems analysis. In particular, there is a clear need to examine and assess more precisely than hitherto the inter-relationships of each of the inputs in a field system. The broad trend of the spatial pattern is suggestive of the connection between them but only the detailed analysis of specific field systems will enable us to test the validity of these suggestions.

FURTHER READING

Allison, K. J. 'The Sheep-corn Husbandry of Norfolk in the Sixteenth and Seventeenth Centuries', *Agricultural History Review*, 5 (1957), 12–30

Ault, W. O. 'Open-field Husbandry and the Village Community: a Study of Agrarian By-laws in Medieval England', *Transactions of the American Philosophical Society*, 55 (1965)

Baker, A. R. H. and Butlin, R. A. (eds), *Studies of Field Systems: an Evaluation*', *Agricultural History*, 39 (1965), 86–91

Baker, A. R. H. 'Some Fields and Farms in Medieval Kent', *Archaeologia Cantiana*, 80 (1965), 152–75

Baker, A. R. H. and Butlin, R. A. (eds), *Studies in Field Systems in the British Isles*, (Cambridge, 1973)

Bowen, H. C. *Ancient Fields* (1962)

Butlin, R. A. 'Northumberland Field Systems', *Agricultural History Review*, 12 (1964), 99–120

Chambers, J. D. *Laxton: the Last English Open Field Village* (1964)

Gray, H. L. *English Field Systems* (Cambridge, Mass 1915)

Harris, A. 'The Agriculture of the East Riding of Yorkshire Before the Parliamentary Enclosures', *Yorkshire Archaeological Journal*, 40 (1959–62), 119–28

Harvey, P. D. *A Medieval Oxfordshire Village: Cuxham, 1240 to 1400* (Oxford, 1965)

Orwin, C. S. and C. S. *The Open Fields* (3rd edn Oxford, 1967)

Postgate, M. R. 'The Field Systems of Breckland', *Agricultural History Review*, 10 (1962), 80–101

Thirsk, J. 'The Common Fields', *Past and Present*, 29 (1964), 3–25

Thirsk, J. 'The Origin of the Common Fields', *Past and Present*, 33 (1966), 142–7

Thirsk, J. (ed) *The Agrarian History of England and Wales Vol IV 1500–1640* (1967)

Titow, J. Z. 'Medieval England and the Open-Field System', *Past and Present*, 32 (1965), 86–102

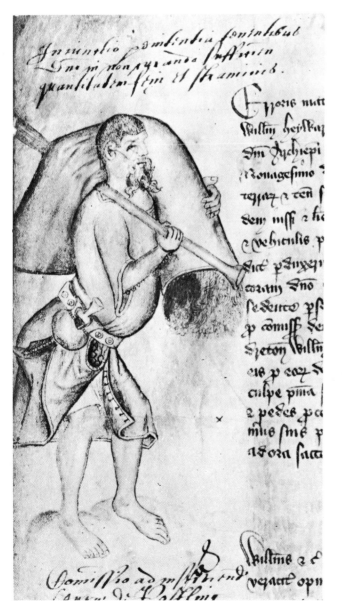

6 GOING TO TOWN IN THIRTEENTH-CENTURY ENGLAND

by H. S. A. FOX

THE thirteenth century saw an unprecedented phase of urban expansion and a proliferation of market-places. Towns already established in 1200 grew rapidly and many newcomers were added to the urban pattern. Some villages acquired town status and at least sixty-five new towns were planted where no previous settlement had existed. In addition, during the course of the thirteenth century, about 2500 market charters were granted, most of them to rural communities. Old-

77 (top)   During the thirteenth century, England's towns multiplied and expanded. In consequence, ever-increasing quantities of agricultural produce had to be transported to feed urban dwellers. The fourteenth-century Luttrell Psalter shows a cart which might have been used on landlord's farms and by the richer peasants.

78   Shouldering his sack of hay or straw is one of the tenants of Wingham in Kent who in 1390 were forced to do penance for failing to perform their carrying services in full for their lord, the Archbishop of Canterbury. Journeys which should have been made by a cart had instead been undertaken on foot.

established towns did not acquire all of their new inhabitants from natural increase: they, and the new towns, grew by attracting immigrants from the countryside. Nor did towns of the thirteenth century exist as isolated communities producing everything for their own needs or engaging only in reciprocal trade – 'taking in each other's washing' as Lewis Mumford put it. They were producers of simple manufactured goods for distribution to rural populations, consumers of agricultural surpluses, and with village market-places functioned as centres of exchange between town and country.

Many parts of the English countryside were over-populated during the thirteenth century and were well able to provide emigrants for urban expansion. In theory, a lord's villeins were bound to inhabit the manor where they had been born, but in practice lords were usually willing to allow non-residence so long as the emigrant paid a small fine. Information on the movements of emigrants can be drawn from the detailed accounts of the manor courts in which these fines, together with fines imposed for illegal flight, were recorded. Court records of the Norfolk village of Forncett, for example, show that about one hundred villeins could be found 'staying outside the manor' in almost every year at the end of the thirteenth century, and the earliest surviving documents of the abbot of Ramsey's East Midland manors reveal that emigration there was a well-established feature of rural life by the 1270s.

Of those who left their home manors, some were women marrying into nearby communities, others became mendicants and casual labourers, and more emigrated to take up land elsewhere. Considerable numbers also left on townward journeys. We know that employment opportunities in trade and manufacture at the city of Norwich attracted emigrants from Forncett, only nineteen kilometres away. One historian who has made a detailed study of the Ramsey Abbey manors in the fifteenth century describes the names of the emigrants as 'almost a tradesman's gazette for many districts'. The same could probably be said of thirteenth-century participants in the rural exodus.

80 *Early migration into Stratford-upon-Avon (after Carus-Wilson 1965).*

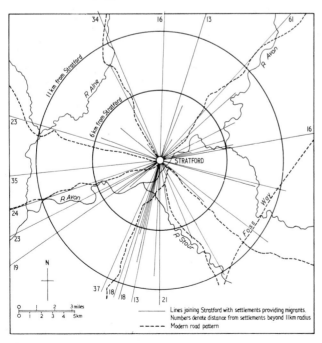

81 The densely-packed spires and buildings of fifteenth-century London probably give a reliable impression of its character throughout the Middle Ages. The lure of the capital was even then attracting immigrants from the whole country.

MIGRATION CLUES FROM PERSONAL NAMES

Medieval migration often involved a change of surname, so that Roger Wain of Tresillian might well come to be called Roger de Tresillian if he took up residence in Truro, or perhaps Roger Cornish if he migrated across the Tamar to Plymouth. For this reason records of the towns themselves, especially records listing the names of inhabitants, can throw light on the part played by rural population mobility in providing the human material for thirteenth-century urban expansion. In a rental of Stratford-upon-Avon dating from 1251–52, when the town had been established for only fifty years, about one third of the 234 householders had names derived from the names of places. When those place-names which can be identified in this sample are plotted on a map, it appears that there was an inverse relationship between migra-

tion and distance: more immigrants came to Stratford from areas close to the town than from more distant places. It is also clear that medieval Stratford's migration field was of limited extent, few immigrants being drawn from settlements more than eleven kilometres from the town.

These two findings accord with the evidence of rural-urban migration patterns in later, better-documented periods, and they are also just what we should expect from our knowledge of the scale of new town foundation in the Middle Ages. After all, when Robert de Tony established a town at South Zeal on the northern flank of Dartmoor in about 1264, with surroundings far less prosperous than Stratford's fertile Feldon, information about the new employment opportunities cannot have spread very far afield. We can be certain that almost all the town's householders, only twenty by 1315, were Devonshire born.

82

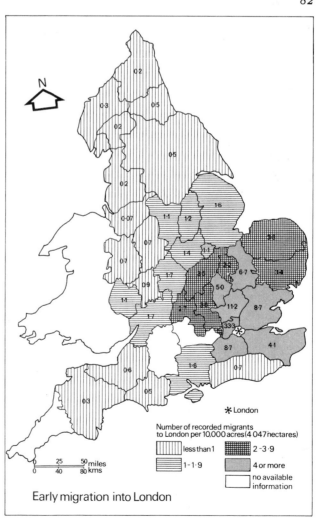

Early migration into London

* London

Number of recorded migrants
to London per 10,000 acres (4 047 hectares)

less than 1

1–1·9

2–3·9

4 or more

no available information

83 *Drawings of medieval provincial towns are rare, but a copy of Geoffrey of Monmouth's* History *includes a picture of Gloucester. A river port, a crossing point of the main route into Wales, a market centre and the site of a number of religious houses, Gloucester was among the twenty richest towns in early fourteenth-century England.*

84 *The Gough map shows the major towns and roads of the fourteenth century. Distances between the towns are given in Roman numerals. This extract is of southern England: the Wash appears at the top left corner and Gloucester at the bottom right.*

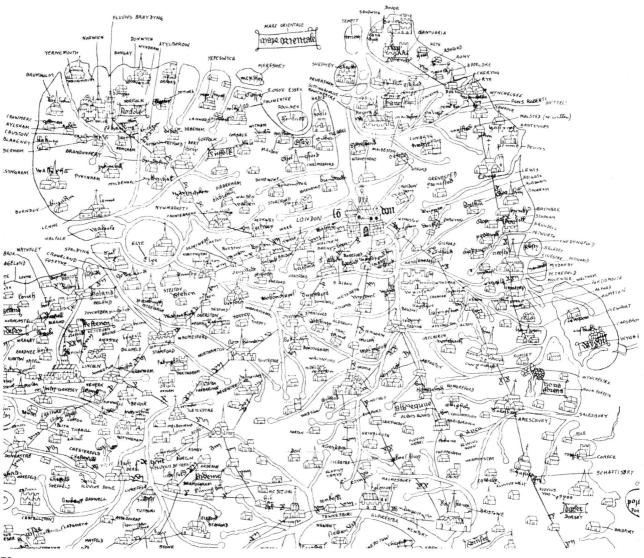

IMMIGRATION TO MEDIEVAL LONDON

Some of the largest and oldest medieval towns, notably London, did have more extensive migration fields. The surnames of many Londoners were indicative of their birth-place or of their ancestors' birth-place, and a thorough survey of names appearing in London records of between 1100 and 1350 has yielded figures relating to the part played by each of the English counties in providing immigrants for the capital. A map compiled from this source does not represent a comprehensive record of early migration to London, but it does give an impression of the capital's far-reaching attraction, and of the relative importance of the Home Counties and of the East Midlands as sources of immigrants.

Just as evidence of considerable mobility among thirteenth-century rural population shows that the early medieval village was not the isolated inward-looking community that it was once thought to be, so when we come to look at the evidence on marketing, we must relinquish at once the traditional idea that the manor was a unit which provided for all of its own requirements and produced no surplus. Exchanges involving agricultural surplus and simple manufactured goods, and the transport of these commodities over short distances were, in fact, the forces which generated the multiplication of towns and markets. Long-distance trade movements did exist but there is no evidence that they dictated the siting of markets. Wool and salt, for example, were transported from areas of production to distant parts of the country; metals, grain and wool were exported in large quantities; and wine, cloths and furs were among the imports. Coastal and river ports, some of the largest inland towns, and numerous yearly fairs flourished as a result of these activities but most towns, and all rural markets, relied on exchanges of goods with a much smaller range.

Much of the thirteenth century was a period of buoyancy for landlord farming. Lords exploited to the full the resources of their demesnes and, although yields were not high, the scale of demesne farming operations ensured the production of large surpluses. These were marketed in the surrounding countryside – *in patria* is the term employed by the estate managers of Canterbury Cathedral Priory – with the aid of carrying services owed by a tenant to his lord. From documents relating to such services, the movement of agricultural produce away from rural manors can be reconstructed. Some documents contain only the terse statement that journeys were to be made 'to all or any of the markets

in the shire', but others are more detailed. We learn that the tenants of Buckland in Gloucestershire should carry to markets at Gloucester, Tewkesbury, Evesham, Chipping Campden and Worcester, and that the men of the Oxfordshire village of Cuxham were bound to carry the lord's grain to Wallingford, Henley and Ibstone, all within nineteen kilometres of their village.

Less well documented is the marketing of produce from peasant holdings. Many peasant families were becoming increasingly impoverished during the thirteenth century, but, even so, surpluses must have been produced in order to raise the cash needed for rents and other payments. Private marketing may have played a part in the disposal of minute surpluses from the smallest holdings, but wealthier peasants no doubt sold their produce in rural and urban market-places where the provision of standard weights and measures reduced the likelihood of fraud, and where buyers were more numerous. A considerable movement of agricultural produce must have existed between these market-places and the farms of peasants and lords alike. Produce would have been transported to market in sacks carried by pack-horses or in carts.

Some agricultural produce sold in market-places was destined for export after having been collected into large consignments by travelling merchants, but a

85 *John Norden's sixteenth-century* Intended Guyde for English Travailers *included the first detailed matrices of distances between towns and important villages.*

Cornewall.	Lancefton	Saltafhe	Stratton	Bofcaftle	Liskerde	Lowe	Bodmyn	Loftithiell	Camelforde	Padftowe	St. Cullombe	Tregney	Peryn	Helfton	St. Ithes	Market Iewe	The Mount	Penfance	Truro	Foye	St. Burien	Iacobftowe	Lands-end	Lantegios	Boconncke	Dauidftowe
Auftell	24	22	20	21	13	12	9	7	18	14	8	6	17	23	28	28	29	31	11	6	36	26	39	8	9	20
Dauidftowe	10	20	12	3	13	20	10	14	2	11	16	26	34	40	43	45	46	48	28	20	53	7	55	19	15	
Boconnocke	18	14	26	16	5	6	4	16	14	13	15	25	32	36	37	38	40	10	6	44	20	48	5			
Lantegios	22	15	30	22	8	4	10	7	18	18	15	14	24	30	37	36	37	39	20	3	44	24	48			
Lands-end	64	66	68	56	54	53	48	46	56	45	39	35	27	20	14	12	12	10	28	46	5	63				
Iacobftowe	7	22	7	6	18	24	17	20	8	17	23	32	40	48	50	50	50	52	34	26	55					
St. Burien	58	58	65	52	48	48	44	43	48	41	35	30	22	16	10	8	8	6	24	42						
Foye	24	17	33	23	10	7	10	7	18	17	12	13	22	29	34	38	38	40	18							
Truro	34	34	40	30	27	24	20	17	26	19	11	6	6	13	17	17	19									
Penfance	53	54	57	46	44	43	38	37	44	35	30	25	16	10	6	2	3									
The Mount	50	50	57	45	44	40	38	34	32	34	28	23	14	8	4	÷										
Market Iewe	53	50	55	45	41	40	37	34	41	33	27	22	13	7	4											
St. Ithes	50	50	56	43	40	40	35	33	40	31	28	22	14	10												
Helfton	43	45	52	41	36	34	32	30	38	30	24	17	7													
Peryn	40	38	46	30	29	28	24	23	32	24	17	10														
Tregney	30	28	36	27	20	9	16	13	24	17	11															
St. Cullombe	24	26	27	19	16	18	10	9	14	7																
Padftowe	19	26	24	12	16	20	9	11	10																	
Camelforde	10	20	14	5	12	18	9	12																		
Loftithiell	18	18	26	18	8	10	4																			
Bodmyn	16	18	23	14	7	11																				
Lowe	20	11	28	23	6																					
Liskerde	14	10	23	16																						
Bofcaftle	10	24	10																							
Stratton	9	27																								
Saltafhe	16																									

The vfe of this Table.

THe Townes or places betweene which you defire to know the diftance, you may finde in the names of the Townes in the vpper part, and in the fide, and bring them in a fquare, as the lines will guide you: and in the fquare you fhall finde the figures which declare the diftance of the miles.

And if you finde any place in the fide which will not extend to make a fquare with that aboue, then feeking that aboue which will not extend to make a fquare, and fee that in the vpper, and the other in the fide, and it will fhowe you the diftance. It is familiar and eafie.

Beare with defectes, the vfe is neceffarie.

Invented by IOHN NORDEN.

86 *Stalbridge in Dorset possesses a carved medieval market cross which was a symbol of protection and security for those who came to trade at its weekly market. Many medieval market-places were to be found in villages which never became boroughs, that is towns in the legal sense.*

87 *The weekly market at Steeple Ashton in Wiltshire began in 1266 when the nuns of Romsey obtained a charter to hold a Wednesday market. Its success caused the owner of near-by Market Lavington's Wednesday market to complain, two years later, that he had lost £40 owing to the new centre's competition.*

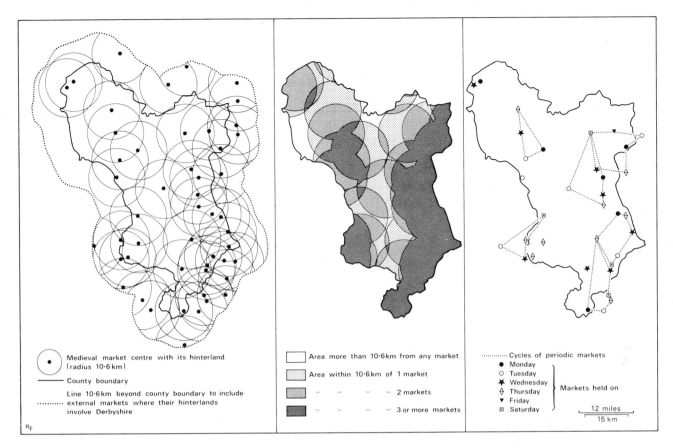

Medieval market centre with its hinterland
(radius 10·6 km)

County boundary

Line 10·6 km beyond county boundary to include
external markets where their hinterlands
involve Derbyshire

Area more than 10·6 km from any market

Area within 10·6 km of 1 market

"   "   "   " 2 markets

"   "   "   " 3 or more markets

Cycles of periodic markets
● Monday
○ Tuesday
✶ Wednesday
⬦ Thursday
▼ Friday
⊡ Saturday

⎫
⎬ Markets held on
⎭

12 miles
15 km

R_F

88 *Medieval marketing patterns in Derbyshire (after Coates, 1965).*

proportion was consumed by local rural populations deficient in certain commodities, and also, of course, by the inhabitants of nearby towns. In exchange, town dwellers fashioned and marketed simple manufactured goods for sale in the surrounding countryside. Certain basic trades were to be found in rural settlements with no claim to urban status: bakers, carpenters, cobblers, smiths and brewers were counted among the populations of most villages. By contrast, the towns contained less common trades indicating that, for some of their needs, rural communities relied on town-made goods. Compared with the average Midland village of the period, even the small town of Stratford stands out as a settlement of considerable functional complexity. In addition to artisans carrying on trades which could be found in the countryside, Stratford possessed glovers, a worker in skins, dyers, tailors, a locksmith, a spicer, a farrier and a whitesmith, all with surnames indicative of their occupation. Their wares, we can be sure, were hawked by merchants in the rural market-places of the surrounding countryside,

and were purchased by peasants on day trips to town.

Henry de Bracton, an eminent thirteenth-century lawyer, considered that the length of a 'reasonable day' spent in marketing could be transformed into the linear equivalent of thirty-two kilometres. Buying and selling would occupy at least a third of the day, leaving a third for the journey to market and a third for the return home. The maximum range of a market journey was therefore, in Bracton's own precise phrase, 'six miles and a half and the third part of a half' or just over ten kilometres. The accompanying maps show that in Derbyshire, for example, most parts of the county were within ten kilometres of a market, while many areas were served by three or more. And Derbyshire was by no means as well provided with market places as other Midland counties. Indeed, so many lords entered the market-founding lottery of the thirteenth century that not all the new establishments were ensured success. We hear of decayed and valueless markets, and of disputes about the setting up of new markets too close to existing centres of trade.

75

89 Abbots Bromley in Staffordshire, a small thirteenth-century borough, has a covered market hall situated in a large square where stalls were set up on market days.

THE TRADE CENTRE'S SPHERE OF INFLUENCE

Officials arbitrating in such cases were presented with the task of stipulating the distance within which one market would be detrimental to another. Various estimates were given, but the most authoritative seems to have been Bracton's statement that a market was a 'hurtful and tortious nuisance' if set up within just over ten kilometres of an established centre of trade. Was his calculation a successful early attempt to delimit what is today termed the sphere of influence of a trade centre, or was it, in the words of one historian, 'a typical piece of medieval confusion masquerading as logical exactitude'?

Two points can be made. In the first place, a fundamental error in the calculation tends to diminish the authority of Bracton's statement: if, as he claimed, just over ten kilometres was the maximum range of a market journey, and if the market spheres of influence were not to overlap, which is implied by his argument, then competition would begin only when markets were less than twenty-one kilometres apart. Second, as Bracton realised, the model was formulated from the point of view of country dwellers on market journeys, failing to take into account itinerant merchants and the market periodicities which arose to satisfy their requirements. Most medieval English markets were not places of permanent trading, but, like the periodic markets of primitive economies today, were used only on one specified day of the week. Where population density and economic activity were sufficient to generate more than one market day per week in a given area, this fact would account for the existence, and in most cases, the survival, of markets spaced at distances far less than twenty-one kilometres. However close they were spatially, two neighbouring markets held on different days would, in fact, benefit one another by attracting merchants into the area – an argument put forward in 1252 to justify a Tuesday market at Wingham in Kent, close to the Wednesday markets at Canterbury and Sandwich.

To the itinerant artisan, town-based but spending part of his time trading at village market-places, and to the travelling trader, collecting consignments of grain or wool for the towns or for export, a closely-spaced mesh of periodic markets was ideal. We know of the

90 *The market place in Chipping Campden, Gloucester-shire, was in the broadest part of the main street. The island of buildings is a modern addition.*

91 *Wooler in Northumberland has functioned as a market place from 1199. From its triangular market place, roads radiate through the village and out into the countryside.*

existence of such traders in medieval England, but no documents have come to light which illuminate the details of their itineraries. Nevertheless, a theoretical reconstruction of their movements may be made by analysing the pattern of markets in both a spatial and temporal context. Certainly, most of the periodic markets of medieval Derbyshire can be grouped into a number of four- or five-day cycles, each cycle perhaps frequented by a group of itinerant merchants.

To end on this conjectural note is to emphasise that much still remains to be learned about mobility and marketing in the Middle Ages. For example, it would be interesting to know about the conditions of life on those rural manors from which emigration was heaviest; to discover the relative importance of the attractions of towns and the poverty of the countryside in motivating the migrants; and to ascertain the role of established towns in providing artisans, ready-made as it were, to take up employment in the new urban settlements. Other questions might be asked in relation to marketing. Would a study of the indebtedness which we know was prevalent on rural manors throw light on peasant marketing arrangements? Are there documents which might yield information which supports or refutes Bracton's estimate of the maximum range of market journeys? What were the activities of the small-time itinerant merchants? Only when the often fragmentary and intractable source material from the Middle Ages has been thoroughly sifted shall we be closer to providing answers to such questions.

FURTHER READING

Berry, B. L. J. *Geography of Market Centres and Retail Distribution* (Englewood Cliffs, 1967), especially pt 3, 'Perspectives of time and space'

Britnell, R. H. 'The Making of Witham', *History Studies*, 1 (1962), 13–21

Britnell, R. H. 'Production for the Market on a Small Fourteenth Century Estate', *Economic History Review*, 2nd ser, 19 (1966), 380–7

Cam, H. M. 'The Early Burgesses of Cambridge in Relation to the Surrounding Countryside', *Liberties and Communities in Medieval England* (Cambridge, 1944)

Carus-Wilson, E. M. 'The Medieval Trade of the Ports of the Wash', *Medieval Archaeology*, 6–7 (1962–3), 182–201

Carus-Wilson, E. M. 'The First Half-century of the Borough of Stratford-upon-Avon', *Economic History Review*, 2nd ser, 18 (1965), 46–63

Carus-Wilson, E. M. 'Towns and Trade', *Medieval England* ed A. L. Poole (Oxford, 1958)

Coates, B. E. 'The Origin and Distribution of Markets and Fairs in Medieval Derbyshire', *Derbyshire Archaeological Journal*, 85 (1965), 92–111

Ekwall, E. *Studies on the Population of Medieval London* (Stockholm, 1956)

Fraser, C. M. 'The Pattern of Trade in the North-East of England, 1265–1350', *Northern History*, 4 (1969), 44–66

Harvey, P. D. A. *A Medieval Oxfordshire Village: Cuxham 1240–1400* (Oxford, 1965), especially ch 4, 'The manor and its outside contacts, 1271–1359'

Hilton, R. H. *A Medieval Society: the West Midlands at the End of the Thirteenth Century* (1966), especially ch 7, 'Towns, markets and manufactures'

Jusserand, J. J. *English Wayfaring Life in the Middle Ages* (1889)

Lennard, R. 'Manorial Traffic and Agricultural Trade in Medieval England', *Journal of the Proceedings of the Agricultural Economics Society*, 5 no 3 (1938), 259–75

Postan, M. M. 'Medieval Agrarian Society in its Prime: England', *The Cambridge Economic History of Europe* vol 1, *The Agrarian Life of the Middle Ages* ed M. M. Postan (Cambridge, 1966)

Postan, M. M. and Rich, E. E. (eds) *The Cambridge Economic History of Europe* vol 2, *Trade and Industry in the Middle Ages* (Cambridge, 1952)

Raftis, J. A. *Tenure and Mobility: Studies in the Social History of the Medieval English Village* (Toronto, 1964)

Russell, J. C. 'Medieval Midland and Northern Migrants to London, 1100–1365', *Speculum*, 34 (1959), 641–5

Russell, J. C. *Medieval Regions and their Cities* (Newton Abbot, 1972)

Salzman, L. F. *English Trade in the Middle Ages* (Oxford, 1931)

Salzman, L. F. 'The Legal Status of Markets', *Cambridge Historical Journal*, 2 no 3 (1928), 205–12

Stenton, F. M. 'The Road System of Medieval England', *Economic History Review*, 7 no 1 (1936), 1–21

Tupling, G. H. 'The Origin of Markets and Fairs in Medieval Lancashire', *Transactions of the Lancashire and Cheshire Antiquarian Society*, 49 (1933), 75–94

Willard, J. F. 'Inland Transportation in England During the Fourteenth Century', *Speculum*, 1 (1926), 361–74

Willard, J. F. 'The Use of Carts in the Fourteenth Century', *History*, 17 no 67 (1932), 246–50

Medieval planted towns in England and Wales

92 Between 1066 and the Black Death in 1349 some 400 new towns were planted in England and Wales. The late-developing areas of Wales and south-west England show a particularly rich urban growth.

7

FOUNDED TOWNS AND DESERTED VILLAGES OF THE MIDDLE AGES

by M. W. BERESFORD

ECONOMIC growth brings a need for more settlements, both rural and urban. The medieval colonisation of marginal land, as on Dartmoor, Exmoor or the Pennine Dales, created new clearings, then new fields, and then new villages of all sizes. The same colonisation encouraged further proliferation of market centres for the products of the fields, and colonists were also delving beneath the earth for minerals, so that the new market towns dealt in more commodities than food and animals. So arose Pateley Bridge in the West Riding of Yorkshire and Bere Alston in Devon. With the poor quality and expense of medieval land transport, such points of exchange were needed more frequently than today. Many present villages had medieval markets and fairs, their greens, like that at Sheriff Hutton in Yorkshire, being the former market places.

93 The expansion of settlement in the twelfth and thirteenth centuries reflected the period's economic growth. Richmond in Yorkshire was planted as a new town by the Normans. Called Rougemont, *it guarded the road from York to Carlisle.*

94 *Newtown, Isle of Wight, was founded in 1256 but has declined.*

With land transport so costly and slow, settlement on a navigable river or an estuarine creek had a good chance of being developed as a port, and in the twelfth and thirteenth centuries, when overseas and coastal commerce was developing particularly rapidly, the coastline of England and Wales was a fertile place for the plantation of many new enterprises designed to succeed as ports. It was no accident that when King John projected his new port of Liverpool in 1207 he sought to attract settlers by promising them liberties equal to those of any existing port that they cared to name. Looking in another direction geographically but in the same direction economically, his brother, Richard I, had founded Portsmouth in 1194. Indeed the progress of England as an economy can be charted in the multiplication of its new ports, from Boston, Lincolnshire, in the generation following the Norman Conquest, through to the last of the medieval port

95 *Boston was another Norman addition, serving as river port for central Lincolnshire and becoming a great fair town.*

96 & 97   *Old Romney, an Anglo Saxon port long since silted and decayed, was replaced by the Norman New Romney – from which the sea has also receded.*

98 English medieval urbanisation was also felt in Wales. Pembroke was probably built in 1110 by the first earl. Its design makes a unity of castle, town and walls as in Richmond, Ludlow and New Windsor.

projects, that which Edward III engineered at Queenborough on the Isle of Sheppey in 1361–8 during the Hundred Years War. He named the town in honour of his queen, Philippa. Far from the Thames, Edward I had had the same idea when founding and naming *Burgus Reginae* in 1288 on the Gironde estuary in his Gascon territory. The Gascon port sent wine to England and, like its greater and older neighbours on the Lot, Garonne, and Dordogne, took immense quantities of cloth, manufactures and even wheat from English ports.

Thus the new quays, the newly colonised fields, the newly prospected mines and the new places of customs collection were all topographical and visible signs of an expanding medieval economy. The expansion, which lasted until the last years of the thirteenth century, was not simply one which encouraged novelties. Less spectacular perhaps, and less easy to detect in documentary sources, is the parallel growth of the cultivated areas of older villages, the promotion of villages to boroughs, and the growth of the built-up areas of older towns. Some general indication of this overall expansion is given by the growth of population. In 1086, at the time of Domesday Book, the population was about 1,250,000, but by the late thirteenth century it was probably at least three times as large.

It is significant that among the top-ranking towns of the late thirteenth century some were quite new. The 'new' in the name of Newcastle upon Tyne was as

99 The layout of house plots in Queenborough, Kent, compares with other planted towns such as Pembroke.

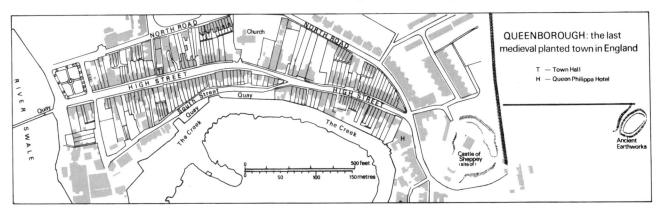

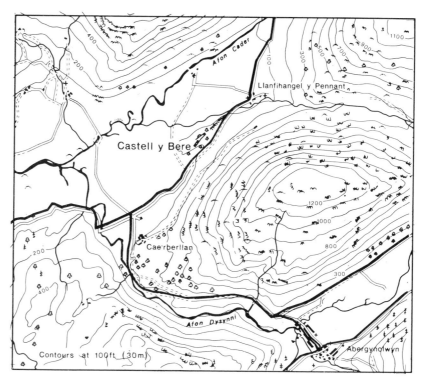

100 At Bere, Merionethshire, Edward I planned a town on the defended site. It received its charter in November 1284, on the same day as those issued to Conway and Caernarvon. The borough did not survive long, and today the castle lies in ruins.

101 Castell y Bere.

genuine, historically, as the 'new' of much smaller ports like Newborough in Anglesey, Newport in the Isle of Wight, New Winchelsea in Sussex, and New Romney in Kent. At the bottom of the scale were such tiny creations as Newton in Warkworth, Northumberland, where 'it was thought good for divers causes that those persons which should trade their traffic by sea as mariners or fishermen should inhabit and dwell together.'

Perhaps most indicative of the opportunities which became apparent in these centuries of economic expansion is the proliferation of river ports in the Humber estuary, dominated in 1066 only by Grimsby. By the end of the thirteenth century the enterprise of the crown, the archbishop, and local seigneurs had added four ports. These included the double-origined port at the junction of the rivers Hull and Humber: the town of Wyke-on-Hull, founded as a speculation by the Cistercian monks of Meaux Abbey and taken over, enlarged and renamed as Kingston by Edward I in 1293. Sometimes, however, the quiet and local creation is as significant as the nationally known. It was obviously with the same expansionist optimism that on quieter estuaries in the south-west rival seigneurs created little ports within an arrow's shot of each other, such as the two Looes in Cornwall,

103 *Four centuries before the Ulster plantations of James I, the Anglo-Norman settlers in southern Ireland were creating new towns, as they had in Wales. Jerpont in County Kelkenny, now deserted, was a borough created by the Cistercian abbey of Jerpoint.*

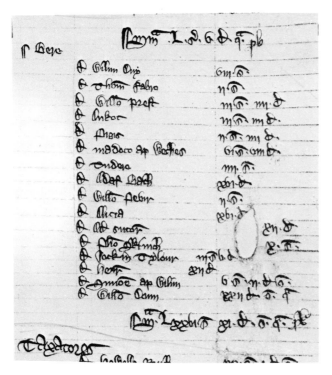

102 *A tax collection of 1292 includes sixteen of the weathier burgesses of the borough of Bene.*

Dodbrooke and Kingsbridge in Devon, and the two rival market settlements that have now amalgamated across the steam that once divided them to make the town of Newton Abbot.

The Latin word for town, *burgus*, has given us 'bourgeois' as well as 'borough', and since with hindsight we can see that the ways of life and thought engendered within town walls were in the long run inimical to the privileges of landed, aristocratic and inherited wealth, it may seem something of a paradox to learn that the founders of towns were the seigneurs. Towns were not founded by the medieval equivalent of Pilgrim Fathers escaping to seek freedom on distant coasts nor by freebooting Robin Hoods throwing up town defences against the established order. It was pillars of the establishment who seized the main chance. It was they who encouraged colonisation of undeveloped lands to augment their rent-rolls, and it was they who augmented their rent-rolls further by encouraging urbanism in the countryside. Indeed, there was more to new towns than the prospect of future dividends from burgage rents, market tolls and the profits of mercantile courts; older towns often purchased exten-

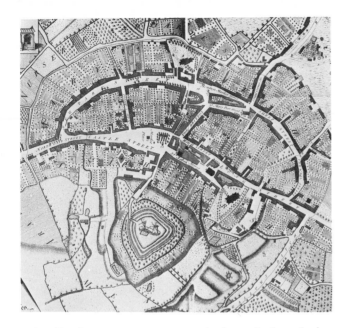

104 *Devizes was a new town sited on the boundaries,* de divisis, *of several rural parishes, next to the castle of the bishop of Salisbury. The plan of 1759 suggests two successive creations, resulting in two street market-places.*

sions of their own liberties from their territorial lord.

In such activities, the king, the most powerful lord of all, was not left behind. For him, in addition to the income from rents and tolls, the development of towns meant the chance of augmented revenues from customs duties and from the taxation of the laity. Thus in 1296 the richest taxpayer in Newcastle upon Tyne paid as much tax as the king obtained from six ordinary villages west of the town. In 1332 the two new towns of Stratford-on-Avon and Henley-in-Arden, Warwickshire, were worth as much to the exchequer in tax collected as the old county town of Warwick. For kings and seigneurs immersed in costly wars and with queens and mistresses tempted by the luxuries of the market place, the inducement to enter into an almost effortless sleeping partnership by extending old towns and creating new ones was irresistible.

PLAGUE AND OTHER ILL-FORTUNES

Few economic historians now doubt that the early fourteenth century showed a pause in population growth, and probably a parallel halt in new economic opportunities. The total population certainly shrank

105 *Boroughbridge, the long narrow settlement on the right, was planted when a new bridge was built about 1145 to take the North Road over the River Ure. It supplanted the Roman bridge at nearby Aldborough, the square settlement on the left.*

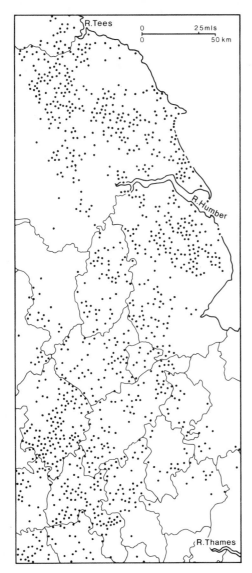

106 Deserted medieval village sites of eastern England. The majority of these disappeared in the fifteenth century.

by between a quarter and a third with the Black Death of 1349, and with the subsequent visitations of the plague that lasted into the 1370s. The plague visited the whole of Europe, and all economic life could not help being affected by it. Economic historians are less in agreement about the long term consequences. When, for example, did population in England begin to move back towards its pre-plague peak – the 1370s or the 1420s? When was that peak reconquered – the 1460s or the 1520s? In the pause before recovery, whatever its duration, there was little incentive to establish new towns and even less to bring new lands into cultivation around the new villages.

As ever in England, there were places and occupations which hardly, if at all, felt the cold wind of change. Cloth making, for home and export, was flourishing in the fourteenth and fifteenth centuries, although the places that benefited were more likely to be the country textile villages of the hills than the old cloth-making towns of the plains. Professor Carus-Wilson has produced a most illuminating study of the development of settlements of country textile workers in the Stroud valley in these very circumstances. In the Pennines, the dales of Aire and Calder were becoming busy. But it cannot be a coincidence that the long line of speculative urban plantions in England, Wales and Gascony was petering out even before the visitations of Black Death, and that in the two centuries following 1349 the list is extended only by Queenborough, essentially a wartime victualling town and not a centre of commerce.

Speculation implies risk and there were failures among medieval urban ventures, even those engineered by Edward I who was generally so successful. In Wales his greatest monument is the string of fortified

107 The adjoining villages of Cestersover, Little Walton, and Newnham in Monks Kirby parish in Warwickshire have all been deserted. Cestersover was depopulated in 1460–7. Only Monks Kirby survives.

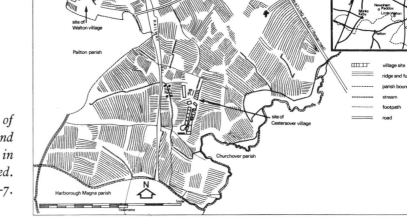

108 *The parish church of St Martin at Wharram
Percy, Yorkshire, is disused as the village is now deserted.
Part of the church tower has fallen.*

109 *Excavation plan of St Martin's, Wharram Percy,
showing its former size when the village was flourishing.
The inner rectangular foundations are Anglo-Saxon.*

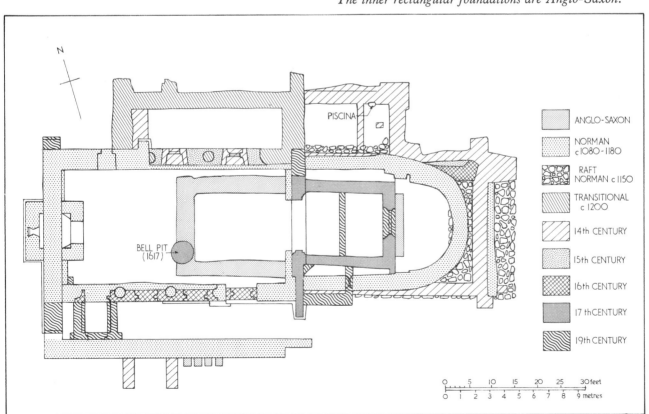

PISCINA

BELL PIT
(1617)

ANGLO-SAXON

NORMAN
c 1080-1180

RAFT
NORMAN c 1150

TRANSITIONAL
c 1200

14th CENTURY

15th CENTURY

16th CENTURY

17th CENTURY

19th CENTURY

0   5   10   15   20   25   30 feet
0 1 2 3 4 5 6 7 8 9 metres

110 (above) Excavations have uncovered the chalk foundations of peasant houses from the last centuries of occupation as well as the Norman manor house, c 1190, of the Percy family.

111 (below) Reconstruction of one of the houses. On the stone foundations were set rough timbers. Walls were made of mud and straw. Peasants and animals would have shared the same roof.

towns along the coastal plain from Flint through Caernarvon to Aberystwyth, but at Bere in Merionethshire the hill of the *castell* carries no town like the hill of Conway or Harlech. At Newton in Purbeck he projected a port for the shipping of the valued 'marble' but nothing is known of it beyond its charter. Of pre-Edwardian towns, New Radnor had a longer life but is now largely over-grown. Newtown, or Francheville on the Isle of Wight, lies along a silted creek of the Solent and is also largely grassed over. With a change in the currents the seas washed away Old Winchelsea as they silted up Old Romney. Strangest of all, the play of the waves threw up a series of shoals and sandbanks off Spurn Point providing a site for the earls of Aumale to found the successful borough of Ravenserod, and then capriciously washed them away again.

If grass growing in the market place, silted creeks, and grassy quays are visible signs that the local bases of economic prosperity were shifting, what then of the changes in rural settlement during the Middle Ages that have given us about 2300 deserted village sites? Once the earthworks of former streets and houses have been recognised, they are not difficult to interpret, and some are authenticated by a ruined or disused village church alongside them. The most satisfactory identification comes from a scrutiny of medieval tax lists. In Leicestershire, for example, the county of Professor Hoskins' classic study, the early fourteenth-century tax collectors recorded contributions from 319 separate villages: thirty-seven of these have completely dis-

appeared and another twenty-five sites were either too small to be separately taxed in 1334 or had already been depopulated. The thirty-seven taxed sites were definitely not pigmies because thirty-three of them were inhabited by at least a dozen families in the early fourteenth century. Most English counties show a similarly high percentage of depopulations.

CAUSES OF VILLAGE DECAY

When and why had the villages been depopulated? In Leicestershire four villages disappeared between Domesday Book and the early fourteenth-century tax lists. This most probably resulted from the operations of the Cistercian abbeys whose rule prescribed solitude and whose farming could be continued from non-village centres. Only three Leicestershire villages disappeared in the post-plague decades of the late fourteenth century. Thus, the easy explanation of the Black Death as the murderer of villages must fail. Too many of them, and not solely in Leicestershire, were still paying substantial contributions to poll taxes collected between 1377 and 1381. This tax, being levied on heads, is not open to any ambiguity. Urban creation had virtually ceased half-a-century before the Black Death and so the villagers had not been tempted away to people the new towns. Our subtractions in England were not simultaneous with our additions.

The first impact of the Black Death would have produced empty holdings everywhere; within a short time the more attractive of these in fertile areas would

112 Kingston, Warwickshire, an old Anglo-Saxon village, was deserted in 1500. The estate plan of 1697 shows a single farm, yet the field name 'town' indicates a memory of settlement.

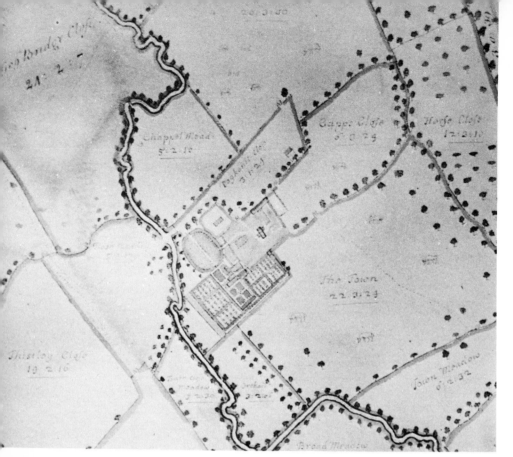

113 *Site of the deserted medieval village of Walton d'Eivil, Warwickshire, is indicated by field names on an eighteenth-century plan of a country house. The village church is now sited on a lawn, having become a family mausoleum.*

be filled again, although shortage of labour would force landlords to make them available on much easier terms. Elsewhere, abandoned arable areas were changed into grass pasture to meet the needs of the still-growing home woollen market and the traditional overseas market for raw wool. Only on the margins of infertile land did areas fall right out of cultivation causing the decay of the village from which the fields had once been tended. Instances of such post-plague depopulations of marginal villages are few and far between. Two authenticated examples are Tusmore in Oxfordshire, where the lord transformed the empty holdings into a deer park, and Bolton, near Bradford in Yorkshire, where the tax collectors of 1379 found 'not a soul remaining'.

The late fourteenth century, then, saw villages smaller than before the plague but still continuing in agriculture, albeit with an increased area of pasture and some overall diminution in arable. The great depopulations were still to come. When they did come, probably from the 1450s onward, they were certainly the result of a massive change in land use, from arable to grass: from a form of agriculture which maintained a substantial number of husbandmen in a village to the

114 *The medieval village of Hardmead, consisting of houses strung on the enormous street loops, or 'ends', was not finally deserted until after 1638, as the extract from the plan of that year shows. The shaded area shows the approximate area of the photograph in figure 115.*

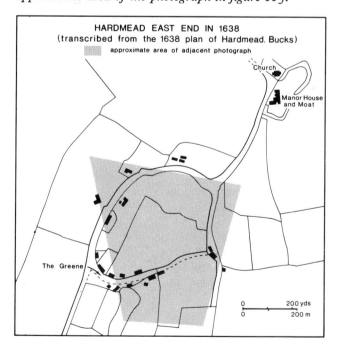

HARDMEAD EAST END IN 1638
(transcribed from the 1638 plan of Hardmead. Bucks)
▓ approximate area of adjacent photograph

Church
Manor House and Moat
The Greene

0   200 yds
0   200 m

90

115 *An aerial photograph reveals in relief the earthworks of the village's former open arable fields and the rectangular crofts or gardens of the farm houses of Hardmead (see figure 114).*

116 *The village of Ogle, Northumberland, is so shrunken as to be virtually deserted. The earthworks on the right reveal a whole street of crofts and houses, together with a back lane separating crofts from open fields. To the left of the modern lane a similar line of earthworks is interrupted by new houses and by two older surviving farms.*

pastoral form with a small labour force – a single shepherd, his boy and his dog, type-figures of the anti-enclosure literature of the early sixteenth century. The stimulus to this change in land use came from a massive and continuing expansion of the demand for wool, principally for home manufacture. The earlier stages of this demand had been met by using the post-plague surplus of former arable land as grazing; the continuation had been met in part by overstocking the commons with sheep; but the full impact could only be met by landlords and tenants deciding to make the complete transition from arable to pastoral husbandry.

In the history of agriculture there have been many changes of mind about the best way to use land as produce prices have altered. The late-medieval swing from corn to grass, however, when it involved the total area of a township's fields, was almost an irreversible action. With the end of arable husbandry the husbandmen were superfluous, and the archaeological evidence shows what happened then to the houses of husbandmen. Without villagers there was no village. The grassed-over sites of the houses remained alongside the ruins of the church. From the late thirteenth century until the late eighteenth century there was little incentive to change back to corn, and when corn was sown again over the sheepwalks there was no return of the natives to a village: improved Hanoverian husbandry made it possible to farm from a small number of farmsteads located conveniently over the township, and the villages did not return with the ploughs.

VALUE OF FOSSILISED COMMUNITIES

Even today, a deserted village site, especially if there is the buried stone of peasant house walls, can lie untouched by the plough, although the temptation of grants for ploughing up the land and the techniques of mechanical earthmoving are annually diminishing the number of deserted medieval village sites. This is why the Inspectorate of Ancient Monuments is taking special measures to preserve some sites. The deserted villages, their cousins the shrunken villages, and their distant relatives the deserted town sites, offer archaeologists an unusual opportunity: here is the material fabric of a community, as fossilised by the onset of economic change as Pompeii was fossilised by the onset of volcanic eruption. Under the shroud of grass, time has stood still.

FURTHER READING

Allison, K. J. *Deserted Villages* (1970)

Allison, K. J. and others *The Deserted Villages of Oxfordshire* (1965)

Allison, K. J. and others *The Deserted Villages of Northamptonshire* (1966)

Beresford, Maurice *History on the Ground* (2nd ed 1971)

Beresford, Maurice *The Lost Villages of England* (1954)

Beresford, Maurice *The New Towns of the Middle Ages* (1967)

Beresford, Maurice and Hurst, John G. eds *Deserted Medieval Villages: Studies* (1971), with gazetteer of 2,263 sites

Biddle, Martin 'The Deserted Medieval Village of Seacourt, Berkshire' *Oxoniensia*, 26–7 (1961–2)

Carus-Wilson, E. M. 'The First Half-Century of the Borough of Stratford-upon-Avon', *Economic History Review*, 2nd series, 18 (1965)

Edwards, J. G. 'Edward I's Castle-building in Wales', *Proceedings of the British Academy*, 32 (1946), 15–81

Finberg, H. P. R. *Gloucestershire Studies* (1957)

Hallam, H. E. *Settlement and Society: a Study of the Early Agrarian History of Lincolnshire* (1965)

Harley, J. B. 'Population Trends and Agricultural Developments from the Warwickshire Hundred Rolls of 1279' *Economic History Review*, 2nd series 11 (1958), 8–18

Hatcher, John *Rural Economy and Society in the Duchy of Cornwall 1300–1500* (1971)

Hilton, R. H. and Rahtz, P. A. 'Upton, Gloucestershire, 1959–64' *Transactions of the Bristol and Gloucester Archaeological Society*, 85 (1966), 70–137

Hoskins, W. G. *The Midland Peasant; the Economic and Social History of a Leicestershire Village* (1957)

Hoskins, W. G. 'Seven Deserted Village Sites in Leicestershire' *Transactions of the Leicestershire Archaeological Society*, 32 (1956), 38–53. Reprinted in his *Provincial England* (1963)

Jarrett, M. G. 'The Deserted Village of West Whelpington, Northumberland' *Archaeologia Aeliana* 4th series 40 (1962), 189–225 and 48 (1970), 183–302

Lewis, E. A. *Medieval Boroughs of Snowdonia* (1912)

Postan, M. M. *Cambridge Economic History of Europe*, I (2nd ed 1966)

Spufford, Margaret *A Cambridgeshire Community: Chippenham* (1965)

Taylor, C. C. 'Whiteparish' *Wiltshire Archaeological and Natural History Magazine*, 12 (1967), 79–102 is a carefully mapped study of expansion and contraction in one settlement

Turner, Hilary L. *Town Defences in England and Wales* (1971)

8 ROOTS OF INDUSTRIAL ENGLAND

by JOAN THIRSK

INDUSTRIES are normally associated with towns and even in the Middle Ages this was considered to be the natural and proper order of things. The policy of the rulers of medieval England was to foster agriculture in

117 A spinning gallery at Yewtree Farm near Coniston. This sixteenth-century farmhouse was the home of a pasture farmer with a domestic handicraft as a side line.

the countryside and to keep industries for the employment of townsmen. Hence they gave support to craft guilds which organised urban craftsmen, supervised their standards of workmanship, and prevented people from practising a craft outside the towns. The activities of the craft guilds, many of which were already in existence by the twelfth century, were in accordance with accepted notions of Christian brotherhood and charity to one's neighbours and fellow workers. They grew immensely strong in the larger towns but when the demand for industrial products ceased to be merely local and markets developed on a national and an international scale, guild restrictions became irksome. Plainly, they held back production and merchants' opportunities in trade were thwarted by lack of workers and the high town prices. In their search for more hands they turned to the countryside and a remarkable expansion of rural industries of all kinds took place between the fifteenth and early eighteenth centuries.

The development and logic of such a process is illustrated by the history of the Wiltshire cloth industry. Wool cloth making was the first industry to develop an export trade. Between the fifteenth and seventeenth centuries wool cloth was the country's principal article of commerce and represented over 75 per cent of English exports in the sixteenth century. In the Middle Ages some of the finest broadcloth was made in the towns of Salisbury and Winchester. The introduction of fulling mills, which took some of the physical labour out of the 'thicking' process, necessitated a supply of fast-flowing water to drive them. Consequently, new mills were built on the banks of streams out in the country. Dyers, fullers and weavers were drawn into villages along the Kennet valley and in the Wylye and Nadder valleys around Salisbury. This change in location liberated large numbers of craftsmen from the control of the guilds. It thus opened up great opportunities for further industrial expansion; soon the market for cloth widened, and yet more workers were needed.

The Wiltshire clothiers failed to find sufficient workers in the neighbourhood of the old cloth centres, for the countryside around Salisbury and Winchester specialised in corn growing. Its peasants and their wives and children were already fully occupied in the labour-consuming tasks of sowing, weeding and harvesting arable crops. So the clothiers shifted their attention to the north-west of the county between Malmesbury and Westbury, and to the south-west around Mere. In these areas of pastoral dairying, where men with small family holdings had time to combine dairying with another occupation, the cloth industry of Wiltshire subsequently made its principal home.

With few exceptions, all the rural industries of the fifteenth, sixteenth and seventeenth centuries throve in pastoral areas where fresh reserves of labour were available on a part-time basis. And this is where many of them remained into the eighteenth, nineteenth, and some even into the twentieth centuries, though the industries themselves ceased to be organised on a domestic basis and moved into mills and factories.

The structure of the rural cloth making communities in Wiltshire serves as a model for many other parts of the country. The Wiltshire cloth area was itself only part of a larger region stretching into east Somerset and Gloucestershire where the same kind of semi-wooded, pastoral country supported dairy farmers and cloth-workers. In Suffolk and Norfolk the partly wooded, partly pasture country in the centre of the two counties also developed a cloth industry at an early date which was combined with dairying. Industrial growth was slower in the Kentish Weald but by the sixteenth century many small farmers – some stock-keepers, some dairy-men – were weaving cloth and seem to have sold both cloth and cheese to itinerant clothiers. In the Lancashire forest of Rossendale cloth working was carried on jointly with stock rearing. Pasture farmers in the valleys radiating from Kendal in the Lake District took up the manufacture of cheaper cloths which sold well in Mediterranean countries.

Wool cloth was not the only domestic handicraft stimulated by an expanding national market. The rapidly increasing population in the Tudor period,

119 Map of the Cloth Industries, c 1500 and c 1700. Based on Bowden, The Wool Trade in Tudor and Stuart England.

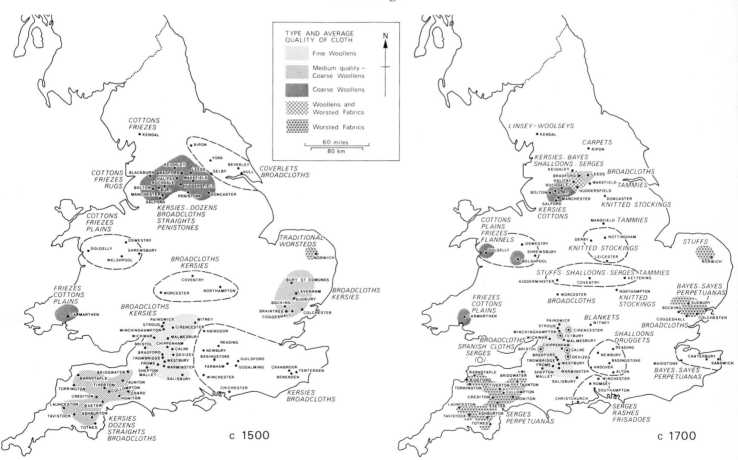

120 *Handknitting flowered into a national industry in the sixteenth century. The men and women of a north Yorkshire village, pictured in the nineteenth century, sit to knit and gossip. A shepherd knits as he leads his four sheep out to the fells to graze.*

together with rising standards of living among the gentry and merchant class, enlarged the demand for all types of textiles and handicraft work. New and ever changing fashions in clothes caught on among the well-to-do. Handicraft industries which had hitherto catered only for local customers became enmeshed in the web of national and overseas trade as merchants scoured all England for goods to supply to the towns of the kingdom and countries abroad.

Stocking knitting was one craft which suddenly flowered into a national industry in the sixteenth century, serving eager buyers in London and Holland with mittens and socks in a great variety of patterns and colours for all ages and sexes. In north Yorkshire it was centred on Richmond and employed a thousand knitters from the dales making 166 dozen pairs of stockings in a week. Northampton employed knitters from the Northamptonshire forests; Norwich found knitters among the fishermen and their wives on the Norfolk coast. Other centres were Doncaster, Rotherham and Nottingham, the latter depending on knitters from Sherwood Forest. Thus, the 'terrible hand-knitters of Dent', as Robert Southey termed them, who flourished in Dentdale in the 1870s were carrying on a tradition that went back at least 300 years. Men and women knitted and farmed, knitting as they led their beasts out to graze, or as they walked to market. Singing quickened the rhythm of their movements so that their needles flew faster than the eye could see. A champion knitter from Cotterdale won renown for her ability to complete a pair of men's stockings on one day's walk to the market at Hawes and back.

121 *William Lee was the inventor of the stocking knitting frame. A broadsheet in his memory shows this intricate machine, said to consist of 3000 pieces.*

TO THE
WORSHIPFUL COMPANY
OF
FRAME-WORK-KNITTERS

In the Year 1589, the Ingenious WILLIAM LEE, Master of Arts, of St. JOHN'S COLLEGE, CAMBRIDGE, devis'd this profitable Art of Knitting Stockings: But his Invention being despis'd, he went to FRANCE, Yet of IRON to himself, but to us and others of GOLD. In Memory of so great a GENIUS this is here depicted.

In antient days, when Dame ELIZA reign'd,
Who prov'd to Infant Arts a nursing Friend,
And, made, by kind Encouragement she gave,
The Scolar studious, & the Soldier brave;
Then ev'ry Genius did his Pow'r exert,
And labour'd to advance some useful Art:
Amongst the rest, LEE of immortal fame,
To learning bred upon the banks of CAM,
By great BELLONA favour'd & inspir'd,
Rais'd a new Engine (even now admir'd)
Whose curious form in ev'ry Part displays
The force of Love in those reforming days;
For Love, enrag'd by cool neglect & spite
First brought this artful Stocking Frame to light,
That pretty Maid, when woo'd might lay aside
Their KNITTING (which was then their only Pride)
And be the more at leisure to attend
The Sighs and flatteries of an am'rous Friend.

Nor is there one Device that can appear
More wondrous than the FRAME depicted here.

NB. Lord Rt CAREY Earl of HUNSDON was admitted a Member of this Company on the 25th of June, 1666, and in 1677 was admitted a * Workhouse Keeper and bound Wm Pope Apprentice.

Three Thousand Pieces doth the whole contain,
Th'unwearyd Task of one poor Scolars Brain;
Who, in revenge of Female slights, was mov'd
To spoil the KNITTING of the Dame he lov'd.

Since such a curious Art that tends to gain,
Its Origin we owe to PROUD DISDAIN,
May each desponding Lover pensive grow,
And when despis'd, the like Resentment show!

Nor is there one MECHANIC Art can name
A PEER a Workman but the KNITTING FRAME;
Who in his Youth was to the Engine bred,
And serv'd seven Years Apprentice to the trade,
Wrought many Years as modern Fame records,
Yet liv'd to sit among his Brethren LORDS.

Since thus this useful FRAME has honour'd been
By a late noble PEER, that work'd therein,
May the famd Art be still more famous made,
And peaceful times with riches bless the trade!

GEORGE SIMMONS, Beadle.

* In the Time of Lord CAREY, no FRAME-WORKE KNITTER was permitted to take an Apprentice, without first giving a specimen of his Ability, and if approv'd, was afterwards call'd a Workhouse keeper.

LONDON. Printed by J. Davis No 10 Brownlow Street Long Acre Citizen and FRAME-WORK-KNITTER.

122 *Flax growing was an important domestic industry in the forests and fens. Flax was prepared for use by being beaten with a wooden blade and passed through a flax breaker. The dressed flax was then either sold or spun and woven by the family.*

123   Hemp dressing involved several separate operations: soaking, stripping, carding. Here a workshop has been provided but cottagers also undertook the processes in their homes, having grown the crop, like flax, in their crofts.

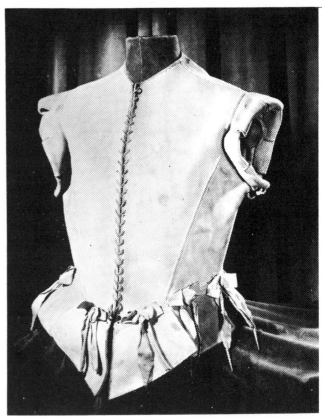

124   Fine doeskin doublet made c 1580. Leather working was a craft which flourished in cattle-keeping country, producing such articles as bags, bottles and straps.

The stocking knitting industry of Sherwood Forest was centred in a stock-keeping, pastoral district, but was led along paths that diverged from those of other areas specialising in hand-knitting by the introduction of the knitting frame. The inventor, William Lee, was brought up in a Sherwood Forest village and invented his first frame in 1589. It was not immediately accepted: Queen Elizabeth discouraged Lee when he sought a patent for his machine, fearing, it is alleged, that it would cause unemployment among the hand knitters. She urged him to construct a machine for knitting silk hose which he completed in 1598. Disappointed by this response, Lee moved to Rouen in France and received the support of the French king.

After Lee's death, his brother and fellow workers returned to England in the 1640s, and the framework knitting industry spread through Nottinghamshire and Leicestershire, the two counties which ever since have remained important as centres of hosiery knitting.

Other handicraft industries which are identified with pastoral economies are lace making and basket making. Lace making was a significant by-employment in Bernwood Forest in Buckinghamshire, in the North-amptonshire forests, and in Somerset, in and around Shepton Mallet. Basket making was an occupation of fenlanders using osiers grown along the dykes and in special osier beds.

125 *An unprecedented expansion of industry of all types took place in rural areas from the fifteenth century. It often led to disputes between land users. This letter to Basil Fielding, and others, of theco unty of Warwick, puts the complaint from John Bugg and Thomas Robinson, 'farmers of the great coalmine at Bedworth', that a customary route for transporting coal from the mine 'into other shires' had been barred to them: 'we pray and require you to take order that the said way may be for the present open and freed from disturbance'.*

126 a & b *Mining techniques are illustrated by engravings from the mid-sixteenth century. The methods of sorting, sieving and washing copper ore were brought from the continent in 1565 when, at the invitation of Elizabeth I, German miners came from Neusohl in Hungary to set up copper mining in Kendal.*

127 At Bentley Grange near Emley in Yorkshire are earthworks formed by medieval iron pits. Waste material was scattered around the openings of shallow shafts leading to the bed of iron ore. The shafts have collapsed and trees and thorn bushes have found a roothold in the loosened soil of the hollows.

128 Bonsall lead mines in Derbyshire were probably worked by a partnership of two or three men who combined mining and farming for subsistence. The small, grass-covered hollows and mounds are shallow workings of the seventeenth century; lighter coloured waste heaps are more recent.

129 *During the Middle Ages, Barnack Quarry near Stamford in Rutland was one of the best-known stone-quarries in England – yet the medieval village of Barnack remained an agricultural community, with 122 taxpayers in 1377, no larger than its neighbours.*

WEAVERS OF HEMP AND FLAX

Less widely publicised, because the market was purely domestic, were the linen and hemp weaving industries. They did not produce goods to compete in foreign markets with the fine quality cloth of Holland and Silesia, but purchasers of this material were not all discriminating connoisseurs prepared to pay for a high priced product. Linen and hempen cloth were needed for a multitude of everyday purposes – for sheets and other household linen, for aprons, and for sacks of all sorts.

Hemp and flax weaving were considerable domestic industries in the forests and fens where the raw materials were already grown: for example, in the fens around the Wash; in the Isle of Axholme where they made hemp cloth for sacks; in the Northamptonshire forests; and in Somerset and Dorset. In the late seventeenth century an energetic propaganda campaign was mounted in favour of growing these crops and weaving them into cloth in order to reduce the scale of foreign imports. This seems to have made some headway in the counties of the West Midlands, particularly in Staffordshire. In other places cloth weaving was fostered on the basis of imported supplies of hemp and flax which could be readily shipped from the Baltic to Hull and thence transported inland along the newly improved rivers. Thus the weavers of Nidderdale changed over from wool to flax in the seventeenth century: inland vessels trading between Boroughbridge and Hull took away their lead and brought them Danzig flax. In the late eighteenth century a cotton weaving industry was set up in mills in the same dale.

Another large group of rural industries which supplemented the livelihood of peasants was based on the use of minerals or other natural resources. Some industries were located in pastoral areas because they utilised local minerals that could not have been exploited economically elsewhere. Most of the seams of coal, lead, iron and copper in England lie in the Highland Zone, while the exceptions are found in pastoral areas of the lowlands. Many such seams were worked by small partnerships of men who mined for a season and then transferred their attention to their land and farm stock. In the forests charcoal burning and glass making flourished alongside a range of timber and wood-turning industries and tanneries, which in their turn supported leather-working crafts in the neighbourhood. Iron working was widespread in the Forest of Dean and in the Sussex Weald. Glass makers settled in the Sussex Weald in the sixteenth century, moved on to the Hampshire Forests when their timber supply diminished in the seventeenth century, and eventually settled in Stourbridge. Local iron-working

130 Woodworking crafts were a by-employment in all forest areas. Bodgers, or chair makers, in the Chiltern beechwoods erected small rough cabins and cut timber to size for chair legs. The industry survived into the twentieth century.

131 Barrel making was an important woodland craft. Coopers in Suffolk used ash trees to make barrels for salted fish from the East Anglian coast.

132 Edge tool makers were especially numerous in north-east Worcestershire. Belbroughton near Stourbridge, boasted seven families of smiths who sent scythes to the grinders by the gross.

133 & 134 Charcoal burners moved ceaselessly around the forests, living in temporary huts. The furnace was a cone-shaped heap of timber, supported by a central pole, and made airtight by a plaster of earth and charcoal dust. When the furnace was lit, vents were opened in the outer clay covering to promote combustion. In the Forest of Dean and Kinver Forest charcoal burning and iron manufacture were mutually dependent; in the Weald, iron and glass making both relied on charcoal for fuel.

supported large numbers of scythe smiths in north east Worcestershire, while nail makers thronged the neighbourhood of Wednesbury. Potters were established in north-west Staffordshire around Burslem. Leather industries were widely dispersed over all cattle-keeping country: hence the glove making in Wychwood Forest, Oxfordshire. Timber industries included the making of furniture in the Chilterns, the making of coopers' barrels from ash in Suffolk, and hurdle and ladder making in Northamptonshire's forests.

With the expansion of rural industries, more and more people were lured to the pastoral districts from corn-growing areas. In the latter the consolidation of farms into larger units and the conversion of some lands to pasture were reducing the demand for labour, while in the traditional pastoral areas land was abundant, rights of common could be acquired without great difficulty, and industries offered by-employments.

INTEGRATION OF FARMING AND INDUSTRIAL WORK

Those who moved to these growth areas became what are known today as peasant workers. For them farming and industrial work were closely integrated in a routine of labour which harnessed the energies of the whole family, afforded variety of occupation, and by yielding

food and a source of cash income represented a good insurance against want. Not many peasant workers are left in England, but they still form a substantial proportion of the peasant population in east European countries, where the advantages of the combination of work on the land and in industry are fully recognised. We have a record of the daily routine of a peasant-weaver in Halifax in 1782 who one day worked out of doors until 3 p.m. and then wove two yards of cloth before sunset. On wet days he could weave eight or nine yards. On Christmas Eve, he wove two yards before 11 a.m. and spent the rest of the day on winter jobs around the house and midden. He also did occasional work for other farmers – hauling timber, preparing a calf stall, and fetching and carrying.

Peasant workers seem to have gained on every side. Although they suffered along with the full time industrial workers during severe trade depressions, it is evident that they suffered a good deal less than those

135 Principal centre of the iron industry in the late Middle Ages was the Weald of Kent and Sussex. At Cowden, the Kent water was dammed to form Furnace Pond which supplied water with sufficient force to work the mechanical bellows and hammers of a furnace and forge. In 1574, thirty-eight forges and thirty-two furnaces were located in Sussex.

136 *Ashburnham Furnace was probably the largest of the Wealden iron works. The steam worked a wheel which provided power for the forge.*

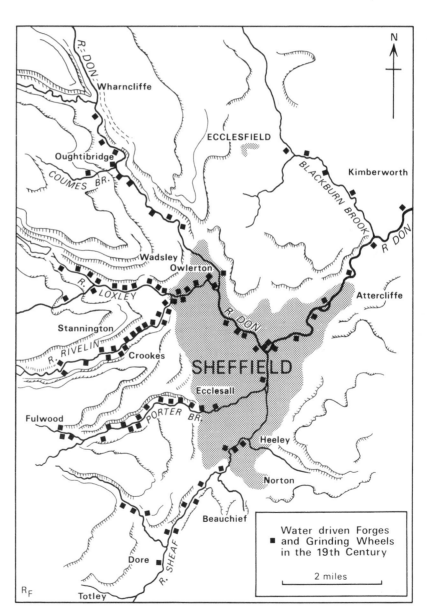

137 *Sketch plan of Sheffield and neighbourhood, showing watercourses and water power formerly employed (from G. I. H. Lloyd, The Cutlery Trades).*

who lived in the cloth towns and were divorced from the land. And in the late seventeenth century their lot was compared favourably with that of peasants and cottagers in arable areas who were then experiencing the hardships of a prolonged depression in grain prices.

The establishment of industries in formerly purely rural areas, however, gradually and imperceptibly brought about a fundamental transformation. The rural industries by their very success intensified competition. Young men from stocking knitting families in Dent and Sedbergh, for example, were apprenticed to craftsmen in the worsted weaving and capping trades in Norwich and learned more advanced techniques and more sophisticated forms of trade. The search for labour spread in the late seventeenth century from pastoral areas into arable districts troubled by overpopulation and unemployment. These problems were especially acute in villages where the absence of a squire had permitted immigration to go unchecked, or where agricultural changes had reduced the demand for labour on the land. Competition in trade and for employment tended to depress the workers' conditions.

DIVISION BETWEEN AGRICULTURE AND INDUSTRY

Eventually, the pressure of demand on rural craftsmen reached a stage where some men depended wholly on work in industry, the movement into factories gathered momentum, and those retaining a stake in the land could no longer compete on equal terms. The scales which had held agriculture and industry in balance tipped to the industrial side and the peasant worker had to relinquish his foothold on the land. This had happened to a large extent in Wiltshire, Somerset, and East Anglia by the early seventeenth century. Daniel Defoe's description of Halifax in the early eighteenth century reveals another community already largely dependent on its industry: the inhabitants hardly sowed enough corn to feed their poultry, and relied on grain supplies from Lincolnshire, Nottinghamshire, and the East Riding. Their butter came from the East and North Ridings, and their cheese from Cheshire and Warwickshire. They bought the winter's supply of meat at the bullock fairs in Halifax in September and October. Later in the century begin the descriptions of domestic handicraftsmen working excessively long hours in their cottages for a pittance. Competition had become unbearably intense and domestic industry was regarded as something akin to slavery.

But for a long period of perhaps two to three hundred years, domestic industries had offered substantial economic and social benefits to rural communities. They are perhaps best illustrated in the words of a not very sympathetic observer.

Whilst travelling in Derbyshire, Defoe watched a man climb out of a lead mine, leather-jacketed, pale, thin, and as grey as the lead he toiled for. He looked like 'an inhabitant of the dark regions'. Defoe rode on and came upon the home of another miner in a cave in the hillside. Again he could not conceal his horror, and yet on going inside he found a clean, neat and pleasantly comfortable home, divided by curtains into three rooms. Earthenware, pewter and brass filled the shelves. The miner's wife was comely and her five children plump and bonny. They had a close of barley at the door, ready to be harvested; bacon hung in the roof of the cave; a lean cow grazed at the door; and a sow and pigs rooted about nearby. The husband earned a daily wage at the mine and his wife washed ore whenever she was free. Defoe grudgingly admitted that their life gave 'the appearance of substance. . . . They seemed to live very pleasantly.'

The advantages of a country life combined with a variety of daily and weekly work are experiences from the past which should not be deemed irrelevant in our economic and social planning for the future.

FURTHER READING

Birrell, Jean 'Peasant Craftsmen in the Medieval Forest' *Agricultural History Review*, 17 (1969), 91–107

Bythell, Duncan *The Handloom Weavers. A Study in the Cotton Industry during the Industrial Revolution* (Cambridge, 1969)

Hartley, Marie and Ingilby, Joan *The Old Handknitters of the Dales* (Clapham via Lancaster, 1969)

Hey, David 'A Dual Economy in South Yorkshire' *Agricultural History Review*, 17 (1969), 108–9

Hunt, C. J. *The Leadminers of the Northern Pennines in the Eighteenth and Nineteenth Centuries* (Manchester, 1970)

Jennings, Bernard *A History of Nidderdale* (Huddersfield, 1967)

Thirsk, Joan 'Industries in the Countryside' *Essays in the Economic and Social History of Tudor and Stuart England in honour of R. H. Tawney* ed Fisher, F. J. (1961)

Weatherill, Lorna *The Pottery Trade and North Staffordshire, 1660–1760* (Manchester, 1970)

9 THE DISTRIBUTION OF WEALTH AND POPULATION IN TUDOR ENGLAND

by JOHN SHEAIL

THE Tudor period of 1485 to 1603 is an interesting phase in the development of the English countryside. The Norman Conquest was as remote from Henry VIII and his daughter Elizabeth as these monarchs are from the present day. During the 450 years since William the Conqueror had arrived in England, extensive areas of woodland had been cleared, and grass, scrub and arable land were more in evidence. There were about 2,500,000 people in England in the early sixteenth century compared with 1,500,000 to 2,000,000 in Norman times. Though the population still depended completely on the corn harvest for survival, large flocks of sheep were being kept for wool. Shepherds were a familiar sight, and the wool trade and industry brought prosperity to many parts of England. Numbers of houses and streets were rebuilt in Tudor times, and a traveller passing through the country would have seen more new houses than ever before. Many fine new churches were constructed. Leading sheep-masters, merchants and traders often paid for the rebuilding of

138 & 139 During Tudor times more new houses were built in England than ever before. At Lavenham, Suffolk, and at Chiddingstone in Kent, the homes of the more prosperous families still survive.

140 One of the few sixteenth-century paintings to show the landscape and the common people of England is this wedding feast in Bermondsey, attributed to Joris Hoefnagel. It shows groups of men and women, ranging from pastry cooks, shipwrights and pedlars to mothers with babies.

their local churches, and the Cotswold 'wool churches', for example, reflect not only the religious fervour of the period, but also the concentration of wealth in that part of England.

Much is known about events in London, life at the royal court and the activities of men of importance, like Sir Francis Drake, but much less about provincial England and the life of the common people. There are the occasional brief glimpses with exceptional events like the serious rebellion in Norfolk in 1549, led by one Robert Ket. The rebels protested against their landlords who overgrazed the common pastures with animals and abused their rights by keeping excessive numbers of pigeons and rabbits which damaged farm crops. Historians have suggested that the population was so high in that part of Norfolk that there was not enough land to grow food and feed the peasants' animals. There is very little reliable information on the population of Norfolk or any other part of the country for that period. It is not known how many people lived in the towns and villages scattered over the countryside and whether there was a large range of wealth in the farming and trading communities. Towns such as Lavenham, famed for its textiles, and the port of Plymouth were very prosperous, but we do not know how they compared with other centres and parts of England.

There were regional differences in the economy and society of Tudor times. Numerous historians have drawn a distinction between the highland and lowland parts of England, but there is no precise way of measur-

ing these regional differences. Very little is known about the diversity in standards of living and, paradoxically, least is known about the men closest to the land – the men who cleared the woods, ploughed the fields and built houses in each village and town. These men left no letters or account books when they died because most of them could not read or write. The few people who could write have recorded little information on the common people: they were much more interested in kings and queens, clerics and seafarers.

The population was never counted, there were no censuses, and priests did not begin to keep parish registers until 1538. Many of the early registers have been lost and, for example, only half the parishes of Huntingdonshire have records going back as far as the sixteenth century. Because of this historians and geographers have experimented with the use of Tudor tax returns in estimating the total population and its distribution. Unfortunately, many of the returns have been lost and some of those which survive are useless because so few paid taxes. But on five occasions, a special tax called a lay subsidy was levied. The Crown was so short of money for fighting wars on the Scottish border and in Europe that it taxed a very large number of people in the years 1524 and 1525, and in 1543, 1544 and 1545. The tax lists included every man owning £1 or more in possessions or earning that amount from landed income. In 1524 and 1525, the Crown also taxed everyone earning £1 or more each year in wages. Since most men earned at least £3 a year, only a small

141 & 142 Illustrations in the Shepheards Calendar *of 1579 showing shepherds and a lumberman. Both wool and timber were expanding trades in the sixteenth century.*

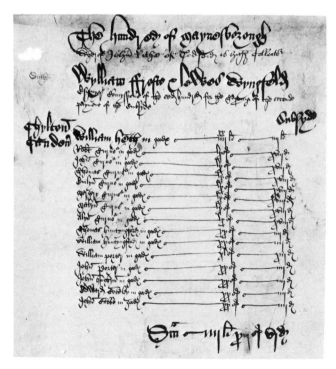

143 *A major source of information on Tudor society is provided by the tax lists compiled in 1524, 1525, 1543 and 1545. The 1525 list of taxpayers for Chilton Candover, a Hampshire village, was prepared by the surveyors Wylliam Ffroste and Lewes Wyngfeld. The tax collector lived in the hamlet of Todford. There were fifteen payers in all, paying a total of £4 13s 6d. Most people owned between £1 and £3 in possessions. The richest man was William Heth, owning £80. Other contributors were Robert, John, Thomas, Emlyn, Mergery, Malyn, and Alys Turnor, Thomas and William Huntyngford, William and John Porter, John Huchyn, Edward Cokeley and John Cabbe.*

proportion of the adult male population was left out of the lists. Fresh surveys of wealth were made in each of the five years, and many of these lists still survive.

The names of the taxpayers were written down by the surveyors in each year. They gave the name of the taxpayer, the character and value of his wealth, and how much tax he owed in that year. Taxpayers were listed under their respective settlements and it is easy to find out the number of taxpayers in each area and how much they paid in taxation. Very often, several taxpayers shared the same surname and may well have lived under the same roof. There was usually a wide range in wealth, with one or two rich men and many more relatively poor. The lists usually included the names of a few women who were widows or had an independent income. There were no clergy because the tax was only imposed on the laity. The lists of each of the five years included most of the men in each community, although they vary in detail according to changes in population and personal wealth.

These tax surveys give a unique insight into the state of the common people in both town and country areas. Often, these lists are the only record of a man's existence. The whole of England was taxed with the exception of the four northernmost counties, Cheshire and the Cinque Ports of Kent and Sussex. Throughout the medieval period, these parts were exempt from the taxes imposed on the remainder of the country. Some parts of Herefordshire and Shropshire were not included in the returns of the 1520s because they were then in Wales, which was not included in the lay subsidy. They do, however, have returns for the 1540s, a few years after the Act of Union when they were transferred to England.

THE NUMBER OF TAXPAYERS

By counting the number of taxpayers and comparing the returns, an assessment of the distribution of population and wealth can be made. When considering the lists for Birmingham and Coventry, for example, it is clear that Coventry was the leading centre at the end of the medieval period – there were 723 taxpayers compared with 153 in Birmingham which also paid twenty times less money in taxation. The number of taxpayers varied between one year and another. There was some difference in the basis for taxation in the 1520s and the 1540s, but the surviving returns for the country show that overall there were only 5 per cent more taxpayers in the 1540s. In the town of Gloucester, there were 466 names in the list of 1524 and 494 names in 1544.

The information contained in the tax surveys can be mapped to show variations in the number of people paying tax and the amount of money paid to the Exchequer. Unfortunately, since many of the lists have been lost or destroyed, such maps are incomplete. All the surviving documents are now stored in the Public Record Office in London. Few places have a complete set of lists for all five years, and for some areas all the relevant documents have been lost. Hence, the distribution of taxpayers cannot be studied in parts of Leicestershire, Lincolnshire, Kent and Somerset. But one or two lists have survived for most villages and towns and have been used to compile a map showing the distribution of taxpayers in Tudor England.

Henry VIII and his Exchequer would probably have been puzzled by maps showing the distribution of men and money. Although they had access to all the lists, it is doubtful whether they ever conceived of the distribution of taxpayers in a cartographic form. They could not have plotted the information accurately on a map since there were no large-scale county maps at that time. Christopher Saxton produced the first series of regional maps from the 1570s onwards, and even then the number of acres in each parish and county remained unknown. England was not accurately measured until the nineteenth century when the Ordnance Survey undertook the work. It has therefore only been possible to plot the density of taxpayers and amount of tax paid per square mile since about 1900.

The lists do not, of course, give the total population of each settlement – there is no complete list of people living in each village and town – but they are a guide to the size of the population. By comparing the number of taxpayers in one village with those in other villages, the relative size of each community can be estimated. The tax surveys also indicate the relative size of towns – in the 1520s there were 784 taxpayers in Canterbury, 523 in Cambridge, 431 in Oxford, 401 in Leicester and 330 in Winchester. These figures suggest how the towns ranked in terms of total population. There were forty-four taxpayers per square mile in the Avon valley of Hampshire, about thirty around Alton and Winchester, and fewer than twenty taxpayers per square mile in north-east Hampshire – an indication of how the density of population varied within one county.

DISTRIBUTION OF WEALTH FROM TAX RETURNS

Analysis of tax returns provides considerable infor-

SAXTON'S MAP OF NORFOLK, 1574

144 Christopher Saxton began his survey of the counties of England in the 1570s. Although the maps give little indication of the size and wealth of the settlements, they do show the location of all habitations and give some topographical details.

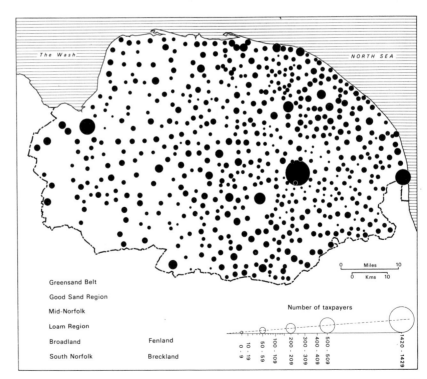

145 The distribution of taxpayers in Norfolk 1524–5 and 1543–5. The area of each circle is proportional to the number of contributors in each taxation unit. Norwich, Kings Lynn and Great Yarmouth had large populations. Many of the taxpayers lived along the north coast in the textile centres of eastern Norfolk.

Greensand Belt

Good Sand Region

Mid-Norfolk

Loam Region

Broadland   Fenland

South Norfolk   Breckland

Number of taxpayers

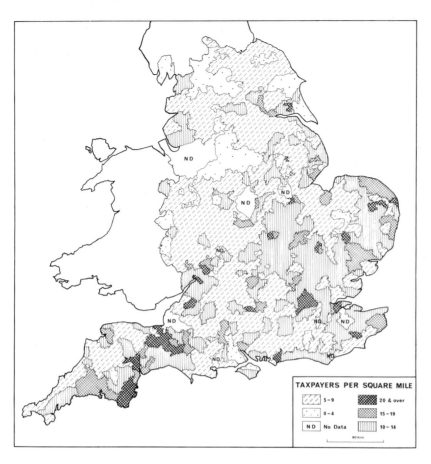

TAXPAYERS PER SQUARE MILE

▨ 5 – 9	◼ 20 & over
⸳ 0 – 4	▨ 15 – 19
N D No Data	▥ 10 – 14

80 Km

146   The spread of taxpayers in 1524–5. Returns for 1543–5 are given where earlier records are missing; the later returns only are used in Yorkshire and Lancashire. The distribution of men and money varied markedly, reflecting the importance of urban centres and indicating the presence of local industries and trade.

mation on the distribution of wealth. In 1524, the City of London contributed £8,263 in tax; followed by Norwich which paid £739; Bristol £465; Coventry £463; Salisbury £405; and Southwark £387. The surveyors wrote down how much money was owed by each borough and hundred, or group of parishes, in two documents, one of which has survived in its entirety. The map based on these returns is almost complete. Parts of Somerset, Northamptonshire and Kent paid over twenty shillings per square mile, compared with under five shillings in the Pennines, New Forest and Breckland. In 1524–5, the returns of the counties of Lancashire, Shropshire and Yorkshire seem to have been compiled in a different way from those of the rest of the country. The towns and villages contained fewer taxpayers and paid less tax than might have been expected. There were many more taxpayers listed in the 1540s returns for those areas.

Hence, such centres as Beverley, Hull, Manchester and York were probably more prosperous than the lists would suggest. The tax surveyors in these parts may have misunderstood their work or they may have tried to deceive the Exchequer in London.

On the basis of these tax returns, East Anglia and the east Midlands were wealthier and more densely populated than the west Midlands and central southern England. Parts of the coastline were exceptionally prosperous and had large centres of population. The Thames estuary and south Devon coast had very high returns, and the coastline of Norfolk, Lindsey and Sussex had higher returns than most places inland. The situation in south Kent is obscured by the fact that the Cinque Ports were excluded from the lay subsidy. The Essex coastline paid a large amount in tax but the number of contributors was relatively small.

Wealth was often concentrated in towns, and in very

The amount of tax paid in each part of the country in 1524–5. An average is taken where the returns for the two years differ and in some cases the records for one year are not available.

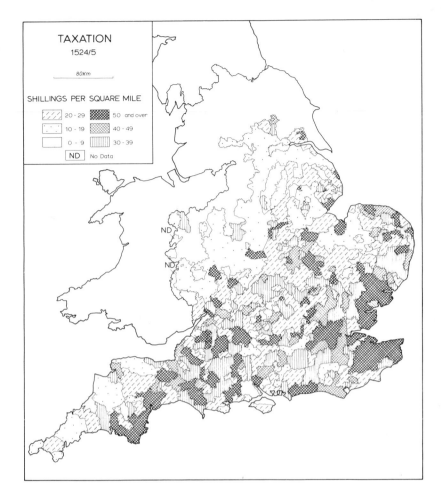

TAXATION
1524/5

80Km

SHILLINGS PER SQUARE MILE

20 - 29   50 and over
10 - 19   40 - 49
0 - 9   30 - 39
ND No Data

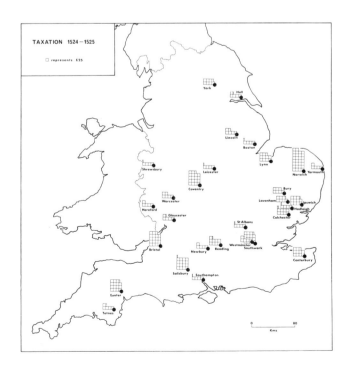

TAXATION 1524 – 1525

☐ represents £25

148 Tax paid by the thirty leading urban centres in 1524–5. The map does not show the return for the City of London, which paid ten times more taxation than Norwich.

few hands. The towns associated with the textile industry, such as Lavenham, Long Melford, Nayland and Sudbury in Suffolk, were very prosperous although the records show that most of the money rested in the hands of only a few of the townspeople. Alice Spring, a widow of Lavenham, was worth £1000 and paid £50 in tax in 1524, a high percentage of the £179 paid in taxes at Lavenham by 199 people. Of the taxpayers, 164 paid £9 and the remaining 35, £170.

In one or two cases, the tax surveyors noted that men owned property in more than one settlement. For instance, they found that five men with possessions in St Ives, Huntingdonshire, lived in other parts of the county and in Cambridgeshire. This pattern of dispersed wealth meant that quite distinctive regions were economically and socially interdependent. The re-

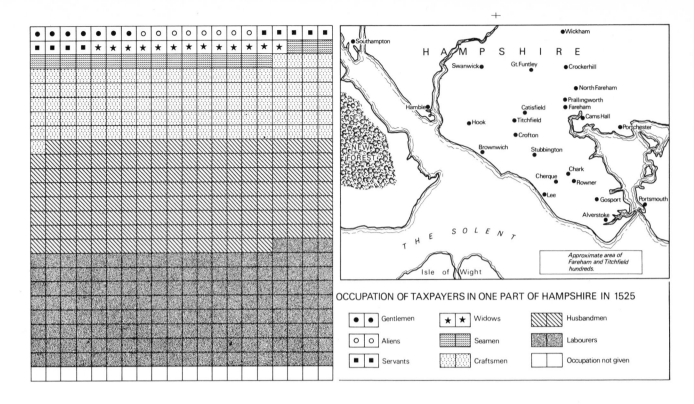

OCCUPATION OF TAXPAYERS IN ONE PART OF HAMPSHIRE IN 1525

● ● Gentlemen	★ ★ Widows	Husbandmen
○ ○ Aliens	Seamen	Labourers
■ ■ Servants	Craftsmen	Occupation not given

149 Two-thirds of the 500 taxpayers in this part of Hampshire, relating approximately to the area of Fareham and Titchfield hundreds, worked on the land. Some were prosperous farmers, but the majority were very poor farm labourers. A few seamen and aliens are found in the coastal villages and towns.

150 Minting coins in the sixteenth century. Debasement of the silver coinage helped to prevent State bankruptcy on several occasions in this era of inflation in England.

sources of the fens, for example, were exploited by villages on the neighbouring uplands of Lincolnshire, Norfolk and Suffolk. The peat fens were used where possible as summer grazing grounds.

The five surveys were all made during the autumn – a good time from the point of view of the Exchequer because the crops had just been harvested and the population was at its most affluent. But, of course, the surveys do not give the situation in other years of the sixteenth century and it is clear that some settlements and taxpayers were going through a bad time in the 1520s and 1540s. Brighton, a town of ninety-six houses, was excluded from the 1520s lay subsidy because it had recently suffered from a calamity: it had been raided and devastated by the French in 1514. Heavy rains in 1524 caused much flooding, ruining crops and encouraging disease among livestock in many parts of the country. In south-east Devon, for example, 3744 sheep, thirty-nine horses, thirty cows, fifteen bullocks and hogs, and thirteen oxen were lost, leaving farmers much the poorer.

The lists rarely give the occupations of people, but the trades of many taxpayers are noted in the surveys of Bristol, Cambridge, Coventry and Northampton A fishmonger, grocer, mercer and draper were among the wealthiest men in Northampton in 1524, and, according to W. G. Hoskins, about 70 per cent of the taxpayers were engaged in the leather, clothing, food and textile trades. The lists also give some information on employment in the hundreds of Fareham and Titchfield, Hampshire, in 1525. This part of Hampshire was predominantly rural with about two-thirds of the taxpayers described as labourers, husbandmen or yeomen. Most people lived in small hamlets which could support only one or two carpenters, thatchers and butchers. Craftsmen and artisans generally lived in the larger centres, such as Fareham and Titchfield, where tailors, weavers, shoemakers and tanners were found. Nineteen seamen paid an average of 1s in taxation, and craftsmen producing clothing and furnishings contributed about 1s 6d. It may be significant that as many as thirteen widows were included in the list of 500 names. They were acting as heads of their households and paid an average of 2s in tax.

ALIENS AND MIGRATION

Aliens paid twice the normal rates of taxation and where they had no wealth at all, they contributed a poll tax of 8d. Laurence Browne, a Scotsman, was in this category in Ashby, Lincolnshire. Aliens were common in London and Middlesex, especially in Smithfield, and among the entries of ports such as Poole and Hull. They came mainly from the Low Countries, northern France and Italy. It is sometimes possible to discover instances of Englishmen moving about the country. William Cheshire was taxed in Preston, Shropshire, in 1524, but the surveyors of 1525 reported that he had moved away. It is difficult to prove cases of migration because the variety of Christian names was small in Tudor times and it is impossible to identify accurately many people in the lists.

The taxation lists are complicated documents to use and they pose more problems than they solve. They do, however, cover the greater part of the country and treat towns and villages, farmers, tradesmen and industrialists in a similar way. They are an extremely important source of information on life in early modern England, midway between the coming of the Normans and the economy and society of today.

FURTHER READING

Beresford, M. W. 'The Lay Subsidies, part II – After 1334', Lay subsidies and poll taxes (1963)

Bindoff, S. T. Tudor England (1950)

Blanchard, I. 'Population Change, Enclosure, and the Early Tudor Economy', Economic History Review, 23 (1970), 427–45

Bowden, P. J. The wool trade in Tudor and Stuart England (1962)

Charman, D. 'Wealth and Trade in Leicester in the Early Sixteenth Century', Transactions of the Leicestershire Archaeological and Historical Society, 15 (1949), 69–97

Chibnell, A. C. and Woodman, A. V. 'Subsidy Roll for the County of Buckingham, Anno 1524', Buckinghamshire Record Society, 8 (1950)

Cornwall, J. 'The Lay Subsidy Rolls for the County of Sussex, 1524–5', Sussex Record Society, 56 (1956–7)

Cornwall, J. 'The People of Rutland in 1522', Transactions of the Leicestershire Archaeological and Historical Society, 37 (1961–2), 7–28

Cornwall, J. 'English Country Towns in the 1520s', Economic History Review, 15 (1962–3), 54–69

Cornwall, J. 'English Population in the Early Sixteenth Century', Economic History Review, 23 (1970), 32–44

Fisher, F. J. 'Influenza and Inflation in Tudor England', Economic History Review, 18 (1965), 120–39

Glasscock, R. E. 'The Distribution of Wealth in East Anglia in the Early Fourteenth Century', Transactions of the Institute of British Geographers, 32 (1963), 113–23

Hervey, S. H. A. 'Suffolk in 1524', Suffolk Green Books, 10 (1910)

Hollingsworth, T. H. Historical demography (1969)

Hoskins, W. G. 'English Provincial Towns in the Early Sixteenth Century', Transactions of the Royal Historical Society, 6 (1956), 1–19

Patten, John, 'Village and town: an Occupational Study', Agricultural History Review, 20 (1972), 1–16

Russell, J. C. British Medieval Population (1948)

Schofield, R. S. 'The Geographical Distribution of Wealth in England, 1334–1649', Economic History Review, 18 (1965), 483–510

Sheail, J. 'The Distribution of Taxable Population and Wealth in England During the Early Sixteenth Century: A Commentary', Transactions of the Institute of British Geographers, 55 (1972), 111–126

Smith, C. T. 'The Cambridge Region: Settlement and Population', The Cambridge Region, ed by J. A. Steers (1965), 133–51

Thirk, Joan 'Sources of Information on Population, 1500–1760', Amateur Historian, 4 (1959), 131

Thirsk, Joan, ed The Agrarian History of England and Wales Vol 4 1500–1640 (1967)

10 THE GREAT AGE OF THE YEOMAN FARMERS

by JAMES YELLING

THE sixteenth and seventeenth centuries stand as the great age of peasant farming in England. By this time the peasantry had progressed from a state of subjection in the middle ages to the greater independence evoked by the term 'yeoman', whilst the inroads of the industrial revolution and large-scale capitalist farming were largely yet to come. The growth in farm sizes had brought a new and more confident class of farmer to the fore. Whatever the state of other social classes, it is generally recognised that farmers were becoming more prosperous, and this new wealth is shown above all in their houses, attractive and substantial buildings which still survive in many areas.

REGIONAL FARMING

Part of the charm of such houses is that whether on the Cotswolds or in the Midland Plain, building material and style reflect the character of the local area. Farmers were still very much part of local communities, and as is normal in peasant societies there was a strong interrelationship between cultural life and the environment. In no other period is the distinctive regional variety of English farming conditions so clearly demonstrated. This regional theme is of course of intrinsic interest to geographers, but it has also been taken up enthusiastically by the local historians.

A tentative map of farming regions in the sixteenth and early seventeenth centuries has been produced by Dr Joan Thirsk figure 73. Particularly important is the distinction between pasture farming and 'mixed' or mainly arable areas. The pastoral districts were characterised by landscapes of enclosure and mainly dispersed settlement, whereas most, but not all, of the arable districts had nucleated villages and common fields. The contrast between these woodland and champion landscapes was noticed by contemporary topographers such as Leland, and is epitomised in the

151 The sixteenth and seventeenth centuries represent a great age of farming in England when cultivable areas were extended, farm holdings became larger, and new crops and techniques were introduced. The attractive homes built by the new yeoman farmers are evidence of a growing prosperity. Middle Bean Hall Farm, a timber framed farmhouse in Worcestershire, dates from 1635, but a large house on this site is on the Feckenham map of 1591.

152 *Excellent contemporary maps and plans of agricultural and settlement features also survive. An eighteenth-century copy of the 1591 map of Feckenham shows the village with its church and court house. The surrounding open fields are being eaten into by piecemeal enclosure. In the north, settlement was later in date, consisting of isolated farms and hamlets, some of them moated. The map also shows land use.*

153 *Records of farming between 1550 and 1750 include inventories of farmer's possessions. That of Margery Stonnall of Huddington in Worcestershire was made in 1579 and lists some of her farm stock.*

Arden and Feldon of Warwickshire, both true English *pays* reflecting a long interplay between man and the land.

Dr Thirsk's map is of necessity a qualitative summary, but documents exist which should eventually enable a more accurate and detailed regionalisation. In particular, there are the probate inventories in which farmers' possessions were recorded. From these it can be learned, for example, that Margery Stonnall who died at Huddington in Worcestershire in 1579 left to her heirs, amongst other things, six oxen, five acres of wheat, ten acres of beans and peas, her apparel worth 40s and a frying pan worth 4d. A study of the crops recorded in sixteenth-century Worcestershire inventories shows that the broad regional distinctions between pastoral and arable areas were repeated in a more intricate pattern in the crop combinations. It was possible to travel within the space of a few miles from a district growing nearly all wheat, barley and beans to another where rye and oats were virtually the exclusive crops. To a lesser extent livestock combinations were similarly differentiated.

CHANGES IN AGRARIAN ORGANISATION

The same documents which provide us with this unique insight into the geography of English peasant farming also reveal its gradual demise. The process took a long time, but already by the end of the seventeenth century many of the old regional differences were becoming less important. From the beginning of the period pressures were at work to convert farming from a traditional cultural activity to one based on general principles of economics and agricultural management. Many writers, including Fitzherbert, Walter Blith and John Norden, attempted to formulate such principles, covering the whole field from medicine to estate plans and surveys. It must be admitted that some of what was written was nonsense, and that the impact of these works on the ordinary farmer is debatable. But they reflect the spirit of the age.

Such writers consistently advocated enclosure as the key to better husbandry, and in this they have been followed by some modern historians such as Ernle. There undoubtedly were enclosures which served this purpose, but the equation of enclosure with progress and

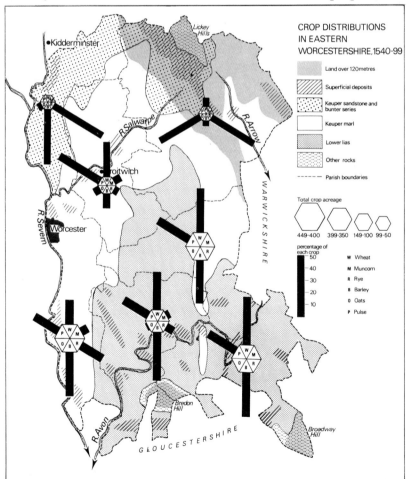

154 Crop distributions in eastern Worcestershire.

open field with stagnation is much too simple. For one thing enclosure had long been a normal feature in certain peasant societies and economies, as in much of the west of England. For another there were common field farmers in many areas who were very commercially minded. These farmers were able to participate in agricultural improvement, although they did not always adopt the same systems as were used on enclosed land.

Most of the period under discussion falls between two highly publicised episodes in enclosure history. It catches only the tail end of the 'lost village' enclosures of the fifteenth century, and precedes the parliamentary enclosures which came mainly after 1750. Enclosure was proceeding rapidly in the interim period, but it provoked less antagonism. The major exception to this was the enclosure of common pasture in the Fenland. In places such as Leicestershire whole parishes were enclosed by agreement, although most of the Midlands

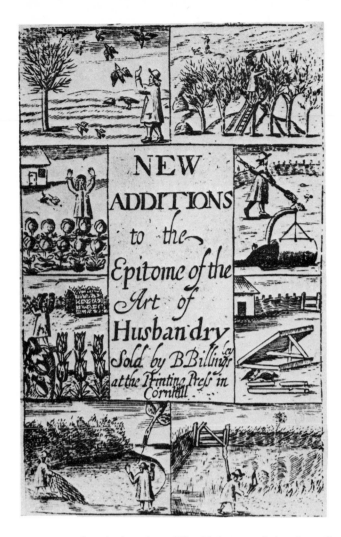

155 *The frontispiece from* The Epitome of the Art of Husbandry *by Jos Blagrave has scenes of peasant life. The growing numbers of such books on farming was one sign of the improvement in agriculture.*

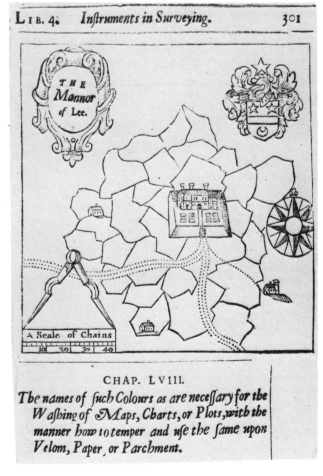

156 *Many works on the techniques of surveying were published during the sixteenth and seventeenth centuries. Some of the most notable are those by Fitzherbert, John Norden and William Leybourn. Leybourn's Plano-metria of 1650 includes a sample survey of a manor.*

157 Bourn Mill in Cambridgeshire, dating from 1636, is a post-mill and was used for grinding corn. Some windmills were also used for drainage in parts of the Fens during the late seventeenth century.

158 The practice of irrigating riverside meadows was a major agricultural improvement of the seventeenth century which had a lasting impact on the landscape. It was of great significance in chalk districts like the Frome Valley in Dorset and involved considerable investment.

remained open at the end of the seventeenth century.

However, the characteristic form of enclosure in this period was piecemeal, a gradual process nibbling bit by bit at the common fields, and most virulent around the fringes of the Midlands in areas like Somerset and Herefordshire. This is perhaps the type of enclosure which most reflects 'grass roots' activities and attitudes. There was no overall plan; farmers enclosed varying proportions of their holdings, and seem to have regarded enclosure and common field not as two totally opposed systems, but as methods of land use which could well be profitably combined.

Equally important changes were brought about through the continued growth in the size of farms and estates. A. H. Johnson in his pioneer study showed that there was no necessary connection between this process and that of enclosure, and that engrossment was taking place in the common fields as well. Moreover, the most decisive changes were at the end of the seventeenth century and the beginning of the eighteenth, a period not especially notable for its enclosures. These conclusions have not since been refuted, and they point to a most important phase not only in the break up of peasant farming but also in the spread of agricultural innovations. A pattern of fewer, larger, farms was more likely to lead to improvement, not least in common-field parishes where much depended on the willingness of farmers to waive the strict rules of communal rotation.

On the whole, larger farms were also more likely to respond to market opportunities, and it seems certain that demand was greater and trade more extensive at the end of our period than at the beginning. Evidence exists of quite long-distance movement of goods, especially to London. The capital, with over 500,000 inhabitants by the end of the seventeenth century, far outstripped other towns in size and rate of expansion. To it came products from the orchards of Kent, the cornfields of East Anglia and the dairies of Cheshire, whilst cattle were driven there on the hoof from as far off as Wales and Scotland. One must add, however, that these movements were merely the more spectacular part of a complicated pattern of local and regional trade that is now beginning to be revealed.

AGRICULTURAL PRODUCTS AND ACHIEVEMENTS

Changes in agricultural organisation were matched by rises in output, as can be deduced from a study of the population figures. In the early fourteenth century the growth of population to over 3 million brought about a severe food shortage. By the year 1550 when the population had again reached this level, it could be fed with relative ease, and a substantial increase in population in the late sixteenth century was accommodated, although not without some difficulty. By the early eighteenth century English farmers were not only supplying the country's own needs, but had a substantial surplus of corn for export, and there was still room for further expansion.

As is normal in these circumstances there was an extension of the cultivated area into former woodland, fen and moorland. Most important was the work of Vermuyden in the Fens, where production rose considerably in the late seventeenth century. A great deal was also achieved in the Weald, but in many other areas the scope for advance was limited. Most of the increase in output must have come therefore from better use of the existing cultivable area. A great variety of improvements were made; indeed a great deal could be achieved simply through more diligent attention to the general routine of farming. But the most spectacular results came from the adoption of new systems which involved a closer integration of crop and livestock farming. By increasing the production of fodder crops and grass larger numbers of livestock could be kept. In turn these would supply increased amounts of manure which could be used to raise arable output even further, so resulting in a continuing upward spiral of productivity.

One way in which this desirable process might be achieved was through convertible husbandry. This was the use of temporary grass, or leys, and tillage in rotation instead of permanent pasture or a succession of crops and fallow. Such practice was advocated by the leading agricultural writers of the period who thought it would raise the yields of both crops and grass. It was certainly in widespread use from the mid sixteenth century when circumstances were especially favourable to its adoption as the quickening growth of population encouraged more intensive farming and brought an end to the long period of low prices and extensive pastoralism.

If, then, convertible husbandry is the backbone of the agricultural revolution – as Dr Kerridge contends – there is certainly a strong case for regarding the late sixteenth and early seventeenth centuries as a decisive period of advance. But some doubts must remain, principally concerning its impact on mainly arable systems. The practice was most famous in districts

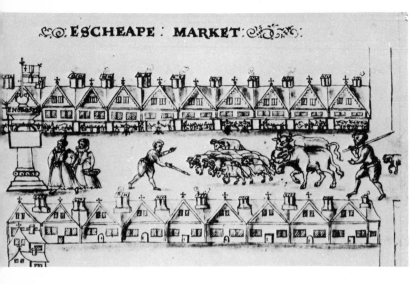

159　In the sixteenth and seventeenth centuries, livestock often made long journeys on the hoof to market to feed a growing urban population. Eastcheap in London was one destination. In 1603 John Stow records in his Survey of London 'Eastcheap is now a flesh market of butchers there dwelling on both sides of the street; it had sometime also cooks . . . as sold victuals readie dressed'.

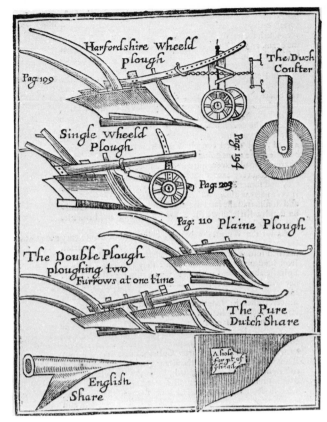

160　A desire to improve agricultural implements was widely felt in the early modern period. Walter Blith showed the various types of ploughs available for different soils in The Improver Improv'd, 1653. Most of them he thought were too heavy and clumsy.

161　Imaginative design for a seed drill by Worlidge. It is unlikely to have been put to practical use.

The Improvement improve
BY
A SECOND EDITION
OF
The great Improvement of Land
BY
CLOVER:
OR,
The Wonderful Advantage by
and right management of
CLOVER.

BY
ANDREW YARRANTON
of *Ashley*, in the County of *Worcester*.

LONDON:
Printed by *J. C.* for *Francis Rea*, Bookseller
in *Worcester*. 1663.

162 The first English books on clover and potatoes were published in the mid-seventeenth century. Both crops were coming into use at that time and clover spread rapidly.

areas of agricultural improvement. It was most advantageous on relatively heavy soils, and practised with greatest success in places like Devonshire and Leicestershire. Livestock, of course, was the chief beneficiary, but the acreage of crops might also be increased in areas like the Warwickshire Arden where permanent pasture had formerly dominated. Where convertible husbandry was practised after the enclosure of common fields the tillage area usually declined, but the extent to which clayland England was tumbling down to grass at this time seems to have been exaggerated. There were specialist grazing and dairying areas, but in general arable production remained at a high level.

Apart from convertible husbandry, the early modern period was also a great age for new crops, some of which, like clover, became of immediate significance whilst others, like the potato, were to have their principal effect in later times. The most famous in the history of agricultural improvement is the turnip, which had the double advantage of reducing the area of fallow and providing winter fodder for livestock. It was

163 Potatoes were cultivated by the mid-seventeenth century but were not a common crop before the 1700s.

ENGLAND'S
Happiness Increased,
OR
A Sure and Easie Remedy against all
succeeding Dear Years;
BY
A Plantation of the Roots called POTATOES,
whereof (with the Addition of Wheat Flower) excellent, good and wholesome Bread may be made, every Year, eight or nine Months together, for half the Charge as formerly.
ALSO
By the Planting of these Roots, Ten Thousand Men in ENGLAND and WALES, who know not how to Live, or what to do to get a Maintenance for their Families, may of One Acre of Ground, make Thirty Pounds per Annum.

Invented and Published for the Good of the Poorer Sort,
By JOHN FORSTER Gent.

Natura beatis omnibus esse dedit, si quis cognoverit uti.
For the Lord hath chosen Sion to be an Habitation for himself, Psal. 132. Ver. 14.
I will bless her Victuals with increase, and will satisfie her Poor with Bread, Verse 16.

LONDON, Printed for *A. Seile*, over against St.
Dunstans Church in *Fleetstreet*, 1664.

where fairly long leys were used. Shorter leys became more widespread from the late seventeenth century when improved grasses were introduced; though William Marshall could still observe of the Vale of Taunton in 1796 that 'it is properly an arable district: the temporary ley which is common in Devonshire, scarcely appears to extend into this vale'. It is doubtful whether convertible husbandry was extensively used in the common fields, which comprised a large proportion of the country's better arable land even in 1750 – far more in 1550. Hoskins and Havinden, amongst others, have argued that it was, but the balance of evidence seems against this.

From the geographical point of view a corollary of the stress now placed on convertible husbandry is that it brings the claylands more to the centre of the stage as widely grown as a field crop in parts of East Anglia from the mid seventeenth century, but its overall advance was slow since it was only really suited to light and medium soils. In the late seventeenth century it appeared in small quantities in most districts, but was only generally adopted during the eighteenth century.

There are many other signs that the lighter soils were being put to more intensive use, particularly from the 1650s onwards. The range of crops increased and the proportion of fallow declined. Leguminous crops such as peas, beans and vetches, were more widely used. Other new fodder crops were introduced, such as sanfoin in the limestone uplands, where the technique of floating water meadows also increased yields of hay. On the poorer soils of the south and Midlands, wheat was grown increasingly in place of rye. Most of these innovations appear to have been adopted in common-field parishes as well as on enclosed land. The communal system was reasonably adaptable to more intensive arable economies but was less able to move from arable to pastoral systems.

Of all the new crops clover was probably the most important. It can be cultivated on a wider variety of soils than the turnip, and it occupied various positions in rotation systems, sometimes replacing fallow, sometimes peas and beans. In the 1660s and 1670s its use spread rapidly across the country both on enclosed and open ground, indicating the speed with which innovations and information on agricultural advances could sometimes be disseminated to the ordinary farmer at this time.

All these improvements in fodder supplies must have brought about a corresponding increase in the numbers and quality of livestock. The more intensive farming also produced changes in livestock combinations. In many areas oxen were replaced by horses, and sheep were another animal to benefit from the new husbandry. The key position in the intensive mixed farming system which they came to occupy was not to end until the depression of the late nineteenth century.

The great age of yeoman farmers must therefore be regarded as one of considerable achievement, even if the pace of change remains debatable. Dr Kerridge contends that it is the age of agricultural revolution; others believe that this process was only firmly under-way in the late seventeenth century, and that it took some further time to run its course. From another point of view the period represents the final flowering of a traditional peasant culture with roots extending deep into the past. Since World War II there has been a great upsurge of interest in the agriculture of early modern England, but specialist geographical work is only in an early stage of development. There is much to be done not only in regional studies but also in systematic investigation of topics such as the distribution of large and small farms, crop and livestock combinations, and the diffusion of innovations.

FURTHER READING

Campbell, M. *The English Yeoman in the Tudor and Stuart Age* (1942)

Chalklin, C. W. *Seventeenth Century Kent* (1965)

Darby, H. C. *The Draining of the Fens* (1940)

Ernle, Lord *English Farming Past and Present* (1912, new ed 1961)

Fisher, F. J. (ed) *Essays in the Economic and Social History of Tudor and Stuart England* (1961)

Fussell, G. *The Old English Farming Books from Fitzherbert to Tull* (1947)

Fussell, G. *The English Dairy Farmer 1500–1900* (1966)

Gonner, E. C. K. *Common Land and Enclosure* (1912)

Gray, H. L. *English Field Systems* (Cambridge, Mass, 1915)

Hoskins, W. G. (ed) *Studies in Leicestershire Agrarian History* (1949)

Hoskins, W. G. (ed) *The Midland Peasant* (1957)

Johnson, A. H. *The Disappearance of the Small Landowner* (1909)

Kerridge, E. *The Agricultural Revolution* (1967)

Kerridge, E. *Agrarian Problems in the Sixteenth Century and After* (1969)

Minchinton, W. (ed) *Essays in Agrarian History*, Vol I (1968)

Sheppard, J. A. 'Vernacular Buildings in England and Wales' *Trans Inst Br Geog*, 40 (1966), 21–37

Skipp, V. H. T. 'Economic and Social Change in the Forest of Arden 1530–1649' *Ag Hist Rev*, 18 (1970), 84–112

Tawney, R. H. *The Agrarian Problem in the Sixteenth Century* (1912)

Thirsk, J. *English Peasant Farming* (1957)

Thirsk, J. (ed) *The Agrarian History of England and Wales IV 1540–1640* (1967)

Yelling, J. A. 'The Combination and Rotation of Crops in East Worcestershire 1540–1750' *Ag Hist Rev*, 17 (1969), 24–43

Yelling, J. A. 'Probate Inventories and the Geography of Livestock Farming' *Tr Inst Brit Geog*, 51 (1970) 111–127

11 URBAN LIFE BEFORE THE INDUSTRIAL REVOLUTION

by JOHN PATTEN

EMERGING slowly and uncertainly from the great economic recession of the later Middle Ages, English towns at the beginning of the sixteenth century began to regain some of their lost prosperity. People filled up long empty and dilapidated houses, while only a stone's throw from the centre of towns like Lincoln rebuilding started on waste ground within the walls, areas which had remained empty in some cases since the demographic and economic disasters of the fourteenth

164 *Sir Christopher Wren's plan for the rebuilding of London after the Great Fire of 1666. It was never put into effect and the winding streets of the old city persist to today. Despite the effects of fire and plague, enormous increases in the size and population of London occured during the sixteenth and seventeenth centuries. Though provincial towns were becoming increasingly prosperous, they could never compete with the capital as the major centre of manufacture and business.*

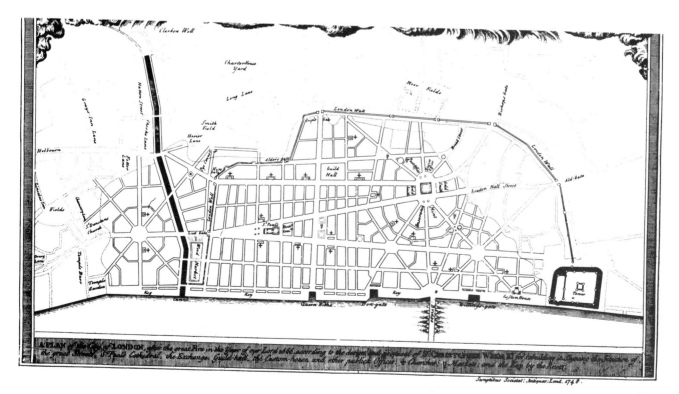

Sumptibus Societat: Antiquar: Lond. 1748.

127

165 *In York the medieval guildhall and many warehouses built along the Ouse in the seventeenth and eighteenth centuries still survive. Small boats played a vital role in carrying cloth and grain on the river.*

century. Markets and fairs, traders and craft manufacturers entered a renewed phase of real if sometimes erratic growth. With the exception of London, which was experiencing dramatic growth in size and wealth as a great capital city, the majority of towns were still essentially traditional in their trade structure and marketing facilities, even if the powers of craft and town guilds and corporations were on the wane, and some older, non-corporate manufacturing towns like Birmingham were rising to ever greater prominence.

It appears that the size and growth rate of the national population of England was holding fairly steady in the sixteenth century, but tremors of the great explosion in numbers to come were being felt in towns which were products of perhaps 900 years of continuous urban growth. The first manifestations of the great transformation of the Industrial Revolution were becoming apparent. Already some small country towns of the west Midlands, even during the middle of the sixteenth century, only differed in scale from the 'Black Country' urban landscape of 1850. Most of the towns of pre-industrial England were small in both area and population but their centres were characterised by crowded, tightly-packed and insani-

tary streets which ended quite abruptly at the edge of the town fields. They generally lacked the urban sprawl that Elizabeth I had sensed beginning in London and had legislated vigorously against.

THE GREAT CAPITAL

In 1500 London's population was probably nearing 100,000 and had increased rapidly to about 450,000 by 1660, although the effects of the great plague and fire a few years later carried away an estimated 100,000 people. Even after this terrible setback the population of London recovered quickly and reached at least 700,000 by the mid eighteenth century, a far greater actual order of growth than was experienced by any other town in the country whose government, law, finance and trade it so completely dominated. Gregory King writing in 1688 estimated that at least 10 per cent of the population lived in the capital, while only 16 per cent lived in what he termed 'the market towns', the remaining 74 per cent inhabiting the villages.

Provincial towns attempted increasingly to copy the capital's style but they were never able to compete with its rate of growth. London was the self-generating metropolitan nucleus of a country that was, in many ways, being increasingly bound to it. The countryside was the capital's source of agricultural produce, for example, creating a demand that was gradually integrating the regional farming economies. In return, many things flowed out of London – judges on assize, fashion, imported luxury goods like silks, spices and the recently introduced chocolate and tobacco. The youth of the nation came to the capital in search of education or a fortune. But London's relatively sudden acceleration is not characteristic of even the greatest provincial town for no other centre had the monarch and his court, parliament, the inns of court and a growing, centralised bureaucracy to which the inhabitants of the country had increasing occasion to turn.

THE PROVINCIAL CENTRES

These factors, and the capital's undoubted importance as a centre of manufacture and trade, largely explain the rapid growth of London compared to that of the three greatest towns in the kingdom – York, Bristol and Norwich. Bristol was opening up its links with the New World and maintaining its traditional trade with mainland Europe, Ireland and Iceland in the early sixteenth century and had a population of about 10,000. By 1750, even with the continued expansion of overseas trade, it had been overtaken by Liverpool, its more northerly competitor, which had grown rapidly to include about 60,000 people, some 10,000 more than Bristol. Norwich, the centre of a wealthy East Anglian region whose economy was based both on arable and pastoral farming and the manufacture of cloth, contained only about 13,000 persons in 1524 and had not fully recovered from the slump of the fifteenth century. Grass was still growing in the streets of Norwich in the early sixteenth century and the city fathers introduced ordinances forcing people to maintain their empty properties. Yet some fifty years later problems of vagrancy and of a substantial sector of the population needing relief were sure indicators of demographic as well as economic pressures. Such 'stop-go' cycles of urban growth were common during the sixteenth and seventeenth centuries. Under such conditions Norwich had only attained a population of some 30,000 by the mid eighteenth century. Even the most prosperous of the larger cities of pre-industrial England, lacking self-sustaining population growth, were unable to break out of the constraints on manufacturing industries which were carried out in small craft shops and which utilised organic raw materials like leather, wood and wool with the aid of human

166 *A mayor of Bristol in the late fifteenth century taking his oath. A town's commercial activities were controlled by a mayor and corporation chosen from wealthy manufacturers and merchants.*

skills and man or animal power.

The major urban centres were beyond the everyday horizon of the majority of countryfolk in England, who looked first to a whole network of medium-sized county towns, like Leicester, Northampton or Exeter, with their important local markets, annual livestock fairs and supplies of staples like woollen and leather goods. Even by the Industrial Revolution such towns contained less than 12,000 people each. On the coast remote from London's immediate influence ports of the size of Newcastle and Ipswich were important for the coastal shipping of coal and agricultural goods from their hinterlands. The presence of the universities in Oxford and Cambridge served to retard the growth of these county towns to a certain extent as the vice-chancellors were able to dominate the administration and economic development of both places. The absence of any such centralised control or town corporation enabled

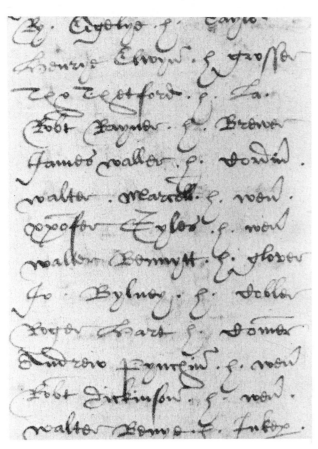

Birmingham to expand its manufacture of metal goods and, free of restrictive legislation, to grow substantially.

Every English county had, at the lowest level, a varying number of small towns and centres, each 'barely accounted more than a village' by contemporaries and resembling in many ways an overgrown version of some of the surrounding rural settlements for which it provided a focus. Places like Tonbridge in Kent and Eccleshall in Staffordshire with populations numbering from 800 to only a few thousand must have been very sleepy, coming to life only on the weekly market day or during the annual Michaelmas fair. The bustle of shire towns like Worcester was absent in these little,

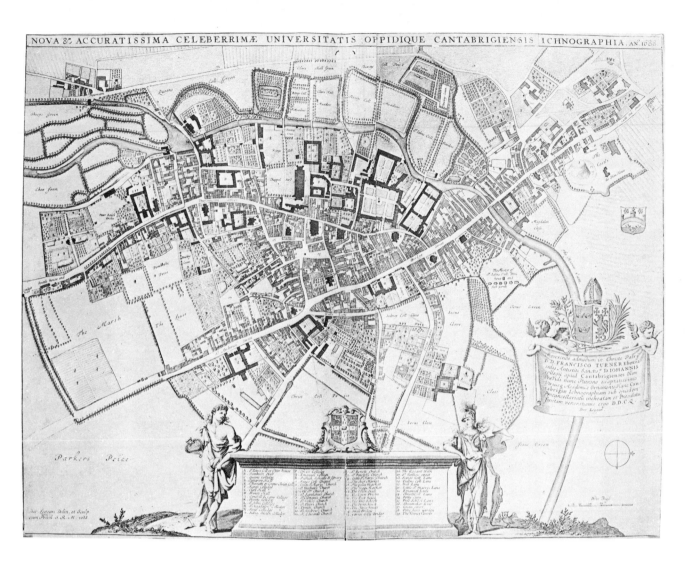

169 *A 1688 survey of Cambridge reveals how the college courts and quadrangles dominated the street scene, just as university authorities dominated town life.*

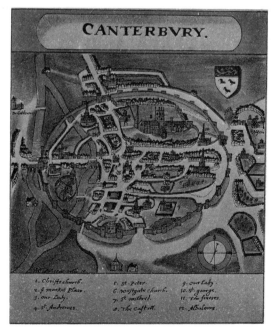

170 *The sixteenth century saw great development in the drawing of town plans, although many still lacked detail and scales. A perspective view of Canterbury illustrates its small extent, the considerable amount of open space within the walls and the growing suburbs outside.*

unwalled market towns. Their short streets ran out into the surrounding countryside and their inhabitants were often as much concerned with the prices of sheep and corn as with the simple craft and service occupations which supplied the immediate needs of other townsfolk and surrounding country areas. Some places, however, were prosperous centres of industry in their own right. The small towns of the Cotswolds and East Anglia are examples, and today rich and substantial churches and sizeable clothiers' houses bear witness to the profitable activities that were once carried on there.

THREATS FROM FIRE, DISEASE AND MALNUTRITION

Although during the sixteenth century the country escaped the dreadful decimation of population that struck medieval England, a large part of the erratic urban development of early modern England is attributable to a regular series of setbacks in population growth. Town dwellers, besides living in far from sanitary surroundings, were particularly prone both to attack by the various forms of plague and to the consequences of an uncertain supply of food in years of harvest failure,

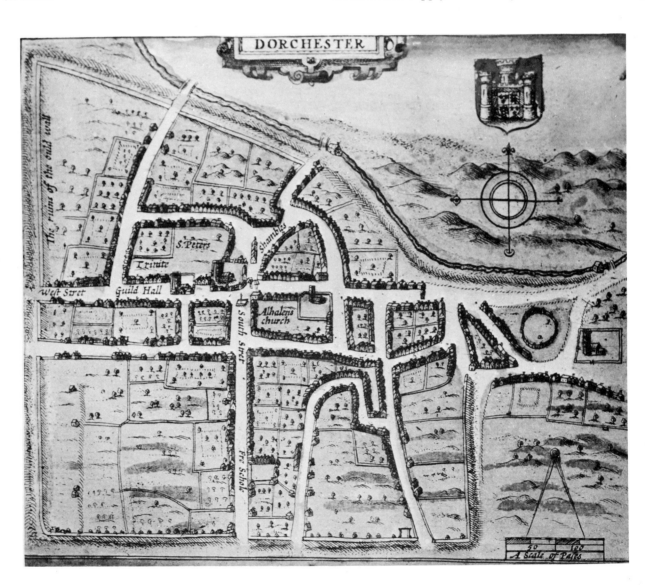

171 Dorchester drawn by Speed at the beginning of the seventeenth century. It still possessed a fairly regular plan; much of the original site laid out by the Romans had never been built over.

132

172 *From* Britannia Depicta. *Road travel, still slow and difficult, particularly in bad weather, was made easier with such detailed maps.*

this despite the farming interests of many occupants.

The last great plague outbreak in England was largely over by 1666, having had a devastating effect on London, but also having struck savagely in earlier years. The coastal town of Southwold, in Suffolk, had 429 baptisms but 792 burials between 1602 and 1611, with 373 deaths recorded in the year 1602 alone. A warning of plague was enough to send the better-off inhabitants to their farms; those left behind suffered terribly. Within the crowded and filthy streets of the average shire town there was little chance of escape and every encouragement for the disease-carrying organisms to spread through the overhanging timber-framed houses that crowded in on the narrow lanes. Household refuse flowed down the streets to be joined by offal thrown out by butchers, despite the prohibiting town ordinances. This garbage could find its way into a stream that was simultaneously a source of drinking water, a place for domestic laundering and perhaps the site of the rather unsavoury industrial activity of a fuller whose collecting pots by the wayside were the nearest equivalent to a present-day public urinal.

Even when the plague abruptly ceased its depredations in England during the later seventeenth century, smallpox was to replace it as a serious threat. The miseries so induced were heightened by the occurrence of quickly spreading fires which devastated London and attacked smaller places with equal ferocity. The county of Suffolk, for example, attempted to raise relief for the stricken inhabitants of two small market towns, Beccles and Bungay, on more than one occasion in the seventeenth century. Malnutrition and near starvation were also threats, particularly to the old and infirm, and a series of bad harvests in the region of a large town some-

173 *The site of the ancient market beside the town wall at Canterbury has become part of a major highway. Livestock and local agricultural produce poured in to town markets for the growing urban consumption.*

times led to appalling hardship, as in the starvation decade of the 1590s. Town corporations such as that at Great Yarmouth set up stores of grain to counteract uncertain supply and distribution.

Towns of all sizes had an excess of deaths over births in many years, and were only able to maintain and increase their population by the ever growing immigration of rural people. London in particular but also lesser towns like Southampton, as its registers of apprentice enrolment demonstrate, depended on such regular inflows of young people coming to domestic service and craft apprenticeships. These apprentices were to some extent the life blood of the urban industries, for they eventually became journeymen or perhaps master craftsmen as cordwainers, apothecaries or even goldsmiths. The records of the livery companies of London bear witness to the great distances which had been travelled by apprentices to find work, though these represent only one sector, albeit an economically important one, of total urban immigration.

The indentures of such young people also illustrate the close relationship between town and country. They sometimes gave an apprentice leave to return home for the harvest month: '. . . to suffer the said Thomas in harveste tyme yerely to go home to his frendes in Bedforthshere and to Remayne there one month.' Equally, the wills and inventories of the husbandmen and yeomen show the essentially rural nature of many smaller towns. There were often gardens and orchards within fairly large towns, though they had been built over by the eighteenth century as pressure on available urban land increased. With this expansion the town walls frequently fell into disrepair and were used as house foundations or as sources of building material.

Rural occupations of urban dwellers became markedly fewer in later seventeenth-century Norwich and Bury St Edmunds, although in smaller towns like Guildford the journey to the surrounding fields was still a feature of daily life. Rich merchants in Worcester owned farms in the surrounding county and the butchers and cordwainers of Leicester were also substantial graziers, ensuring supply from rural areas of the raw materials their urban craft interests demanded. Thomas Spring, a townsman of Lavenham in Suffolk and probably the richest commoner in all England at the time of the early sixteenth-century Musters and Lay Subsidies, owned lands all over East Anglia and in nearly half of the thirty-two parishes of the hundred in which his home town stood. His great wealth was derived initially from the manufacture of woollen cloth and he was proud to be recorded as 'clothier' when he might easily have aspired to 'gentleman', a generally more desirable classification in an age obsessed with status. Indeed, social consciousness undoubtedly caused some younger sons, or their descendants, to leave booming urban businesses in order to set up as country gentry. The pull of land ownership and the status it bestowed thus dampened the entrepreneurial spirit of rich townsmen time and time again, unlike the ironmasters and potters of the late eighteenth and nineteenth centuries, who built country houses but still controlled industries and were not ashamed to do so.

174 Shoemaking. Craft activities to meet everyday needs for clothing, shoes and household goods usually took place in the home of the craftsman himself. Production was essentially on a small scale, even though the cost to an apprentice or journeyman of setting up as a master was high.

175 *The shearing of cloth was often concentrated in towns as it depended on specialised skills. The unfinished woven cloth was brought from the countryside or from other urban workshops.*

176 *Furniture making. The increasing demand of the country gentry for more elaborate furniture to modernise their country homes encouraged the growth of yet more specialised skills in the towns.*

TOWN WORKSHOPS, TRADE AND MARKETING

The prosperity of the towns, away from London with its unique functions, was based largely on manufacturing and service industry within a traditional framework, and their importance as both official and informal market places. The activities of the urban workshop were most important, whether in the humble home of some poor tailor or cobbler, or in the rigid and traditionally controlled cutlery industry of Sheffield with its masters, journeymen and apprentices labouring long hours. The apprentices worked four or five together in a shop attached to the Master's house, where they would also eat and sometimes sleep. The busy streets of Birmingham, noisy with hawkers and pedlars, were divided into specialised trading districts of, for example, gunsmiths, makers of metal buttons, and makers of needles and pins.

From urban workshops in towns like Exeter and Coventry poured some of the cloth that was so important to England's export trade. The prosperity of weaving towns and of the ports handling cloth largely depended on ever changing commercial relations abroad, and on the state of trade in London itself. Hull and Newcastle declined for a while in the early seventeenth century as their trade in cloth with the Baltic dropped, but later, when new markets were found in the Low Countries, Hull and Exeter, in particular, successfully wrested a little of London's dominance.

The importance of foreign trade to the merchant clothiers of inland manufacturing towns is illustrated by examples of apprentices who were sent abroad to learn Dutch or French. Some towns specialised in certain products, as did Leicester in leather goods and little Wymondham in Norfolk in the manufacture of wooden spoons and taps. Others failed to contribute much to export overseas and, lacking any speciality, concentrated simply on supplying the daily and occa-

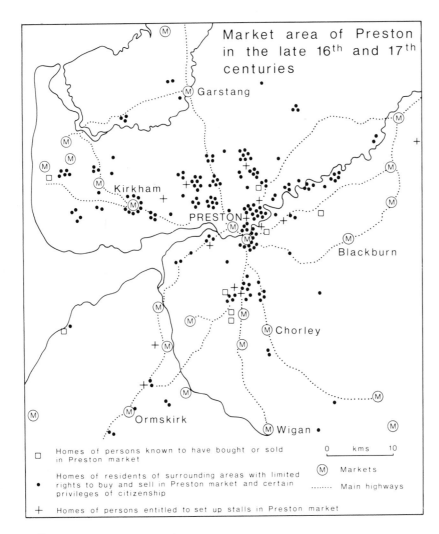

Market area of Preston in the late 16th and 17th centuries

□ Homes of persons known to have bought or sold in Preston market

• Homes of residents of surrounding areas with limited rights to buy and sell in Preston market and certain privileges of citizenship

+ Homes of persons entitled to set up stalls in Preston market

Ⓜ Markets

.... Main highways

0   kms   10

177 By using guild records which give details of those renting stalls in the market-place, the extent of the influence of Preston over the surrounding countryside can be estimated (after Rodgers).

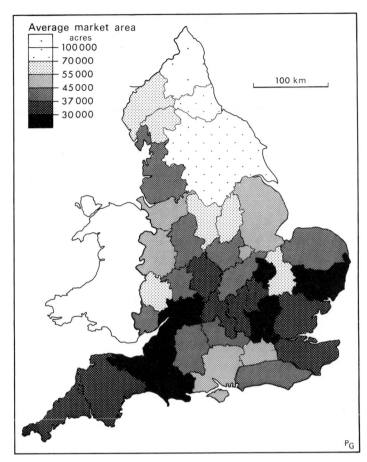

178 *The market areas of English towns grew larger in the less populated and prosperous north which had fewer such centres (after Everitt).*

179 *In southern and eastern England, market towns were fairly regularly spaced except in areas like the Weald or the Fens. However, they often differed widely in size and importance (after Everitt).*

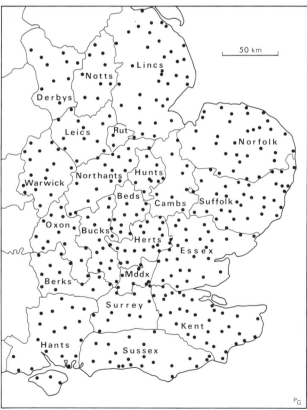

sional needs of their own inhabitants and those of the countryfolk who flocked in to sell their produce on market day.

Not all of a town's inhabitants were gainfully employed in manufacturing, buying or selling. The rich merchants and manufacturers with their processions, guild 'drinkings' and other festivities, some of which were preserved into the eighteenth century, represented the top of the socio-economic structure supported by day and apprentice workers. As much as a third of the population of some towns was too poor to take a very significant part in any economic activities. The aged, infirm, vagrant and work shy, who made a perilous living as sweepers or as pedlars of cheap drink, were susceptible to the frequent short-term fluctuations in the prosperity of the pre-industrial town. They represented the lower portion of the economy of such towns and forced the city fathers into hasty measures. Rarely noted in tax lists due to their poverty, they warranted in the hearth taxes of the later seventeenth century mention only as a class 'that doe receve collection' – in other words, charity.

The other source of a town's prosperity was undoubtedly found in its markets. Agricultural goods were bought and sold for local consumption, and changed hands *en route* for one of the important provincial towns like York, or eventually London. Centres increasingly specialised in livestock or local agricultural produce: Canterbury and Maidstone in hops and fruit, Devizes and Banbury in horses, and Kings Lynn in malt and corn. Much of this trade took place in open market, but often, and sometimes unlawfully, such transactions went on informally in taverns and inns. Urban products like shoes and pewter plates changed hands as farmers and their wives shopped for these and luxury goods from London and abroad in new specialised shops as well as from the market stalls. A number of the towns which relied solely on their market function suffered like their medieval forebears, especially where several were close together; the fortunes of Needham Market in Suffolk declined as the influence of Stowmarket, some six kilometres away, increased.

The towns of early modern England, in size, layout and social and economic structure, represent the stable end product of centuries of continuity – a continuity that was only to be shattered by the effects of the Industrial Revolution.

FURTHER READING

Bartlett, N. 'The Expansion and Decline of York in the Late Middle Ages'. *Economic History Review* 2nd series, 12 (1959), 17–33

Bridbury, A. R. *England in the Later Middle Ages* (1962)

Buckatzsch, E. J. 'Occupations in the Parish Registers of Sheffield, 1655–1719' *Economic History Review*, 2nd series (1949), 145–150

Buckatzsch, E. J. 'Places of Origin of a Group of Immigrants into Sheffield, 1624–1799' *Economic History Review*, 2nd series, 2 (1950), 303–6

Carter, H. 'The Urban Hierarchy and Historical Geography: A Consideration with Reference to North-East Wales' *Geographical Studies*, 3 (1956), 85–101

Chalklin, C. W. *Seventeenth Century Kent* (1965); and 'A Seventeenth Century Market Town, Tonbridge' *Archaeologia Cantiana*, 76 (1961), 152–162

Clarke, P. and Slack, P. *Crisis and Order in English Towns 1500–1700* (1972)

Coleman, O. 'Trade and Prosperity in the Fifteenth Century: Some Aspects of the Trade of Southampton' *Economic History Review*, 2nd series, 16 (1963), 9–22

Cornwall, J. 'English Country Towns in the Fifteen-twenties' *Economic History Review*, 2nd series, 15, (1962–3), 54–69

Cressey, D. 'Occupations, Migration and Literacy in East London, 1580–1640' *Local Population Studies*, No 5 (1970), 53–60

Cowgill, U. M. 'Life and Death in the Sixteenth Century in the City of York' *Population Studies*, 21 (1967), 53–62

Dyer, D. *The Economy of Tudor Worcester*, University of Birmingham *Hist Jnl*, 10 (1965–6), 117–136

Dyer, D. *The City of Worcester in the Sixteenth Century* (Leicester, 1973)

Everitt, A. 'Urban Growth, 1570–1770', *The Local Historian*, 8 (1968), 118–125

Everitt, A. 'Urban Growth and Inland Trade, 1570–1770; Sources', *The Local Historian*, 8 (1969), 196–204

Fisher, F. J. 'Development of the London Food Market, 1540–1640' *Economic History Review*, 1st series, 2 (1935), 46–64

Fisher, F. J. 'The Development of London as a Centre of Conspicuous Consumption in the Sixteenth and Seventeenth Centuries' *Transactions of the Royal Historical Society*, 4th series, 30 (1948), 37–50

Hill, J. W. F. *Tudor and Stuart Lincoln* (Cambridge, 1956)

Hoskins, W. G. 'An Elizabethan Provincial Town: Leicester' *Studies in Social History* ed J. H. Plumb (1955)

Hoskins, W. G. 'English Provincial Towns in the Sixteenth Century, *Transactions of the Royal Historical Society*, 5th series, 6 (1956), 1–19

Hoskins, W. G. *Industry, Trade and People in Exeter, 1688–1800* (Manchester, 1935)

Lloyd-Pritchard, M. F. 'The Decline of Norwich' *Economic History Review*, 2nd series, 3 (1950–1), 371–377

MacCaffrey, W. T. *Exeter, 1540–1640* (Cambridge, 1958)

Pound, J. F. 'An Elizabethan Census of the Poor. The Treatment of Vagrancy in Norwich, 1570–80' *University of Birmingham Historical Journal*, 8 (1962), 135–161

Pound, J. F. 'The Social and Trade Structure of Norwich, 1525–75' *Past and Present*, no 34 (1966), 49–69

Ramsey, P. *Tudor Economic Problems* (1963), esp Chap III, Industry and the Towns

Rodgers, H. B. 'The Market Area of Preston in the Sixteenth and Seventeenth Centuries' *Geographical Studies*, Vol 3, (1956), 46–55

Thirsk, Joan *The Agrarian History of England and Wales, 1500–1640*, Vol IV (Cambridge, 1967), especially Everitt, A. 'The Market Town', 466–90

Unwin, George *Industrial Organisation in the Sixteenth and Seventeenth Centuries* (1904, reprinted, 1957, with an introductory note by T. S. Ashton)

Wrigley, E. A. 'A Simple Model of London's Importance in Changing English Society and Economy, 1650–1750', *Past and Present*, no 37, 44–70

12 AGRICULTURAL IMPROVEMENT AND CHANGING REGIONAL ECONOMIES IN THE EIGHTEENTH CENTURY

by ROBERT I. HODGSON

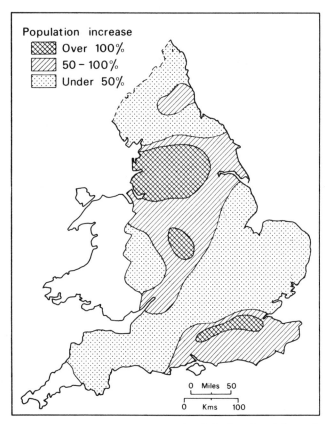

Population increase

Over 100%

50 - 100%

Under 50%

0   Miles   50

0   Kms   100

180   Population change in England during the eighteenth century.

THE view that industrial is the opposite of agricultural has a strong emotional appeal to most people and appears to be based on sound geographical principles. Landscapes of industrial blight and urban decay in northern England and the west Midlands are contrasted with areas of rural tranquillity in parts of the south and east. According to the popular view, this is a pattern that emerged in the eighteenth and nineteenth centuries as a result of the impact of the Agricultural Revolution in the south and east, and of the Industrial Revolution in the north and west. The eighteenth century was a critical period in which marked regional distinctions did emerge. Thus it is necessary to outline the progress and spatial impact of both revolutions before demonstrating that the economic and geographical ties between agriculture and industry were strengthened rather than weakened at this time.

Throughout the eighteenth century and with increasing vigour towards its close there was an acceleration in the rate of population growth, in agricultural and industrial output and in transport development. Such mutually reinforcing achievements, backed by large-scale capital investment and changing social attitudes, were to produce a so-called 'Industrial' Revolution. Phyllis Deane and W. A. Cole have put forward statistical evidence to suggest that the population of

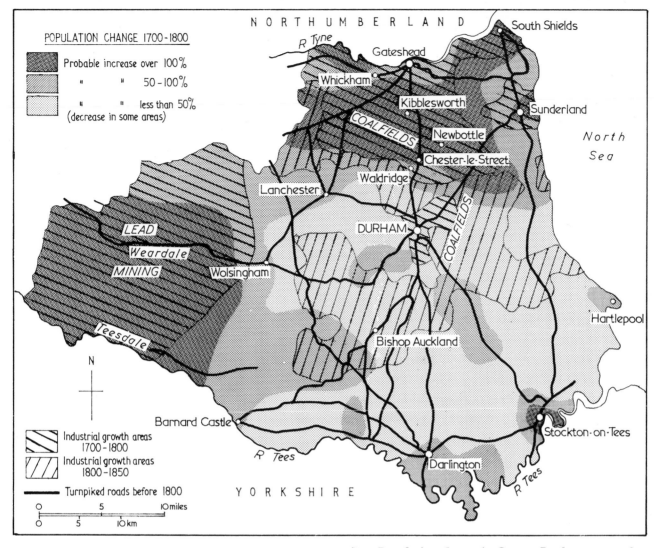

POPULATION CHANGE 1700-1800

Probable increase over 100%
" " 50-100%
" " less than 50%
(decrease in some areas)

Industrial growth areas 1700-1800
Industrial growth areas 1800-1850
Turnpiked roads before 1800

0   5   10 miles
0 5   10 km

181 Population change in County Durham 1700–1800.

England rose from c 5.4 millions in 1700 to 5.6 by 1750 and then to 8.6 in 1801. Growth was particularly noticeable in those parts of northern England and the west Midlands that were associated with either increasing industrialisation on or near the coalfields, or some town growth in regional centres such as Liverpool, Manchester and Birmingham. Recognition of this pattern encouraged the once cherished view that population growth was a result of a south to north migration, with the capitalist forces of industry at work in the rural lowlands of the south and east enclosing the common or open-fields by act of parliament and banishing peasants to the horrors and poverty of Manchester. However, this picture does not accord with much historical evidence. First, any discernible long-distance migration was from north to south, not the reverse.

London rather than Manchester grew at the expense of Norfolk or Lincolnshire. Second, growth in the north and west was largely an outcome of high rates of natural increase – the excess of births over deaths – which reflected attractive conditions in these areas. High wages, a wide range of economic opportunity, and ample food and clothing encouraged earlier marriage and larger families and gave better chances of survival. The mass of people in England probably enjoyed a far higher standard of living in 1800 than they had a century earlier, especially those in the industrialising areas where marked urbanisation and its attendant poverty had yet to emerge.

The agricultural sector of the economy had the task of making food readily available and at a sufficiently cheap price to allow surplus spending power to go on

141

182 Pit villages like Waldridge were the spontaneous creation of mining colonisation. In 1800 Waldridge Fell remained open and exploited for minerals when surrounding fell land was converted to tillage.

183 Many apparently nineteenth-century Durham villages are in fact of greater antiquity, adapted to new circumstances. Newbottle successfully absorbed industrial labourers without forsaking its agricultural roots.

manufactured goods such as clothing. Little wonder that the Industrial Revolution has been seen as originating in an agricultural revolution. How and when did this other revolution come about? Where did it have greatest impact? Seemingly its products were needed most in the industrialising north and west.

184 The terraced housing at Newbottle points to the arrival of industry in a previously agricultural community.

THE AGRICULTURAL REVOLUTION

Although the eighteenth century failed to see either the beginning or end of the Agricultural Revolution, it did witness an important and agitated phase. Its progress can be judged by recognising two essential ingredients distinguished by E. L. Jones: changes of husbandry technique and improvements in agrarian organisation. Technical innovations included the adoption of new fodder crops such as turnips, clover, ryegrass and sainfoin, and, new crop rotations which eliminated the

wastage of bare-fallowing. The idea was to alternate crops like grains which exhaust the soil with those like clover which build up its nutrient content. Whereas in the celebrated and particularist Norfolk system a strict rotation of wheat, turnips, barley and clover might be maintained, many areas of heavier land, needing longer periods for soil recovery, practised convertible husbandry whereby grass leys were laid down for several successive years in the rotation. The progress of such schemes was aided by the application of lime, marl and animal manure as fertilisers and by the adoption of

185 Parliamentary enclosures in upland west Durham promoted agricultural improvement. In 1781–4, when 6100 hectares of Lanchester Fell were enclosed, a 'paradise where the inhabitants were greatly multiplied, cheerful and prosperous' was created out of a 'barren, desert and dreary common'. Allotment boundaries were laid out with precision and regularity and highways were often defined by carefully constructed walls twenty metres apart. Such breadth gave ease of access to driven cattle and carriages whilst roadside verges remained as common pasture. Twentieth-century transport has done little to erode the common grazing but encroaching fences succeed.

186 The Lanchester enclosures sought to increase grain production even on remote uplands described as 'less improvable'. Reclamation was directed from newly built farmsteads which in the case of 'Eliza' stood at an altitude of almost 300 metres.

improved implements such as the seed drill associated with the name of Jethro Tull. Another improvement, the irrigation or 'floating' of meadow lands, provided extra supplies of hay fodder which supplemented root crops as winter feed for livestock. Once the necessity to kill off animals in winter through lack of feedstuffs had been removed, attention could be given to livestock improvement.

One aspect of the new husbandry tended to support the other, and in a similar way the new techniques were often reinforced by changes in agrarian organisation which eliminated social and tenurial restraints on agricultural improvement. Enclosures carried out by act of parliament in the eighteenth and early nineteenth centuries extinguished communal practices and fragmented land holdings in common and open-field areas of lowland England. They also fenced in for the first time large tracts of upland waste in the north and west. Parliamentary enclosures represent only the best documented examples of a process which had gone on

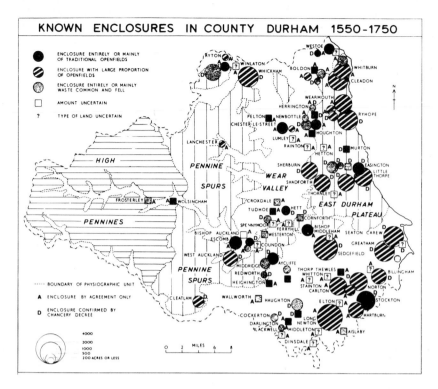

187 (a and b)   Townships in south and east Durham were enclosed by agreement before 1750 with a view to increasing pastoral farming. Upland wastes in the north and west awaited demands for more grain in the late eighteenth and early nineteenth centuries and were enclosed by act of parliament.

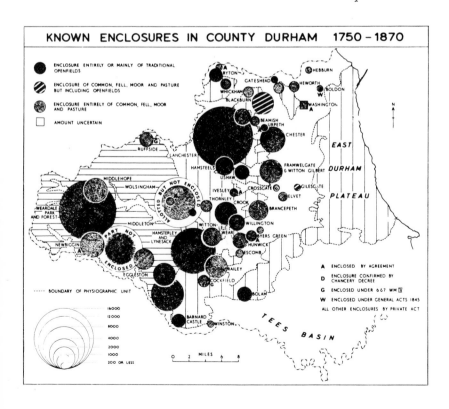

for centuries and with increasing vigour since the seventeenth century.

While the main ingredients of the Agricultural Revolution can be identified with some confidence, its chronology has been the subject of much debate in recent years, with claims for sixteenth- and seventeenth-century innovation being countered by the view that eighteenth- and nineteenth-century changes were far more significant. If the progress of agriculture is judged by its ability to feed the native population without relying upon imports, then the years before 1750 were more successful than those following. Yet there was undoubtedly greater output and wider acceptance of new techniques after 1750. One fact stands out above all others; the success of the Agricultural Revolution did not depend upon the sudden efforts of the famous four – Jethro Tull, 'Turnip' Town-shend, Thomas Coke and Robert Bakewell. Their achievements have not been discredited, despite suggestions that Tull was nothing less than a crank and that Bakewell's Leicester sheep produced 'coal-heavers' mutton', but it would be fair to say that their haloes have become tarnished. They may be regarded as popularisers of new ideas rather than originators.

Economic historians and historical geographers have rightly stressed the need to recognise regional differences in the extent and timing of agrarian change and their arguments suggest that 'revolution' is an inappropriate word for a process which varied so markedly in time and space. In East Anglia it would seem that the new techniques had been widely adopted before the eighteenth century and in Wiltshire, Dr Kerridge is able to ascribe the critical period of change to the years 1575 to 1675. Yet in other parts of the south and east, the revolutionary movement had scarcely begun by the close of the eighteenth century. In 1794 a reporter to the Board of Agriculture described Cambridgeshire as the worst farmed county in the whole of England, and increased productivity on its fenland soils had to await effective drainage in the nineteenth century. Studies of Lincolnshire farming by Dr Thirsk and David Grigg, and of East Yorkshire farming by Dr Harris, have shown that even within a single county or a part of that county the 'spirit of improvement' was strikingly more advanced in certain localities. This condition might reflect difference in landownership or accessibility of markets, but above all it reflected differences in the type of soil.

There is always a need to draw useful generalisations from a mass of complex and often contradictory evidence, and most research findings suggest that the new techniques came first to the light soils on chalk, limestone and sandstone in the lowlands of southern and eastern England, and subsequently spread to the heavier soils of the Midland clay vales where social barriers to improvement had to be broken down at the time of enclosure. Their impact came lastly and least effectively to the pastoral farming districts of the north and west. Thus it may be argued that, in general terms, the Agricultural Revolution, as defined above, was a feature of the lowland south and east. And, since population growth and industrialisation was greatest in the north and west, the idea gains acceptance that the agricultural lowlands fed the industrial uplands in return for the provision of manufactured goods. If this was the case, the long-term capital investment in river, canal and turnpike projects in the eighteenth century, aimed at cheapening and speeding the flow of goods and information, made good sense. A type of regionalism based upon marked self-sufficiency and diversity of economic interest gave way to a regionalism founded on exchange economies and specialisation. Lancashire became synonymous with cotton, Yorkshire's West Riding with wool, while in both the people were fed.

AGRICULTURE AND THE INDUSTRIAL REGIONS

This model of eighteenth-century trends has value when studying problems at a national scale but researchers are also engaged in detailed regional studies with a view to uncovering significant events obscured by the general interpretation. The Agricultural Revolution may have been a feature of the lowlands but it is wrong to imagine that the industrial uplands experienced no agrarian change. Rather it seems that in decisions on land use priorities, agriculture played a vital if secondary role.

In a study of the Vale of Trent, J. D. Chambers has shown that a continuing and strengthening relationship between agriculture and industry was to be found in the critical early stages of the Industrial Revolution. Such studies are all too few, particularly for the north and west. T. W. Fletcher has demonstrated that even in Lancashire, 'the cradle of the Industrial Revolution', agriculture made rapid strides in the period 1750–1850. However, progress was not to be identified with an openfield enclosure movement or the adoption of a Norfolk rotation, both of which symbolised the new orthodoxy of the eighteenth century and assumed the status of holy writ in the eyes of early nineteenth-

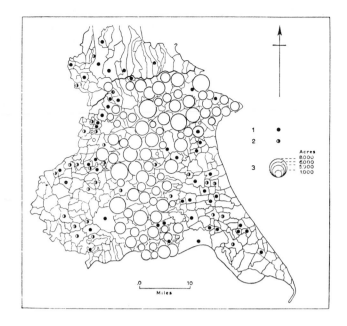

188 On the light soils of the Yorkshire Wolds, parliamentary enclosures after 1750 (shown by proportional circles) facilitated adoption of the new husbandry; while on the heavier lowland soils to the south and east, where enclosure had occured prior to 1750, agriculture remained backward. (After A. Harris.)

189 (2 maps) In a classic study of 1912, Gonner mapped the extent and density of parliamentary enclosures in the eighteenth and nineteenth centuries. These maps are still the most comprehensive available for a study of general patterns despite the passage of sixty years, during which some major regional studies of enclosures have appeared. It is well to remember that in many cases, parliamentary enclosure merely rationalised and finalised a process of piecemeal enclosure covering several decades or even centuries.

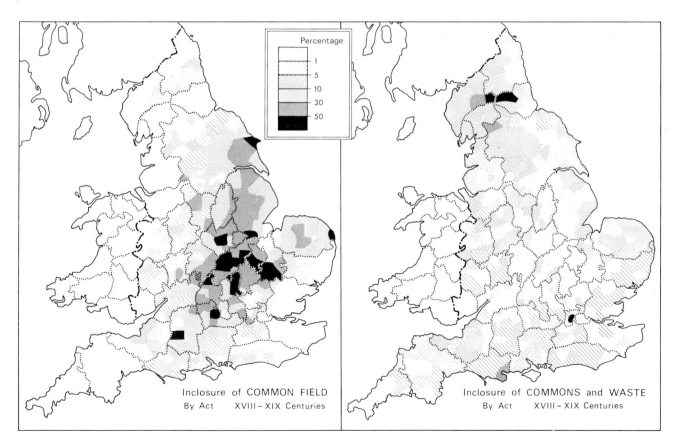

Inclosure of COMMON FIELD
By Act   XVIII – XIX Centuries

Inclosure of COMMONS and WASTE
By Act   XVIII – XIX Centuries

century agriculturists and some modern historians. The basic ingredient of arable Lancashire's 'agricultural revolution' was not the turnip but the potato, not the large landed estate but the expensively rented small-holding, not a strict rotation but a flexible system geared to environmental restraints and market prices. An extremely active and productive system it proved to be. The common night soil of Manchester was carried along improved roads and new canals and poured onto the newly reclaimed mosslands. In return large quantities of corn, hay, straw and potatoes fed a growing urban population, its horses, dairy cattle and those large numbers of Scots and Irish beasts that were fattened for market.

A REGIONAL CASE STUDY: COUNTY DURHAM

Work currently in progress on County Durham serves to demonstrate the intimate and complex relationship between agriculture, industry and population growth. County Durham gained national importance from the middle of the sixteenth century as the supplier of vast quantities of cheap coal to the London and south-east market, and by the end of the seventeenth century two core areas, centred on the upper Tyne valley and the lower Wear (east of Chester-le-Street), were supplying about 40 per cent of the national output. Over the next 150 years the areal spread of mining operations continued with the extension of a wagon-way network into north-west and central Durham and the gradual opening up of east Durham by the application of steam power to drainage problems. Meanwhile the western uplands of Teesdale and Weardale were experiencing a boom in lead mining. About 1850 it was claimed that nearly every parish in the county bore scars of industrial exploitation and that the surface had been sacrificed for the wealth which lay beneath it – not a happy prospect for agriculture.

Early industrial development in the county had far-reaching implications for population growth. An expanding labour force was required not only in mining but also in such industries as salt-panning and glass-making which took advantage of cheap supplies of coal and grew rapidly. Evidence suggests that extra folk were drawn from Scotland and the Border dales as seasonal migrants who came to settle in keelmen's colonies along the banks of the Tyne at Dunston, and the Wear at Fatfield. The Durham parish registers, while displaying many problems of interpretation, suggest high rates of natural increase among the indigenous population. During the eighteenth century the coal and lead mining areas seem to have experienced relatively high rates of growth and examples are found of families moving from district to district as mines closed in one parish and were opened up in another.

Throughout the period there is evidence of a growing class of proletarians: industrial labourers who were sometimes driven to filling in village greens with a mass of tiny cottages, as in Ryton, Whickham and Winlaton, or to squatting on the open fell as in Gateshead, Heworth, and Eighton, as a means of establishing a home and livelihood. When Gateshead Fell was enclosed in 1809 almost 100 squatter dwellings were pulled down by the enclosure commissioners, though resistance was stern and included the brandishing of pitchforks as well as considerable abuse. The growth of a poverty-striken labouring class must not be exaggerated, however, for many Durham families were prosperously involved in a variety of occupations both industrial and agricultural. Inventories show that yeoman farmers might engage not only in the 'land carriage' of minerals but also in mining, and evidence of this dual economy exists as early as the fifteenth century and as recently as the present. The economic and social welfare of the family unit in Weardale, Teesdale and on the Durham coalfield rested upon the indivisibility of agricultural and industrial interests.

The story of agricultural progress in County Durham presents a paradox. On the one hand, the development of mining and associated industry called for an extra labour force and population growth put pressure on agriculture to be more productive. This was particularly true of periods when the price of exported coal was low and the cost of imported grain high, as in the late eighteenth century. On the other hand, as more and more land was exploited for its mineral wealth it became increasingly difficult to advance agriculture.

AGRICULTURE AND INDUSTRY IN HARMONY

The Durham enclosure movements in the mid seventeenth and late eighteenth centuries provide evidence of the beneficial effects of industry in promoting agrarian reform. While many common and open-field areas in the Midland plain of lowland England were not enclosed till after 1750, those in the south and east of Durham were enclosed mainly in the period 1630–80. They were not merely an automatic response to cries for more grain from a growing industrial population; much more evident was a tendency to take out of cultivation land which had been exhausted with continual ploughing and cropping, and to turn it over to pasture. Such a move, however, did show an acute awareness of market opportunities. While extra hay fed a growing horse population, the dairy produce of the newly enclosed Durham farms found its way to local market centres. By the early years of the eighteenth century large quantities of butter were being shipped from Newcastle-upon-Tyne and Stockton-on-Tees. No doubt the earnings from these butter exports offset the costs of imported barley and rye for landowners such as Lords Ravensworth, Lambton and Lumley who employed and indirectly fed hundreds of miners.

A second wave of enclosures came in the late eighteenth and early nineteenth centuries when the incentive to grow more grain, always present in a county with an expanding industrial labour force, became a necessity. During the Napoleonic wars the high price of imported grain had the effect of increasing labour costs for those mining entrepreneurs whose workers demanded higher wages to support their families. An increase in grain production was only possible when 40,000

190 Prior to the Lanchester enclosure of 1781, the Claverings of Greencroft and Iveston had been surreptitiously encroaching northwards with an eye to extra cropland on the fell and mineral wealth beneath the surface. Copyhold tenants of the Bishop of Durham who held common rights urged the bishop to reassert territorial claims. In 1754 a map was prepared to distinguish the northern boundary claimed by Clavering.

191 Thomas Kitchin's map of County Durham, c 1750, shows salt being packed into wicker baskets after brine pumped from the sea has been evaporated in coal-fired salt pans. Cheap coal aided a boom in salt production in the seventeeth century.

192 Agricultural accounts for Gateshead Park and Shipcote in the 1730s provide weekly details of work undertaken, labourers and expense. Improvements include the use of night-soil and lime on new crops like clover and rye.

hectares of upland west Durham were enclosed, rented or leased out at up to ten times their former value, and put under the plough. On parts of the 6100 hectares of Lanchester Fell, enclosed between 1781 and 1784, wheat was being grown in 1801 with returns of forty to forty-five bushels per hectare compared with sixty on old enclosed lands. Even more ambitious schemes were found at St John's Chapel in Weardale with barley cultivation at 365 metres. No doubt the land-hungry lead miners were distorting the true picture of land capability.

The successful marriage of farming and mining interests was often achieved through the initiative and business sense of an enlightened landlord. William Cotesworth of Gateshead Park, for example, in spite of enormously varied and time-consuming dealings in the coal and salt trade, found time to clear many hectares of pit waste from his estates, enclose land still lying open, lime and manure the soils, and put the greater proportion down to grass and clover. Once improved the land could be either farmed directly or let to tenants at as much as £7 per hectare. The lucrative nature of

193 Landlords were important in determining the use of land in the eighteenth century. William Cotesworth, a Tyneside merchant, cleared pit wastes at Gateshead Park and Shipcote so that knowledge gained on extensive travels could be applied profitably in Durham.

the milk trade and market gardening in this quasi-urban district enabled tenants to afford such sums. Some years after Cotesworth's death in 1727, the impact of his efficiency drive was still being demonstrated in the meticulous keeping of agricultural accounts.

AGRICULTURE AND INDUSTRY IN CONFLICT

Apart from an increase in corn growing, made possible by upland enclosures, the later years of the eighteenth century witnessed a continuing interest in pastoral farming. Livestock improvements were encouraged by the growth of cattle fairs at regional centres such as Morpeth, Newcastle, Durham, Darlington, Barnard Castle and Yarm, and in 1796 Charles Colling of Ketton bred the famous Durham Ox. Yet several schemes for livestock improvement arose from a desire for social prestige, while those of George Baker of Elemore Hall probably sprang from a love of horse racing. Efforts to improve the all-round performance of agriculture, like those of Cotesworth, are hard to find and the range of new husbandry techniques found even as late as 1850 is disappointing. Turnips and potatoes were grown only in a limited area at this date and most of the county retained a basic three-course rotation with bare-fallowing. Contemporary agricultural writers condemned this situation. Aware that the poor soils in the east and high relief in the west put severe restraints on a system of alternate husbandry, they urged the adoption of a rational system of convertible husbandry. Unfortunately their cries often fell on deaf ears. Just at the time when agricultural improvement seemed most urgent and fashionable the spread of mining activities throughout the county presented its most serious challenge. The 'double damage', paid by mining adventures to royalty owners and tenants for permission to take colliery workings and wayleaves through their lands, yielded an annual return that was twice the rental or commercial value of the land. Little wonder that all but the most progressive farmers, whose lands were not threatened by the sudden discovery of mineral wealth, took the easy way out. To demonstrate the commercial superiority of lead or coal it is worth recalling that Lord Londonderry paid £44,000 to the Dean and Chapter of Durham for an eleven year lease of Rainton colliery in 1832. Dean and canons were able to declare a special 'dividend'.

INTERDEPENDENCE OF AGRICULTURE AND INDUSTRY

Evidence for County Durham does suggest that the

194 A day at the races depicted in a notebook of George Baker indicates that many eighteenth-century livestock improvement schemes arose from interest in racing.

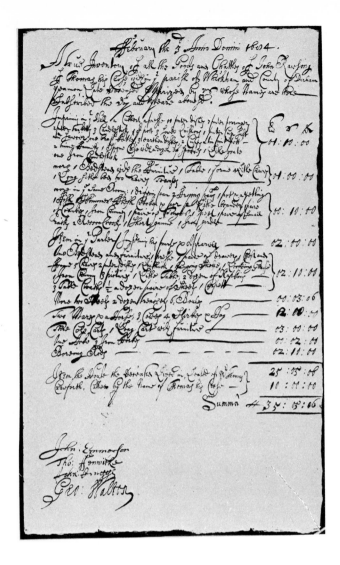

195 On the death of John Rawling of Whickham in 1684, an inventory was prepared of his possessions. Entries reveal that this so-called yeoman owned 'cole' carts and 'boring rods' used in mining as well as livestock and hay. Dual economy was basic to the economic and social welfare of many seventeenth- and eighteenth-century Durham families.

general model of growing regional specialisation in the eighteenth century is in need of some modification, for while early industrialisation and population growth could have a damaging effect on agriculture, they could act also as a stimulant. Agriculture and industry might have progressed side by side, and there is need for further work on the industrialising north and west in the eighteenth century in order to establish the existence of a possible agricultural revolution in the

uplands. No doubt it will possess characteristics different from those of the lowland revolution, reflecting not merely physical conditions but also differences in regional diet, employment opportunities, market trends and land use priorities. Meanwhile, the continuing search in historical documents and some present-day landscapes reveals the close juxtaposition and interdependence of agrarian and industrial interests far beyond the level of rural craft industry.

FURTHER READING

Bairoch, P. 'Agriculture and the Industrial Revolution' *Fontana Economic History of Europe* vol 3, section 8 (1969)

Chambers, J. D. 'Enclosure and Labour Supply in the Industrial Revolution' *Economic History Review* 2nd series, v (1953), 319–43

Chambers, J. D. 'The Vale of Trent, 1670–1800' *Economic History Review Supplement 3* (1957)

Chambers, J. D. and Mingay, G. E. *The Agricultural Revolution, 1750–1880* (1966)

Dean, P. and Cole, W. A. *British Economic Growth, 1688–1959* (2nd edn 1967)

Fletcher, T. W. 'The Agrarian Revolution in Arable Lancashire' *Trans Lancs & Cheshire Antiquarian Soc* (1962)

Grigg, D. *The Agricultural Revolution in South Lincolnshire* (1966), 93–123

Gonner. E. C. K. *Common Land and Inclosure* (1912)

Harris, A. *The Rural Landscape of the East Riding of Yorkshire 1700–1850* (1961)

Hodgson, R. I. 'The Progress of Enclosure in County Durham 1550–1870', *Area, IBG*, No 3 (1970), 67–8

Hughes, E. *North Country Life in the Eighteenth Century: The North East 1700–1750* (1952)

Jones, E. L. (ed) *Agriculture and Economic Growth in England 1650–1815* (1967)

Kerridge, E. *The Agricultural Revolution* (1967)

Marshall, T.H. 'Jethro Tull and the "New Husbandry" of the Eighteenth Century' *Economic History Review*, 2 (1929–30), 41–60

Mingay, G. E. 'The Agricultural Revolution in English History: a Reconsideration' *Agricultural History*, 37 (1963), 123–33

Ross, E. D. and Toritz, R. L. 'The Term "Agricultural Revolution" as Used by Economic Historians' *Agricultural History*, 22 (1948), 32–8

Smailes, A. E. *North England* (1960)

Thirsk, J. *English Peasant Farming* (1957)

196 Britain's horizons widened during the eighteenth century. Between 1700 and 1780 the value of overseas trade doubled. During the last twenty years of the eighteenth-century it trebled. Bristol, Queen City of the West shared with the rapidly expanding port of Liverpool the rich rewards of slave trading and of importing tobacco, sugar, cocoa and other tropical products. Its harbour was constantly crowded with shipping.

13 GEORGIAN LANDSCAPES

by HUGH C. PRINCE

THE first copper penny presents images of Britain at the end of the eighteenth century. At no time before or since had the countryside and town looked so tidy and well-groomed. Architecture was governed by classical rules; nature, picturesquely adorned, inspired romantic feelings; agricultural improvements had made fields as neat as gardens; and smoke from factory chimneys had not yet come to darken the skies.

The scenery most characteristic of Britain was that described by the painter J. M. W. Turner as 'elegant pastoral'.

Analogies and metaphors are not the most precise instruments for examining the geography of an area, but they have the power to stimulate our imaginative faculties. For that purpose they may be employed in constructing theoretical models or, alternatively, they

153

197 *England, gibed Napoleon, had become a nation of shopkeepers. In high streets and side streets new shops were opening to display the wares of bakers, drapers, grocers, poulterers, booksellers and candlestickmakers. The effect of this change in the conduct of retail trading may be seen not only in the fashionable shop fronts of St James's Street or Wigmore Street in the west end of London, but also in the dignified bow windows of suburban Bloomsbury's Woburn Walk (above), in Milsom Street, Bath, and in Elm Hill in provincial Norwich.*

198 *By 1793 an authority on coinage observed that silver pennies had become so scarce and so mutilated that there was a growing 'apprehension they may never be renewed'. The issue of millions of copper pieces did much to restore popular confidence in the currency and to bring about a major change in spending habits.*

154

may be used as aids in recalling the past. Knowledge about the past can only be reached through a study of surviving artefacts, but if we are to do more than simply describe them as material objects and are to succeed in interpreting them as expressions of particular cultures we must seek to understand their symbolic significance. We must study them as images or talismans, reading their meanings as we would read metaphors. In this way Paul Vidal de la Blache viewed the imprint of human activities on the French *pays* concluding: 'Thus is a country defined and distinguished, and in time becomes as it were a medal struck in the image of a people.' By reversing the terms of this analogy we may seek fresh insights into the character of Britain 179 years ago by looking at a coin as if it were struck in the likeness of the country of that time.

THE COPPER PENNY

The first copper penny to be minted in Britain is stamped boldly with the date 1797. Unlike a modern penny, it does not declare its value. It is heavy, thick and deeply embossed, a solid ounce to be tumbled with a clatter on a wooden bench, a coin known to collectors as a cartwheel penny. The image it bears is not a thin photographic impression, but robust and virile. It speaks plainly of British tastes and habits at the end of the eighteenth century. It provides enough clues about the lives and activities of the people who made it and handled it to build a picture of the country in which they lived. But in telling much about some aspects of the character of the country, it leaves much unsaid. It is both a token and a cachet of its age.

The disappearance of little silver coins closed a chapter in medieval thinking. Silver pennies richly emblazoned with medieval heraldry, stamped with the stylised heads of playing card kings and queens, ceased to be minted in the seventeenth century. Silver coins with which generations of peasants had paid their rents and fines to feudal lords, upon which merchants had depended for making payments to foreign creditors, the currency which impecunious monarchs had from time to time debased by adulterating silver with base metals, for clipping and forging which men had been hanged, hoards of which had been buried and hidden by people too cautious to entrust their savings to bankers were now scarcely to be had. The few that remained in circulation were so worn and defaced as to be indistinguishable from counterfeits and forgeries,

and the public lost confidence in their value.

With the introduction of the new penny, day wages could be paid in copper, either in coins of the realm or in tokens issued by manufacturers and tradesmen. It was also an age in which joint-stock banks began to issue paper money in the form of promissory notes, in which bankers and moneylenders came to play an increasingly powerful role in the nation's commerce and industry, in which investors hazarded fortunes in perilous ventures. That is not to say that the penny was a sophisticated instrument of finance, but it was important in facilitating thousands of everyday transactions by ordinary families. Pennies could buy all kinds of things that had been either prohibitively expensive or unobtainable at any price a century earlier: China tea, Jamaica rum, silk twist, plugs of tobacco, sisal rope, coal tar, whale oil, soap, printed broadsheets, seats at the theatre, metal spoons, teacups, buttons, brooches, calico, velvet, ginger biscuits, scuttles of sea-coal, legs of mutton, jugs of beer. As pennies circulated more freely household spending changed in character, and products from distant parts of the world entered British homes in increasing quantities. Labourers began to drink imported tea instead of beer and to wear manufactured cottons as well as homespun woollens. Things once bargained for at weekly markets or bartered from itinerant traders were now bought in shops and in place of temporary stalls permanent buildings began to arise in medieval market places. Commercial transactions were being conducted in secure and comfortable surroundings. Hundreds of towns might boast a solid Georgian bank, a row of well-appointed shops, a coffee house and perhaps auction rooms or a corn exchange of the same period.

CAESAR'S PROVINCE

The words of the parable recounted in St Luke's Gospel: 'Show me a penny. Whose image and superscription hath it? They answered and said, Caesar's', might have been exactly the words addressed to an eighteenth-century congregation. Look at the face of the penny. Its image and superscription are indeed Caesar's – of a republican rather than an imperial cast. The outline is not mechanically perfect; it seems not to be quite circular. The lettering is Roman, not as chaste and refined as on the Trajan column, but stamped in a heavy mould, firmly like a label on a decanter. Each letter is inscribed boldly, spaced

199 *At Bath flights of terraces, such as the Royal Crescent begun by the elder and younger John Woods, swept gracefully into new crescents and circuses and edged their way without emphatic divisions towards blocks of public buildings. The balance of all the parts seems to have been achieved effortlessly, so complete was the mastery of the classical style. The result is the most satisfying and harmonious urban scene ever produced in England.*

200 *The Palladian Chiswick House, flawless as an example of classical building, remains alien in its English surroundings, too exact a replica of Palladio's Villa Rotonda to have been transferred from Vicenza successfully. For most of the winter the interior is cold and draughty, the rooms dark and the steps leading to the front door inadequately protected from wind and rain.*

correctly, and the legend fitting comfortably and compactly into the whole design reads GEORGIUS III DEI GRATIA REX. Shorn of the flattering titles to which an absolute monarch might have presumed, bowing senatorially, not obsequiously towards the established forms of the Church of England, it is the inscription of a constitutional monarch, noble but not divine.

The king does not stare at you like the gimlet-eyed Henry VIII. He does not present a bearded, bewigged head, surmounted by an imperial crown, holding orb and sceptre. His head is shown in profile, as if in the movement of turning his back towards you. He wears a crown of laurels; his face is clean shaven; over his shoulder is draped a simple toga, falling loosely away from a broad expanse of neck. It is an unaffectedly classical portrait of a man. Its muscular modelling, laurels and toga are all of a piece with the Roman lettering. Its purity of expression is a remarkable achievement; it betrays not the slightest hint that the subject might have been represented in a manner other than classical. Its rendering is a dutiful tribute to the Augustan age, strict and uncompromising in its adherence to classical rules.

The rule of taste was absolute. Architects, painters, writers and statesmen did not seek guidance; they submitted themselves to the dictates of the classical orders, classical proportions, classical grammar and classical logic. In architecture, submission could go no farther than in the design of the Palladian villas built at Chiswick, Marble Hill, Holkham and Mereworth. Chiswick was the work of a team whose patron, Lord Burlington, was not only a wealthy nobleman and a connoisseur but also a practising architect. Charles Bridgeman, William Kent and the poet, Alexander Pope, helped in the planning and execution of the building and in the landscaping of the grounds. As individuals they were all versatile artists: Charles Bridgeman was not only an innovator in landscape design but also a land surveyor and author of a fen draining scheme; Kent was an interior decorator, painted ceilings, designed furniture and coaches, in addition to being an architect and a landscape gardener; Pope himself was an amateur garden designer. The accomplishments of later artists were no less catholic. Lancelot Brown, the landscape gardener, turned his hand to architecture, whilst James and Robert Adam not only planned whole streets and squares of private houses and public buildings but also designed the carpets, fireplaces and vases that adorned their interiors. As the principles of classical art were applied to more

and more objects, designers gained in confidence and expressed their ideas with greater freedom.

Early classical buildings in Portland stone were extended by the addition of wings stuccoed to look like limestone. Later, whitish bricks were substituted for stone and by the end of the century entire terraces and neighbourhoods were erected in red brick. Classicism discarded its carapace of stone and presented itself in a variety of materials, and the exquisite proportions of these later structures were even more elegant and refined than previous works. Everywhere designers were striving to impose order and seemliness on their material surroundings. In towns they tidied the jumble of old buildings and composed streets of harmonious facades. Market towns such as Hertford, Aylesbury, Farnham, Calne and many others, racing centres such as Newmarket, Marlborough, Newbury and Malton, canal frontages at Wisbech and Bewdley, spas at Buxton, Cheltenham and Tunbridge Wells, seaside resorts at Sidmouth and Weymouth, naval dockyards at Chatham and Portsmouth were given face-lifts, and some places, such as Blandford Forum, arose anew from the ashes of devastating fires. In the countryside landscape gardeners, land agents and enclosure commissioners redrew the lines of roads and field boundaries in regular patterns, and replanned entire farms and villages.

Classicism was as much concerned with planning as with decoration. It was formal and geometrical without the pomp and ceremony of Baroque planning. The squares and parks of London were regular and uniform but retained an air of intimacy and domesticity. The first semi-detached houses appeared in classical guise in London's suburbs at Highgate, at Kennington and in the Paragon at Blackheath. The Thames was spanned by two classical bridges at Westminster and Blackfriars, and the City and Westminster were linked by new streets and government buildings from Somerset House to the Horse Guards Parade. The capital and provincial cities were furnished with new theatres, clubs, academies, museums, hospitals, gaols and a few churches in the same idiom. In Bristol, Liverpool, Dublin and Newcastle builders put up neat rows of artisans' dwellings, and enlightened manufacturers commissioned entire model villages. The creator of Jasper Ware, Josiah Wedgwood, laid out a compact residential estate for his work-people at Etruria in the Potteries; and pioneer cotton mill owners housed their apprentices and spinners in decent cottages of good design and

201 *Farmer George was a familiar figure to be seen out riding in all weathers, in top boots and greatcoat, sometimes alone inspecting newly created farms on the estate, sometimes accompanied by a pack of hounds and huntsmen. At the time of his accession, in 1760 Windsor was no paradise. The castle was a crumbling medieval fortress, lacking the comforts and refinements of contemporary houses; but the stables were rebuilt to provide superior accommodation for the king's horses, Sir Joseph Banks was commissioned to introduce a flock of Merino sheep, the management of the estate was greatly improved under the king's direction, the results of experiments with plough oxen were reported in the* Annals of Agriculture, *and the king himself contributed to that journal under a pseudonym.*

202 *In the selection of cattle, the cult of corpulence prevailed over every other consideration. 'Nothing would please', wrote George Culley in 1786, 'but Elephants or Giants'. Whether or not the weight of cattle doubled or trebled during the eighteenth century is open to dispute, but the idea that size was the criterion of merit cannot be challenged. The greatest fat beasts, such as the Durham Ox (shown here), won all the prizes at competitions, were exhibited as prodigies, were illustrated in the press and eulogised in verse.*

158

203 An 'unmannerly, imperious lord', as Viscount Milton was described, succeeded after twenty years in removing an ancient town from the precincts of his house. It was rebuilt as a model village in an adjoining valley The rustic thatched cottages, the mock Gothick church, charity school and almshouses have all the patronising artificiality of Marie Antoinette's hamlet in the grounds of the Petit Trianon, except that the villagers in Milton Abbas were not courtiers but labouring countrymen.

classical proportions, such as are still to be seen at Cromford, Mellor and Styal. The early factories themselves were severely classical; so too were dock gates and warehouses, customs houses and lighthouses, tunnel entrances and aqueducts on the new inland navigations. By 1797 most towns had taken on a classical look or had been embellished by some public monument – an equestrian statue, a town hall, an assembly room, a new bridge, an hotel or a courthouse. But classical taste found its fullest and most elegant expression in the building and rebuilding of country houses and in the landscaping of their parks. The most generous and influential patrons of the arts, the final arbiters of taste were a few Whig families who, between them, owned much the largest share of the land of Britain. They could well afford to be generous; secure as no previous generation of landowners had been in possession of such wealth, holding not only extensive estates in the country but also some of the most valuable land in towns as well as much of the nation's minerals. Having tasted the pleasures of building, planting and gardening, they devoted themselves unsparingly to what they regarded both as an absorbing recreation and as a means of improving their estates for their descendants. Questions of design and construction were discussed in the hunting field, in estate offices and in parliament; they were the subject of gossip in clubs and in drawing rooms; they filled pages of diaries and private correspondence. 'How does my good Howard do?' writes Mrs Campbell to the owner of Marble Hill, 'Methinks I long to hear from you; but I suppose you are up to the ears in bricks and mortar, and talk of frieze and cornice like any little woman! I am going in a few days to Colonel Fane's, where I intend to improve myself in the terms of art, in order to keep pace with you in the winter.' A friendly rivalry in matters of building and landscaping animated letters and conversations between landowners and was kept alive by frequent visits to each other's houses. The neat composure of

204 The tableau on the side of the monument in Holkham Park, erected in honour of Lord Leicester by his grateful tenants, portrays a memorable event in agricultural history. It represents the granting of the lease of a newly reclaimed farm at Castle Acre to the teenage John Hudson. The almost legendary improvement of that farm during Hudson's lifetime added a special lustre to the prestige of Norfolk husbandry, and a descendant of the boy-farmer became Minister of Agriculture.

the countryside owed something to these exchanges of ideas, as well as to the professional skills of Kent, Brown and Repton.

HANOVER FARM

Look at the head of George III. The portrait is Roman, but the man is not a severe tight-lipped consul nor a philosopher. He falls short of Arthur Young's ideal of a man 'who might love Greek yet ride well to hounds,' but to do him justice, it must be acknowledged that his understanding of Georgical employments made up for his ignorance of Virgil. The petulant mouth, the baggy jowl, the massive bull-like neck personify the bucolic features of John Bull. It is the stout figure Paul Sandby sketched, astride a pony riding alone down a heathland track in Windsor Great Park. It is a likeness of the querulous landowner whom Gillray frequently caricatured in his rural pursuits, the stingy peasant who made apple dumplings, prepared his own breakfast, toasted muffins and took tea without sugar, the monarch who was ridiculed for making a profit from farming, haggling with tradesmen and striking a hard bargain with salesmen in Windsor market. His mannerisms are savagely parodied in Peter Pindar's rhyme:

A batch of bullocks! – see great Caesar run:
He stops the drover – bargain is begun.
He feels their ribs and rumps – he shakes his head –
'Poor, drover, poor – poor, very poor indeed!'

Whatever else the ruling landowners might have expected their king to be, they expected him to dine well, to ride well and to take an active lead in agricultural improvements. In this they were not entirely disappointed. The work of reclaiming heathland at Windsor was a notable achievement, although on a much smaller scale than on the great estates of west Norfolk. The king paid a warm tribute to the Norfolk improvers by naming one of his new farms Norfolk Farm, and the compliment was returned on scores of estates in Norfolk and elsewhere by naming farms, newly won from wastes, Hanover Farm and Windsor Farm.

The spirit of improvement that seized the inhabitants of Norfolk in the early eighteenth century infected the whole kingdom by 1797. West Norfolk itself was completely transformed from a district of barren sands into the Good Sand region of which Arthur Young wrote, 'instead of boundless wilds and uncultivated wastes, inhabited by scarce anything but sheep,

the country is all cut up into inclosures, cultivated in a most husband-like manner, richly manured, well-peopled and yielding one hundred times the produce that it did in its former state'. The conversion of heaths into arable land was prosecuted with missionary fervour. Noblemen renounced life at court and offices of state in order to dedicate themselves to the work of reclaiming their estates, agronomists loathed the sight of ling, furze and fern, whilst travellers rejoiced at the sight of 'England smiling with cultivation; the grounds exhibiting all the perfection of agriculture, parcelled into beautiful enclosures'. The appearance of new crops was welcomed as an adornment to the countryside. 'Turnips, clover, coleworts and other green winter food', wrote the Suffolk farmer, Thomas Ruggles, 'break the dreariness of the winter prospect and relieve the eye from a boundless expanse of dirty soil and extinguished verdure'. Arthur Young declared that he 'would at any time, with utmost pleasure, ride forty miles to view such another landscape as that from Mr Tucker's cabbage field, situated on the top of a hill' near Rotherham and many writers praised the picturesque beauties of the newly formed landscapes of hedgerows and corn fields. Clover and Saint Foin were regarded as performers of miracles whilst carrots and potatoes were praised as 'admirable roots'. Yet there was still much to be done. Very extensive wastes remained in the eastern counties and in southern England, in regions where progress had been most rapid. In the fens of Cambridgeshire the peat was shrinking to levels lower than those from which windmills could be relied upon to raise water, but elsewhere in the eastern counties patches of fenland were drained and brought into cultivation for the first time and extensive areas were embanked and drained not only in the Somerset Levels but also in northern England. Throughout the country substantial gains in productivity were achieved by irrigating water meadows, particularly in Hampshire and Wiltshire, by warping in the flood plain of the Trent and by underdraining in many different localities.

Not only were crop harvests greatly enlarged but livestock production was dramatically increased. No less energy and enthusiasm was devoted to the task of improving animal husbandry than to the cultivation of new arable land. Robert Bakewell and George Culley accomplished for stock-breeding and grazing what Coke and Townshend accomplished for arable farming. The improvement of beef production was the principal objective of cattle breeding, taking priority

205 *Ralph Allen, whose quarries supplied the golden stone for building Georgian Bath, created an enchanting landscape garden overlooked by his fine house at the top of the hill. By the end of the century the mineral railway had been removed, the bottom of the valley was submerged beneath an ornamental lake, and a charming Palladian covered bridge spanned a cascade.*

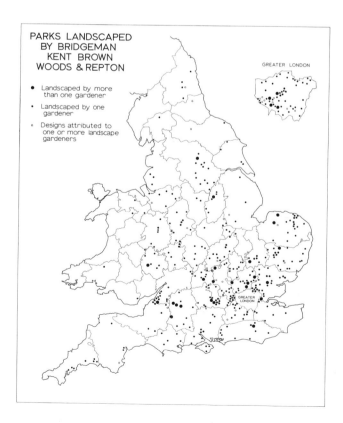

PARKS LANDSCAPED
BY BRIDGEMAN
KENT BROWN
WOODS & REPTON

GREATER LONDON

● Landscaped by more than one gardener

• Landscaped by one gardener

○ Designs attributed to one or more landscape gardeners

GREATER LONDON

206 *Although apparently so artless that they may be mistaken for the works of nature, eighteenth-century landscape gardens were contrived with no less artifice and subtlety than the most elegant town plans. Informality was raised to a fine art by Charles Bridgeman (c 1680–1738), William Kent (1685–1748) and Lancelot Brown (1716–1783), all of whom learned their craft at Stowe under the patronage of Lord Cobham. Capability Brown, the most celebrated landscape gardener, was succeeded by Humphry Repton (1752–1818), whose practice was even more extensive than his predecessor's. During the same period, a number of other designers, including Richard Woods (d 1793), also flourished.*

over the claims of dairying. In breeding sheep a combination of qualities was sought after: hardiness, fecundity, rapidity of growth, fineness of fleece. Fixing two or more of these qualities in a stock was a very high achievement. Arthur Young describes holding a party at his house to discuss ways of improving South Down sheep which were less hardy because born more naked than the Norfolk breed. 'I wrote to Mr Ellman, in Sussex, and to Mr Boys, in Kent, to inform them that South Down sheep would be the subject of a farming party at Bradfield; that objections would be urged, and ought to be answered; they mounted their horses, and rode 130 miles for a *single batch* of farming'. The annual sheep shearings at Holkham, Petworth and Woburn were stock-breeders' congresses of international importance, the toast drunk at Holkham to 'Symmetry well-covered', their high aspiration. A great deal of attention was paid to the propagation of new 'artificial' grasses and fodder crops. On stiff clay soils arable land was laid down to grass and the permanent pastures of the fattening districts in Cheshire, Leicestershire and Middlesex were managed with care.

In the midland shires open fields fast disappeared under neatly trimmed thorn hedges, the acreage of green sward expanded, and the hunting of the hare gave way to the hunting of the fox with large packs of hounds. Cramped little farms in villages were converted into smithies, alehouses and shops. Square brick farmhouses with fashionable parlours that Gillray lampooned and Cobbett detested, sprang up in the midst of newly enclosed fields and on large estates labourers were rehoused in small well-designed cottages. The vast scale of the rebuilding and re-organisation of the countryside is evident not only from estate accounts of the period but also from the visible marks of planning inscribed on the pattern of fields, roads and on the layout of model villages such as Houghton, Lowther, Milton Abbas, Harewood, Blanchland, Coneysthorpe and Tremadoc. Equally impressive is the legacy of eighteenth-century tree planting. The inroads made by agriculture, industry and shipbuilding left Britain one of the least wooded countries in western Europe, but the losses were now being made good. During the last quarter of the century millions of trees were planted annually by large landowners. At Welbeck in Nottinghamshire, for example, the Duke of Portland's gardener, Mr Speechly, reported: 'We sometimes follow a chain of hills to a very great distance; so that what we

plant in one season, which perhaps is sixty, eighty and sometimes an hundred acres, is no more than part of one great design'. By 1780 it was apparent that these exertions were bringing about widespread changes. 'What landscapes will dignify every quarter of our island', exclaimed Horace Walpole, 'when the daily plantations that are making have attained venerable maturity!'

BRITANNIA'S WORKSHOP

Turn the coin over and look at the reverse side. It bears the simple inscription BRITANNIA and the date, 1797. The centre-piece is a voluminous, high breasted figure of Britannia seated on a rock with her target representing the union flag, supporting Neptune's trident in her left hand, holding out an olive branch in her right hand. Britannia is idolised in eighteenth-century popular art, on inn signs, ships' figure-heads and the most jingoistic of popular songs. A seascape occupies the background and on the horizon a three-masted ship lies low in the water; whilst at the base of the rock on which Britannia sits is inscribed the manufacturer's mark, SOHO. Thus are commerce and industry joined together under the emblem of Britannia. The copper penny was a product of the works which manufactured Britannia plate, supplied the king with silver candelabra, ormolu clocks, cameos designed by Josiah Wedgwood, served a growing market with buckles, buttons and toys, and held the patents for the improved Boulton and Watt steam engines.

Soho! – where GENIUS and the ARTS preside,
EUROPA's wonder and BRITANNIA's pride;
Thy matchless works have raised Old England's fame;
THINE! ever blended with a BOULTON's name.

An attentive Boswell, visiting Soho with Dr Johnson in 1776, was rewarded with an epigram freshly minted by their host, Matthew Boulton: 'I sell here, Sir, what all the world desires to have – Power.' With the aid of steam-driven presses, Boulton secured the contract to make 480 tons of penny pieces in June 1797. By August 1799 he had coined over 45 million pieces, weighing 1266 tons, 18 cwt, 3 qr, 25 lb, 10 oz, an outstanding feat of mass production by any standard.

Machinery and the power of steam were revolutionising many branches of manufacturing. During the last quarter of the century William Radcliffe of Mellor remarked upon the complete change which had come about in northern England in the spinning of yarns:

207　*The Thames at Twickenham, painted by Richard Wilson, recalls 'the peculiar happiness' experienced by another observer viewing that stretch of river at that period. For R. S. Cambridge, its charm arose from the sight of 'prospects opened, the country called in, nature rescued and improved, and art decently concealing herself'. Miraculously, the peace and repose of the scene have been little disturbed by the expansion of London.*

208　*By the end of the century a great variety of exotic and eccentric structures had invaded the countryside as picturesque ornaments. Grotesque hermitages, rustic pavilions, sham ruins and other eyecatchers had been introduced into the earliest landscape gardens. Swiss Cottage, illustrated in an aquatint by Hill, was built shortly after 1800 to house a lock-keeper at Cassiobury Park, Watford.*

163

'That of wool had disappeared altogether, and that of linen was also nearly gone; cotton, cotton, cotton has become the almost universal material for employment'. John Aikin, describing the country around Manchester in 1795, viewed the rapid and prodigious increase in cotton manufacturing as 'absolutely unparalleled in the annals of trading nations'. At the same time the manufacture of iron was revolutionised by the use of coke for smelting and the application of steam power to pumping, forging, rolling and turning. After 1780 the output of pig iron doubled in each decade, and the west midlands was transformed from a backward state into a thriving centre of industrial activity. Similar changes were taking place in southern Yorkshire, in south Wales and in Lanarkshire. In 1791 Arthur Young observed that 'all the activity and industry of this kingdom is fast concentrating where there are coal pits'. The industrial revolution had not yet scored deep scars on the face of the countryside. The flares from new furnaces added a touch of sublimity to Coalbrookdale which still, in 1785, retained the charms of a 'very romantic spot'; while the poet John Dyer scanned with unalloyed pleasure the West Riding scene:

> And ruddy roofs and chimney-tops appear
> Of busy Leeds, up-wafting to the clouds
> The incense of thanks-giving: all is joy:
> And trade and business guide the living scene.

On the other hand, the effect of the seven-storey cotton mills recently erected in the Derwent valley and on other streams near Matlock deeply offended Uvedale Price, author of *An Essay on the Picturesque* (1796). He protested that 'nothing can equal them for the purpose of dis-beautifying an enchanting piece of scenery'.

Only a very small part of Britain's manufacturing activities were carried on in ironworks and cotton mills. To find the great majority of industrial workers and the largest share of industrial wealth we should have had to journey through the countryside. The woollen and worsted industries, brewing and the leather trades, still the leading industries by value of output and volume of employment, were for the most part located in rural areas. In addition to rural flour mills, maltings, sawmills and slaughterhouses processing the produce of farms and forests, the countryside supplied the nation with a large part of its building materials, implements and tools. The Board of Agriculture Reports, mentioning only the most specialised and highly localised industries, indicate how diverse the manufacturing activities of the countryside were, and the first census in 1801 reported large concentrations of workers engaged in trade and manufactures in south-west England and in East Anglia.

REALITY AND ROMANCE

The coin is an expressive token. Its imagery summons many associations that help us to visualise and to understand the fabric of the environment at the time it was minted; but many aspects of the eighteenth century are only vaguely alluded to. Abstract ideas may be proclaimed on coins as slogans, but the French revolutionary ideas of Liberty, Equality and Fraternity were alien and subversive. The British way was pragmatic and realistic. The king is no mere figurehead, but a suffering mortal. Look at his bulging eyes; they are nearly sightless. Look at his high, arched eyebrows, the taut high bridge of his nose, the upward curve of the corner of his mouth. The artist has studied the royal physiognomy dispassionately and recorded his observations with complete candour. The same unflinching respect for reality and individuality illuminates the highest poetry, painting and scholarship of the late eighteenth century.

By the end of the century, artists were striving to free themselves from the excessive symmetry and uniformity of classical styles in architecture and in literature. A flood of emotional energy was released in a search for natural truth, some of this energy being deflected into a strenuous effort to synthesise nature in picturesque views. Where suitably irregular scenes were not to be found, they were ingeniously improvised. The new style displayed as many tricks and mannerisms as the old, but it had the compelling attraction of being original and romantic. The landscape was furnished with sham ruins, with Gothick dairies, with Chinese pagodas, with Doric temples, with folly towers and shellwork grottoes. Imagination was called in to relieve the weight of conformity, romance to enliven the dull edge of regularity. The greatest extravagances of the age have been mellowed by the passage of time, but the magic of Stourhead and a hundred other landscapes is as potent now as it ever was.

Landscaping and rural ornament were partly paid for out of the profits of agricultural and industrial improvements. The rich were conspicuously enriched, but the poverty of the masses was no less evident. Enclosure deprived many cottagers of their grazing

rights over commons, wages of farm labourers were regularly supplemented by outdoor relief following a decision of the Speenhamland justices in 1795, whilst the laws of settlement and the game laws worked harshly against families made destitute by depressions in handloom weaving and other declining crafts. The productivity of agriculture was substantially increased; but still too little was produced in years of harvest failure in 1795 and 1799 to avert famine. Despite unremitting efforts, the area of land remaining unimproved at the end of the century was acknowledged to be 'a national disgrace'. Large parts of Scotland, Wales, northern and western England lay dormant, their farms ageing and growing mossy, the lanes leading to them becoming more deeply rutted. This slumbering half-tamed countryside had its devotees. The scenes loved by Clare, Crabbe, Cowper, Burns and Wordsworth were not the harsh newly enclosed tracts of farmland, but

209 Throughout the eighteenth century the overwhelming majority of manufacturing enterprises remained small family concerns, and most of them conducted their businesses in the depths of the countryside. Joseph Wright of Derby, a painter fascinated by the massive strength and strange firelight of the new industrial machines, depicted the interior of an Iron Forge, *as an intimate domestic scene. The tilt hammer, like other technical innovations, was turned by a water wheel, not a steam engine.*

the downs, moors, fells and heaths, remote from the haunts of men. Thomas Bewick, the engraver and ornithologist, is one of many who recalled with gratitude childhood experiences among untamed commons: 'It was mostly fine, green sward, or pasturage, broken, or divided, indeed, with clumps of

165

210 *Whole regions of Britain seem to have escaped the hand of the improver. In 1795 a Parliamentary Select Committee estimated that waste land covered no fewer than 7,888,977 acres in England, 1,628,307 acres in Wales, 14,218,224 acres in Scotland and an unknown amount in Ireland. Much of that unproductive land was high moorland, some was undrained marsh and fen, and some was unreclaimed lowland heath. In Surrey some of the most desolate and villainous heaths, lairs of brigands and vagrants, reached to the outskirts of London.*

"blossom'd whins", foxgloves, fern and some junipers, and with heather in profusion, sufficient to scent the whole air . . . On this common – the poor man's heritage for ages past, where he kept a few sheep, or a Kyloe cow, perhaps a flock of geese, and mostly a stock of bee-hives – it was with infinite pleasure that I lay and beheld the beautiful wild scenery . . . and it is with the opposite feelings of regret that I now find all swept away'. Samuel Palmer, John Constable and the Norwich watercolourists returned again and again to the unspoilt corners of the country and from these scenes drew their inspiration.

The copper penny has now itself entered into legend. After 174 years in circulation it has joined the groat, the noble and the half-crown as an archaeological relic, to be replaced by a decimal penny 2.4 times the value but only a fraction of the weight of its predecessor.

FURTHER READING

Albion, R. G. *Forests and Sea Power* (Harvard, 1926)

British Association for the Advancement of Science *Birmingham and its Regional Setting* (Birmingham, 1950)

Carter, H. B. *His Majesty's Spanish Flock* (Sydney, 1964)

Clare, John *Selected Poems* (1968)

Clark, H. F. *The English Landscape Garden* (1948)

Clark, Kenneth *The Gothic Revival* (1929, Harmondsworth 1964)

Crabbe, George *Tales, 1812, and Other Selected Poems* (Cambridge, 1967)

Deane, Phyllis *The First Industrial Revolution* (Cambridge, 1965)

Gilbert, E. W. *Brighton, Old Ocean's Bauble* (1954)

Higgs, John *The Land: a Visual History of Modern Britain* (1964)

Hudson, Kenneth *Industrial Archaeology* (1963)

Hussey, Christopher *The Picturesque* (1927, 1967)

Hussey, Christopher *English Gardens and Landscapes 1700–1750* (1967)

Marshall, William *The Rural Economy of the West of England* (1796)

Mingay, G. E. *English Landed Society in the Eighteenth Century* (1963)

Monk, Samuel Holt, *The Sublime* (1953, Michigan 1960)

Musson, A. E. and Robinson, Eric *Science and Technology in the Industrial Revolution* (Manchester, 1969)

Prince, Hugh C. *Parks in England* (Shalfleet, 1967)

Richards, J. M. *The Functional Tradition in Early Industrial Buildings* (1958)

Smith, R. A. L. *Bath* (1944)

Smith, Robert Trow *A History of British Livestock Husbandry 1700–1900* (1959)

Stroud, Dorothy *Capability Brown* (1950)

Stroud, Dorothy *Humphry Repton* (1962)

Summerson, John *Architecture in Britain 1558 to 1830* (1953)

White, Gilbert *Natural History and Antiquities of Selborne* (1789)

Wordsworth, William *A Guide Through the District of the Lakes* with introduction by W. M. Merchant (1951)

14 FROM MANPOWER TO STEAM: CHANGES IN THE EARLY INDUSTRIAL REVOLUTION

by J. B. HARLEY

A
TOUR
Thro' the Whole ISLAND of
GREAT BRITAIN,
Divided into
Circuits *or* Journies.

Giving a Particular and Diverting
ACCOUNT of Whatever is CURIOUS, and
worth OBSERVATION, *Viz.*

I. A Description of the principal Cities and Towns, their Situation, Magnitude, Government, and Commerce.
II. The Customs, Manners, Speech, as also the Exercises, Diversions, and Employment of the People.
III. The Produce and Improvement of the Lands, the Trade and Manufactures.
IV. The Sea-Ports and Fortifications, the Course of Rivers, and the Inland Navigation.
V. The Publick Edifices, Seats, and Palaces of the NOBILITY and GENTRY.

With *Useful* Observations *upon the Whole.*
Particularly fitted for the Reading of such as desire to Travel over the ISLAND.

VOL. III.
Which completes this Work, and contains a
TOUR thro' *SCOTLAND*, &c.

With a Map of SCOTLAND, *by Mr.* MOLL.

By *a* GENTLEMAN.

LONDON,
Printed : And Sold by G. STRAHAN, in *Cornhill.*
W. MEARS, at the *Lamb* without *Temple-Bar.*
And J. STAGG, in *Westminster-Hall.*
M DCC XXVII.

THE pulse of the Industrial Revolution can be taken from eye-witness reports of contemporaries whose imagination was fired by the mounting spectacle of industrial change. Topographical writers from Daniel Defoe to Thomas Pennant devoted much space to the description of industry, as did peripatetic diarists such as the Honourable John Byng. European visitors to Britain, notebooks in hand, made pilgrimages to shrines of industrial innovation: some, including painters and poets, were bent on delineating the picturesque but others, such as Eric Thomas Svedenstierna, sent to Britain by the Swedish Iron Bureau in 1802, came as industrial spies. Even the authors of the Board of Agriculture Reports, with an agrarian axe to grind, noted the main seats of industry,

211 '. . . *every New View of Great Britain would require a New Description; the improvements that encrease; the New Buildings erected, the Old Buildings taken down; New Discoveries in Metals, Mines, Minerals; new Undertakings in Trade; Inventions, Engines, Manufactures, in a Nation, pushing and improving as we are; These things open new Scenes every Day and Make England especially shew a new differing Face in many Places, on every occasion of Surveying it' wrote Daniel Defoe in the 1720s. His* Tour *showed remarkable insight into changes that were to accelerate in the second half of the century.*

County of LANCASTER—*continued.*

HUNDRED, &c.	PARISH, TOWNSHIP, or Extra-parochial Place	HOUSES			PERSONS		OCCUPATIONS			TOTAL or PERSONS
		Inhabited.	By how many Families occupied.	Uninhabited.	Males.	Females.	Persons chiefly employed in Agriculture.	Persons chiefly employed in Trade, Manufactures, or Handicraft.	All other Persons not comprized in the Two preceding Classes.	
Town of MANCHESTER — *(Districts.)*	N° 1 A	789	1,171	8	2,620	2,752	—	3,545	1,827	5,372
	1 B	810	1,005	20	2,683	2,984	5	4,062	1,660	5,667
	2 A	279	389	15	823	1,017	—	1,143	697	1,840
	2 B	505	662	16	1,583	1,745	6	1,393	1,929	3,328
	2 C	181	345	6	670	732	—	931	471	1,402
	3 A	373	652	5	1,234	1,379	—	1,637	974	2,613
	3 B	408	681	13	1,412	1,712	—	2,167	1,018	3,124
	3 C	322	554	16	985	1,206	—	1,315	876	2,191
	4 A	509	739	6	1,510	1,766	10	1,442	1,824	3,276
	4 B	697	1,043	33	2,126	2,534	2	2,055	2,602	4,660
	5 A	344	580	8	1,144	1,290	—	1,637	797	2,434
	5 B	663	1,151	19	2,179	2,736	—	3,448	1,467	4,915
	6 —	357	444	19	978	1,129	1	788	1,318	2,107
	7 A	435	632	—	1,213	1,548	14	1,293	1,454	2,761
	7 B	124	170	—	353	416	—	426	363	769
	7 C	212	361	6	721	860	—	1,178	403	1,581

212 Population Census shows increase in industrial workers.

213 Turnpike roads and tollhouses were innovations. Toll board at the Steanor Bottom Bar, on the Rochdale-Todmorton road, survives today and gives a list of dues payable on its negotiation.

and Arthur Young, whose mission was improvement in the countryside, seldom lost a chance to eulogise the great engineering works of his day.

Looking at industrial landscapes through contemporary eyes may help us to assess the role of their attitudes in shaping historical change. But the historical events themselves, in mining, manufacturing and transport, provide evidence of their own birth and expansion. In today's landscape, the physical remains of early industries survive, and their tramways, canals, factories, furnaces and waterwheels now form the subject matter of industrial archaeology.

Documents are also fundamental, the estate papers, notebooks, deeds and letters of the entrepreneurs showing the reasons for their decisions as well as the reality of new industrial processes. Where local manuscript or field evidence fails, the student turns to national sources such as newspapers and parish registers, in which the occupations of marriage partners are often given, or to the Acts of Parliament which established new roads and canals, and their detailed maps and plans. A fuller statistical age began with the first Census of Population in 1801; its printed tables contain figures – albeit extremely imperfect – of the numbers of people engaged in trade, manufactures and handicraft in each parish.

Several abortive attempts were made after 1750 to set up a government map-making agency in Britain but private county map makers surveyed most of the country at the relatively large one inch to one mile scale between 1750 and 1800. In the following year, the Ordnance Survey began the publication of its First Edition maps. By the yardstick of earlier periods, the mass of sources describing the early Industrial Revolution is unprecedented and it enables a detailed historical geography to be written. Much remains to be done, however, in reconstructing simple changes in the distribution of industry and people in the eighteenth century, even before we can assess their impact on the landscape in the visual sense or on the delicate balance of local ecosystems. A debate also continues about the causes, chronology – in particular the times of 'take-off' and 'maturity' – and the consequences of the Industrial Revolution for the lives of ordinary people. The amassing of new knowledge and offering of new interpretations has been linked in recent years with attempts to find a more satisfactory conceptual framework for the study of the Industrial Revolution as a whole. But the building of even a simple process model is an extremely complex task. Any dynamic system must include a large number of variables – not just the well-known inventions in machinery, sources of power and transport, each of which interracted with the basic endowments of raw materials, but also related questions of capital availability, the growth of home and international markets,

214 John Cary surveyed post roads for the government – a page from his Survey of the High Roads from London, 1790. *Such new surveys and maps provide important information on the landscape.*

215 The growth of London and the industrial revolution in England. The model demonstrates the effect of the rapid growth of London upon English economy and society in the eighteenth century. There were close links between a wide range of demographic, economic and sociological changes. Where an arrow points in both directions it indicates that the relationship was a reciprocal one. All the developments in the boxes helped either directly or indirectly to produce the industrial revolution in England. After E. A. Wrigley (1969).

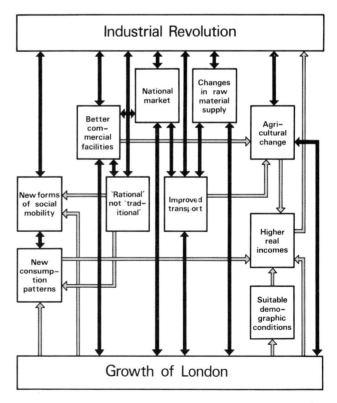

and of more intangible influences such as the long-term changes in economic attitudes which culminated in *laissez faire*. These variables are hard to define and isolate; they are more difficult to measure. To inter-relate them and establish their functional connections may be impossible except in a qualitative sense. The search for order continues, but meanwhile historians and geographers have agreed on certain salient patterns in the early Industrial Revolution.

CANAL MANIA AND TURNPIKES

There is a consensus that improvements in transport were critical among the forces making for industrial growth. In the eighteenth century, however, the sea was still the principal industrial highway. Everywhere, small ports and rivers flourished through trade in agriculture and industrial commodities. The costs of land transport were prohibitive and manufacturers went to great lengths to forward goods by coastal shipping. In 1775 the Horsehay Company, near Wellington in

Shropshire, was sending pig iron to Chester by carting it to the Severn, putting it on river craft to Bristol and then on to sailing ships to round the coast of Wales into the Dee estuary. For the same reason, the spate of schemes to improve river navigation, initiated after the Restoration, gained a fresh impetus especially in industrial England. From 1719 to 1721 works were put in hand to modify the River Douglas, carrying Wigan coal, the River Weaver, exporting Cheshire Salt, and the River Derwent, transporting Derbyshire lead and iron.

Thomas Telford, the civil engineer, wrote in 1804 that 'Canals are chiefly useful for . . . Conveying Fuel and Raw Materials to . . . Manufacturing Towns and Districts, and Exporting the Manufactured Goods'. Born in 1757, the year in which the canal age was inaugurated by the opening of the Sankey Navigation between St Helens and the Mersey, he had worked during the canal mania of 1791 to 1796, and his observations were rooted in experience. The famous Bridge-

216 *The principal waterways c 1830. After Dyos and Aldcroft. Such improvements to the infrastructure of industrial development were one of the critical investments of the age, and performed the essential economic function of carrying goods and raw materials between producers and consumers.*

170

217 *Stourport. Peter Mazell's 1776 engraving is from a local surveyor's drawing. The canal age gave birth not only to a system of inland communications but also to new settlements such as Stourport, which sprang up after the opening of the Staffordshire and Worcestershire canal in 1772.*

218 *The small-scale and primitive techniques of the coal industry in the 1780s are shown in a Paul Sanby sketch of a 'Pit head of a coal mine with a horse-gin' c 1786. Sanby began his career as a military draughtsman.*

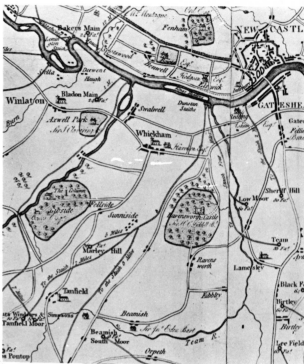

219 & 220 The mining landscape in England and Wales included wooden tramways, waterside staithes and horse drawn waggons. Title cartouche of John Gibson's 1787 map was a guide to the coal mining districts of Durham and Northumberland. Lines marked 'To the Staith' on the detail from his map show tramways from collieries to navigable water.

water Canal, which was a bulk carrier of coal from the Duke's mines at Worsley to the embryo conurbation of Manchester, set a pattern. Of the 165 canal bills approved between 1758 and 1802, over half were primarily concerned with carrying coal. The network was densest in the West Midlands, where Birmingham formed the hub of a wheel of canal communications, in Lancashire, West Yorkshire and South Wales; and these major manufacturing areas were linked by cross-country canals such as the Trent and Mersey, the Grand Union and the Leeds and Liverpool. A canal site became a primary factor in the location of industrial activity and collieries distant from canals were linked to water transport by horse-drawn tramways of up to twenty-four to thirty-two kilometres in length. Today's monuments of this canal system are especially numerous and range from the actual waterways with their

aqueducts, bridges, tunnels, spectacular flights of locks and lockkeepers' houses to urban warehouses and mushroom towns like Stourport which sprang up at the opening of the Staffordshire and Worcestershire Canal in 1772.

'This infernal road' was Arthur Young's verdict on the turnpike from Preston to Wigan. Many turnpikes were miry and impassable in winter, but such polemics cannot detract from the real improvements in the eighteenth century road system. As with the canals, there was a national network of improved roads and bridges, carefully surveyed for the popular road books of John Cary and Daniel Paterson, with inter-city stage-coach services constantly improving their travel times and, from 1785, serving the regular mail coaches. Between 1750 and 1830 the travel time between London and many provincial towns was changed into a question of hours rather than of days.

There were also the industrial turnpikes. The towns of south Lancashire were connected by such roads, along which heavy wagons and commercial carriers as well as pack horse trains could move. Yates's map of Staffordshire shows that in 1775 Birmingham was already coupled to its industrial hinterland by turnpikes radiating to Walsall, Wednesbury, Dudley and Stourbridge. Towards the end of the century, men such as Metcalf and Telford began to apply the principles of modern engineering to road construction.

COAL AND IRON

Compared with other industries, the physical survivals of the century's coal mining are slight, difficult to date and have often been obliterated by later working. The historian must rely on contemporary evidence which points to the continued ascendancy of the Great Northern Coalfield, centred on Tyneside and Wearside, in terms of both output and technique. Pits were relatively large, sometimes employing up to 300 men, shafts reached a depth of ninety-one metres and were drained by atmospheric engines, while most inland collieries of importance were linked to waterside staithes – and hence the sea and the urban markets of South-east England – by an extensively developed system of wooden tramways. There were fewer changes in the land-locked coalfields, although overall production continued to rise – perhaps fourfold in the course of the century. With exceptions, as in the thick coal seams of south Staffordshire, the pits were smaller and less endowed with expensive equipment. A primitive technology was still widespread. Pick and shovel, human muscle, circular horse gin or whimsey, shallow adit and 'bell' pit, and a handful of men in semi-rural surroundings characterised much of the industry.

Iron was the basic raw material of industrial growth, underpinning all other technologies, but its history more closely matches the concept of a revolution. Towards the end of the century, iron production rose dramatically and the culmination of an important shift in location took place. The output of pig iron in Great Britain jumped from 68,000 tons in 1788 to over 250,000 tons in 1806 and in the same period the number of furnaces increased from eighty-five to two hundred and twenty-one. New blast furnaces were set up on the coalfields, where iron ores were abundant. A final retreat from the classic areas of the charcoal-smelting

221 *An embryo industrial landscape as portrayed in William Yates' map of Staffordshire (1775). The cartographer employs special symbols for canals with bridges, milestones and locks, water-mills, forges, lead and copper mines, coal-pits and limeworks.*

era – the Weald and the Forest of Dean – and from mountain streams in Yorkshire, Derbyshire, Shropshire and Wales, was also evident.

Coalbrookdale, famous in its own age, occupies a special place in these events. It was here in 1709 that the first Abraham Darby successfully used the local 'clod' coal for smelting iron. His process was not widely disseminated until about 1770, but thereafter the rapid emergence of new areas of manufacture can be traced on several major coalfields as in Scotland, South Wales, Monmouthshire and in south Staffordshire which, although not yet dubbed a Black Country, already contained many furnaces in blast. The secondary iron trades stimulated by inventions in puddling and rolling, such as that of Henry Cort, were also drawn towards the coalfields. The 'industry of this kingdom', as Arthur Young noted in 1791, 'is fast concentrating where there are coal pits'.

Iron replaced wood for many everyday purposes. This was the age of the first iron bridge and the first iron ship. The archaeological remains consist not only of derelict furnaces and forges but also of ironwork in houses, churches and warehouses, to which must be added hundreds of unspectacular manufactured objects, fashioned at small forges by blacksmiths, cutlers, nailers and button makers – to name a few – working by traditional methods in Birmingham, Sheffield and south-west Lancashire. By the end of the century, an estimated 500,000 people were dependent mainly on the metal trades in the sixteen kilometres around Birmingham.

THE FACTORY SYSTEM

The appearance of the factory most forcibly epitomises the Industrial Revolution; its ultimate effects on the social and economic geography of Britain were profound. The basic innovation in the factory system was to transfer manufacture from the homes of the workers – the domestic system – to the mill or factory, where mechanised mass production could be effectively organised. This took place first in the textile trades, initially in the silk and cotton branches rather than in the older woollen trades, and in the East Midlands rather than in Lancashire. The earliest known factory was the five-storey Derby silk throwing mill, built during 1717 to 1721 for Sir Thomas Lombe. This served as a model for similar establishments in Macclesfield and Stockport, but not until the second half of the century did a series of inventions in spinning, culminating in Samuel Crompton's Mule, hasten its

application to cotton. In 1769, Richard Arkwright established his first cotton mill in Nottingham, but then moved to the Derwent Valley in search of water power and built factories in rapid succession at Cromford, Matlock Bath and Belper. So isolated were the sites that it was necessary to add houses for the workers and also chapels, schools and shops. These small, paternalistic communities can be regarded as the first company settlements in Britain. By 1787 there were twenty-two cotton factories in Derbyshire and another twenty-five in the rest of the East Midlands.

Only after the application of steam power to factory machinery were factories built in large numbers in towns. This was to happen in Lancashire, which quickly overtook its rival. Already, in 1795, Dr John Aikin described Manchester as the capital of the cotton

222 Based on a map by William Yates of 1786, the original provided a census of late eighteenth-century water- and wind-mills. The symbols for colleries and coal pits only give a general indication of the areas of active mining.

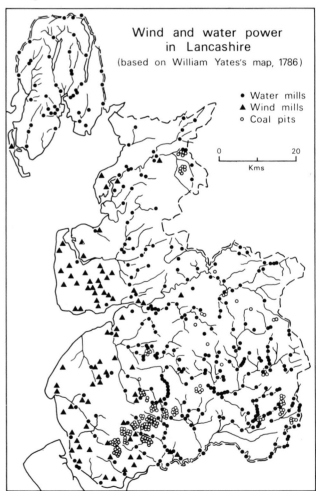

Wind and water power
in Lancashire
(based on William Yates's map, 1786)

• Water mills
▲ Wind mills
◦ Coal pits

223 *The Ironworks at Coalbrookdale,
shown in P. J. Loutherbourg's aquatint
of 1805, was a technological shrine to
which foreign industrialists and artists
made pilgrimages. Iron was the basic
raw material of the tremendous industrial
growth. Production increased by 182,000
tons in only eighteen years.*

224 *Smelting from local coal was a
technical advance, first achieved by
Arbaham Darby in 1709. A smelting
furnace is preserved at Coalbrookdale.*

225 *Causey Arch, near Tanfield, County Durham, built in 1727 for a tramway, is the first railway bridge.*

kingdom, 'the rapid and prodigious increase of which is, perhaps, absolutely unparalleled in the annals of trading nations'. But not all cotton was produced in factories for much was still put out on a domestic basis; nor were the mills mainly steam driven for water generated the bulk of the power. However, the available statistics support the popular view of mushrooming factory industry around Manchester and towns such as Bury, Preston, Chorley, Oldham and Stockport.

Neither Lancashire nor the cotton industry had a monopoly of factory production; in the booming worsted and woollen trades of the West Riding it was developing more slowly. Josiah Wedgwood's Etruria works were a textbook example of the division of labour; in Birmingham, Matthew Boulton had learned the lesson of standard mass production in his Soho Manufactory; and some factories were erected in other industrial areas, such as the West Country woollen region. But in Lancashire the shape of the future had most clearly emerged by 1800.

226 *Iron Bridge at Coalbrookdale. Civil engineering was one of the revolutionary uses to which iron was put in the late eighteenth century.*

WATERWHEELS AND STEAM ENGINES

The waterwheel remained the primary source of industrial power throughout the early Industrial Revolution and by the end of the eighteenth century had reached its moment of greatest relative importance. Millwrights such as Smeaton and Rennie were constantly striving to improve its efficiency in relation to the horsepower required, the seasonal regime and flow of streams, and the topography of individual sites.

176

227 *Illustrations from Enoch Wood's Manufactory, 1827, show the exterior of a pottery and two of the specialised stages in pottery manufacture. As the domestic system gave way to the factory system, leading industrialists, including Josiah Wedgwood, took note of Adam Smith's widely read theories of the division of labour, published in 1776.*

228 *Planting factories in the country-side resulted in the creation of self-contained industrial communities. The three-storey worker's houses at Belper were built close to the cotton mills.*

229 When Arkwright's water-powered cotton mill was established at Cromford, Derbyshire, in 1771, the transformation from village to company town became inevitable.

230 Token coinage issued by industrialists often showed their own plant. A penny struck by Priestfield Collieries and Ironworks, near Bilston.

231 Overshot waterwheels were highly efficient and capable of turning heavy machinery. Kirkby Ireleth, Lancashire, stands today as a monument to the Industrial Revolution.

232 Boulton and Watt rotative beam engines were installed throughout the country to drive industrial machinery.

Engines were sometimes used to pump water back on to the wheels, the diameters, widths and designs of which were modified. The simplest wheels were undershot, with open paddles; they had a calculated efficiency as low as 30 per cent of the total input of kinetic energy of the immediate water supply. The breast wheel, where the water struck the wheel between two o'clock and five o'clock, and which sometimes had buckets added to the paddles to retain the water, could reach a 40 per cent to 70 per cent efficiency, while the overshot wheel, best sited in steep valleys, could attain 80 per cent efficiency.

Hardly a valley in the early industrial districts is without evidence of former waterwheels, if not mill buildings and machinery at least weirs and streams diverted to mill races. These survivals, together with the county maps of the period on which mills were marked by a special symbol, confirm the universality of water power in industrial activity. William Yates's 1786 map of Lancashire provides an example: no less than 330 water mills are depicted throughout the county. In the floors of some valleys lay an almost continuous tier of mill houses, wheels, dams and sluices. One to three mills per kilometre of stream were not uncommon in favourable situations, such as on the Douglas at

Wigan, the Irk at Manchester or the Irwell north-west of Manchester, while the more remote Pennine valleys were being colonised in search of fresh mill sites. In 1795 Aikin wrote: 'There is scarcely a stream that will turn a wheel through the north of England that has not a cotton mill upon it' and the inventory of other industrial uses – such as the manufacture of wool, paper, bobbins, iron and gunpowder – would be a long one.

Many waterwheels rumbled on into the nineteenth century, yet the steam engine, like the factory, is the quintessence of the Industrial Revolution. A common catalyst in technical innovation, it emphasised the interdependence of the main industries and was to become 'a universal motor destined to transform the whole economy'. From the early eighteenth century, the engines of Thomas Savery and Thomas Newcomen had made an important contribution towards solving the problem of mine drainage. By the 1780s, probably more than 300 Newcomen engines had been installed in the tin and copper mines of Devon and Cornwall and in the main coalfields.

233 Distribution of Boulton and Watt engines.

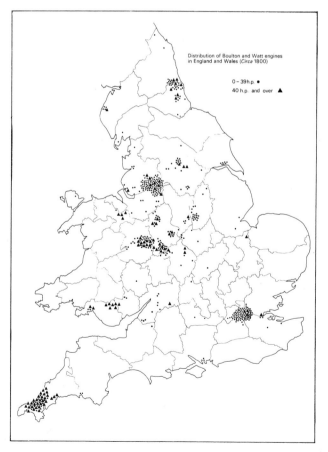

Distribution of Boulton and Watt engines in England and Wales (Circa 1800)

0 – 39 h.p. ●
40 h.p. and over ▲

The description of only a few factors in this chapter is not intended to elevate them as the 'main' causes of geographical change in the eighteenth century. They were all important aspects but many of them could be regarded as manifestations, as much as causes, of industrial growth. Yet while a satisfactory model will have to embrace many more variables, there is likely to be a continuing justification for stressing the contribution of a few innovations which stand head and shoulders above the rest. In the category of such critical inventions, the engine patented by James Watt was a major breakthrough. It succeeded in reducing fuel consumption by some two-thirds and, from the early 1780s, in developing a rotary engine applied directly to the driving of machinery.

The earliest Watt engines were set up in the Cornish mining districts, where the cost of coal was an important factor. In the next two decades they found employment in all the major industries, in the breweries and distilleries of London, the Potteries, the deep collieries of the west Midlands and Northumberland, canal pumping, the iron works of Shropshire, south Staffordshire and south Wales and in the textile factories of Lancastria where half the capacity was installed. As early as 1781, Boulton wrote to Watt: 'The people of London, Manchester and Birmingham are *steam mill mad*'; by about 1800, when their original patent expired, several hundred engines had been installed. The distribution, plotted from the sales noted in their engine book, monitors the location of the more advanced industries towards the end of the heroic period of the Industrial Revolution. Even if the major changes transforming the face of the coalfield districts were far from complete, the age of steam was on the move with profound consequences for the social and economic geography of the nation.

FURTHER READING

Aikin, J. *A Description of the Country from Thirty to Forty Miles Round Manchester* (1795, reprinted Newton Abbout, 1969)

Albert, William *The Turnpike Road System in England 1663–1840* (Cambridge, 1972)

Ashmore, Owen *The Industrial Archaeology of Lancashire* (Newton Abbot, 1969)

Ashton, T. S. *The Industrial Revolution 1760–1830* (1948)

Bowden, W. *Industrial Society in England Towards the End of the Eighteenth Century* (New York, 1925)

Byng, John *The Torrington Diaries, Containing the Tours through England and Wales of the Hon. John Byng, later fifth Viscount Torrington, Between the Years 1781 and 1794.* Edited with an introduction by C. Bruyn Andrews 4 vols (1934–8)

Chaloner, W. H. and Musson, A. E. *Industry and Technology*, A Visual History of Modern Britain (1963)

Chambers, J. D. and Chapman, S. D. *The Beginnings of Industrial Britain* (1970)

Defoe, Daniel *A Tour through England and Wales* (Everyman edition 1928)

Dyos, H. J. and Aldcroft, D. H. *British Transport. An Economic Survey from the Seventeenth Century to the Twentieth* (Leicester, 1969)

Hadfield, E. C. R. *British Canals* (Newton Abbot, 1971)

Harris, Helen *Industrial Archaeology of Dartmoor* (Newton Abbot, 1968)

Hartwell, R. M. 'The Causes of the Industrial Revolution. An Essay in Methodology' *The Economic History Review*, 2nd series, 18 (1965), 164–82

Klingender, F. *Art and the Industrial Revolution* (1947)

Lawton, R. 'Historical Geography: The Industrial Revolution' *The British Isles: A Systematic Geography* Watson, J. Wreford and Sissons, J. B. (eds) (1964), 221–44

Mantoux, P. J. *The Industrial Revolution in the Eighteenth Century* (1928)

Marshall, J. D. and Shiel, M. Davies *The Industrial Archaeology of the Lake Counties* (Newton Abbot, 1969)

Mathias, P. *The First Industrial Nation. An Economic History of Britain 1700–1914* (1969)

Raistrick, A. *Industrial Archaeology: an Historical Survey* (1972)

Simmons, Jack *Transport* A Visual History of Modern Britain (1962)

Smith, David M. *The Industrial Archaeology of the East Midlands* (Newton Abbot, 1965)

Svedenstierna, Eric T. *Svedenstierna's Tour in Great Britain 1802–3: The Travel Diary of an Industrial Spy*, with a new introduction by Flinn, M. W. (Translation Newton Abbot, 1973)

Wrigley, E. A. *Population and History* (1969)

Yates, William *A Map of the County of Lancashire 1786* (reprinted in facsimile with an introduction by Harley, J. B. (The Historic Society of Lancashire and Cheshire, 1968)

15 FARMING IN AN INDUSTRIAL AGE

by J. T. COPPOCK

THE nineteenth century spans two major phases in the evolution of English agriculture. The 100 years before 1860 were a period of improvement, in which new land was brought into cultivation, new techniques were adopted and the remaining links with the medieval world broken. But between the 1870s and the 1930s farmers were forced to make painful adjustments in the face of increasing imports of foreign produce, and the years between World Wars I and II marked the nadir of modern farming. Of course, neither improvement before 1860 nor decline after 1870 were continuous,

nor were all parts of England equally affected.

Both the national and international contexts in which farmers made their decisions changed during the nineteenth century. Although industrialisation and urbanisation were making rapid progress, the England

234 Dry stone walls define rectilinear fields near Alston Cumberland, enclosed in 1820. Enclosure of land had largely been completed by 1850. It was generally beneficial; although, for some marginal land, it merely meant a change of status.

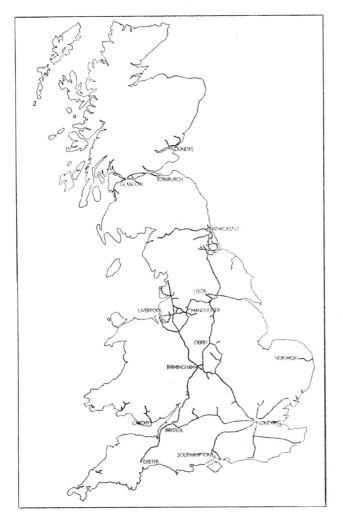

235(a) *Railway network in 1840.*

235(b) *Railway network in 1852.*

of 1800 was still predominantly rural. It is true that less than a third of the population were agriculturalists, but probably three out of every four people lived in the countryside. By 1851 the population had risen from just over 9,000,000 to almost 17,000,000, 50 per cent of whom lived in towns. Although the number of those living in the countryside rose throughout the first half of the century with many parishes reaching their peak population in 1841 or 1851, rural migration was already widespread, and was encouraged by changes in the administration of the Poor Law in 1834 and by relaxation of the laws of settlement. By 1901, the population of England exceeded 30,000,000, more than 75 per cent of whom lived in towns. Rural depopulation was almost universal, stimulated by the disparity between rural and urban wages and by the depressed state of agriculture, which led farmers to economise on labour.

The impact of rapidly growing towns on the agriculture of the surrounding countryside would have been much greater but for the revolution in transport which not only reduced any advantages which those English farmers who were near their markets might enjoy, but also enabled farmers in countries where natural conditions were more favourable for agriculture to undercut the prices received by English farmers. Within England, it was above all the railways which, by lowering the cost of transport and by speeding the movement of perishable produce, had the most profound impact. Instead of making the long journey from Wales, Scotland or northern England on the hoof, cattle could be transported by rail without loss of

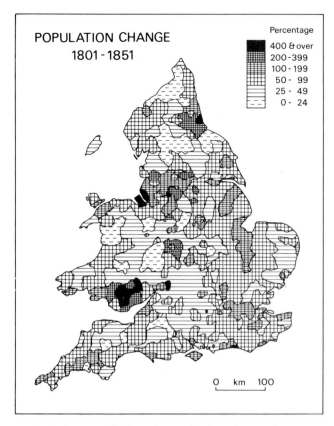

POPULATION CHANGE
1801-1851

Percentage
400 & over
200-399
100-199
50-99
25-49
0-24

0   km   100

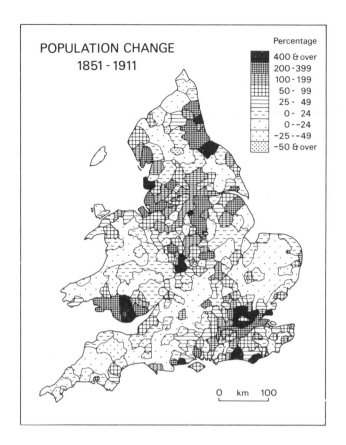

POPULATION CHANGE
1851-1911

Percentage
400 & over
200-399
100-199
50-99
25-49
0-24
0--24
-25--49
-50 & over

0   km   100

236(a&b)   Population change in the nineteenth century.

237   The railways carried an ever increasing volume of milk from the 1860s – especially to London, the most important market.

238 This was the period of the emergence of the large dairy companies; although some urban cowhouses and small dairies survived to the end of the century.

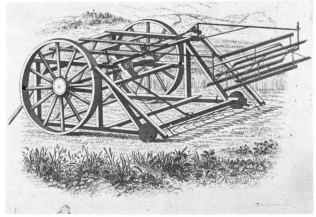

239 Much agricultural machinery was invented in the nineteenth century; new drills, harrows, hoes, mowers, ploughs and reapers lightened the task of the farm worker. In 1826, the Rev Patrick Bell invented this reaper pushed by horses; but a generation passed before it was fully appreciated.

240 Lighter machines of American design followed Bell's reaper. The first version of the McCormack reaper appeared in 1831.

weight. The railways also influenced the supply of milk to London, which had formerly depended mainly on urban cowhouses or on farms in the immediate vicinity of the metropolis. Only 4 per cent of supplies was transported by rail in 1864, and that from farms within a fifty-mile radius, but by 1891 the proportion had increased to 83 per cent and substantial quantities came from as far afield as Wiltshire and Staffordshire. Change on this scale would not have been possible without the railways, even though the initial cause of this switch was the cattle plague of 1865.

IMPROVEMENTS IN AGRICULTURE

Perhaps the most obvious agricultural improvement was the completion of enclosure, although the process was already far advanced by 1800. Of the 600,000 hectares of common arable fields that survived into the nineteenth century, most were enclosed in the next twenty-five years and by 1850 common fields were rare, only a few relics surviving into the twentieth century.

Much of the arable land was laid down to grass after enclosure, for such conversion could double its value. To replace this ploughed land, a new domain of arable

241 The main application of steam power on farms from the 1850s onwards was in driving threshing machines. Threshing in progress on a farm at Hartington, Middlesex, in 1868.

farming came into being on the light soils through the enclosure and reclamation of heath and down. Turnip Townshend and others had already demonstrated the great improvements possible through the New Husbandry and much light land had been reclaimed during the eighteenth century; but there were still extensive tracts of lowland heath and chalk downland in 1800. Some of this land was ploughed under the stimulus of high prices during the Napoleonic wars and subsequently reverted, but much was brought into permanent cultivation in the first half of the nineteenth century. On the Brocklesby estate on the Lincoln Wolds, for example, the great stretches of gorse, on which Arthur Young had commented adversely, had been replaced by 'good turnip land, divided by clipped hedges of thorn'. Not all the heathland was enclosed; some was too barren to justify the expense and, as the century advanced, enclosure became more difficult, as non-agricultural considerations were given greater weight, and less attractive, as prices for the products of arable farming fell.

Enclosure did not necessarily imply improvement and reclamation was not always contingent upon enclosure. Large tracts of moorland commons were enclosed in the Pennines and elsewhere but, although some land was reclaimed, enclosure often meant little more than a change of status and perhaps the erection of stone walls or post and wire fences to mark new boundary lines. Nor was the enclosure of these moorland commons ever completed, for over 400,000 hectares of common grazings remain today. The much smaller extent of low-lying fen and moss was largely reclaimed and often provided farmland of the highest quality By 1870 four-fifths of the Lancashire mosses had been brought into cultivation and the reclamation of Whittlesea Mere in the 1850s completed the draining of the Fens, though these had been saved from reverting to a watery waste only by the installation of steam pumps about 1820. Reclamation of woodland, too, made a small contribution; the disafforestation of

Wychwood Forest in Oxfordshire led to the creation of four new farms.

Other major improvements were made to the land already in cultivation. Farming on the claylands still presented major difficulties, and from the 1840s to the 1870s a major attack on the problems was made through under-draining, which was encouraged by government, sponsored by improving landowners and facilitated by the development of machinery for making cheap drains. During the same period some £12,000,000 was advanced under various statutory schemes of land improvement, mostly for drainage, and it was estimated that private landowners spent twice as much. James Caird thought that perhaps 800,000 hectares were drained during this period, although this represented only a fifth of the land requiring drainage in Great Britain.

New farmsteads and new cottages were built, fields rationalised and unwanted hedges removed, though few of these changes are documented. The increasing use of fertilizers was widespread. Imports of guano rose from a mere 1400 tons in 1841 to 220,000 tons in 1847 and the opening of a factory for the manufacture of superphosphate at Bow in 1843 was no less significant. At the same time, the railways greatly extended the distances over which it was economic to transport

242 Lotz's steam plough. Steam power from stationary engines was applied on a smaller scale to cultivation, especially on heavy soils. Some 80,000 hectares were cultivated in this way in 1867.

243 Denver Sluice occupies a key role in Fenland drainage. Its reconstruction in 1832 was part of an attempt to improve drainage in the southern Fenland.

244 Appold's centrifugal pump at work on Whittlesea Mere. Reclamation of this, the last of the Meres, was made possible by improvements in the outfalls and more powerful pumps.

town manure and the rise of market gardening on the light soils around Biggleswade was largely due to the two-way exchange of produce and manure that the railway made possible. Improvements in farm machinery and in crops and livestock also contributed to the advance of agriculture, as did the increasing practice of supplying purchased feedingstuffs to livestock. In the 1830s, crops were still cut by hand, although Bell's reaper had been invented in 1826; by the 1850s, the use of machinery was widespread and steam power was applied to threshing and even to ploughing.

During the next decade, these developments culminated in a period of high farming which marks a watershed in English agricultural history. New methods were widely applied and the area of arable land was greater, and that of unimproved land smaller, than ever before or after. But this golden age was short-lived, and the last quarter of the nineteenth century was marked by changes in farming systems in response to competition from farmers overseas; for, unlike their continental neighbours, English farmers were left unprotected to meet the impact of agricultural development in the New World.

IMPORTS AND AGRICULTURAL CHANGE

In the 1830s the United Kingdom was largely self-sufficient in food and the repeal of the Corn Laws in 1846 did not immediately have the effects that some critics had forecast, largely because trade was disrupted by war in Europe and in North America. Nevertheless, imports of wheat doubled between 1850 and 1872 and doubled again by the end of the century. Imports of animal feedingstuffs showed similar rises, and those of meat and dairy produce also increased sharply, especially after the development of refrigeration in 1882. By the early years of the twentieth century, four-fifths of wheat supplies, nearly three-quarters of dairy produce and fruit, and two-fifths of meat were being imported.

Despite rises in population and living standards, such a change could hardly fail to have a profound impact on English farming. Prices of home produce fell and the value of agricultural output was almost halved between 1880 and 1893. The seriousness of the

245 Whittlesea Mere before drainage. By 1853 corn was growing in an area of 400 hectares which had been water two years earlier.

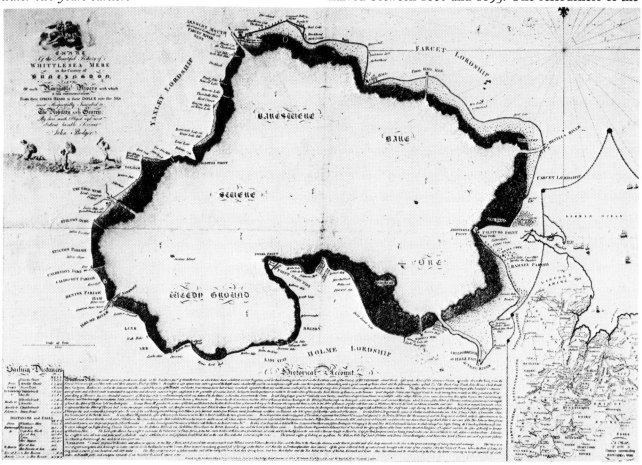

188

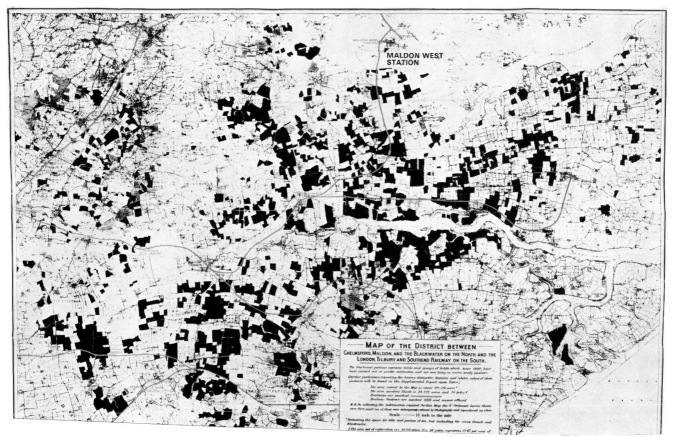

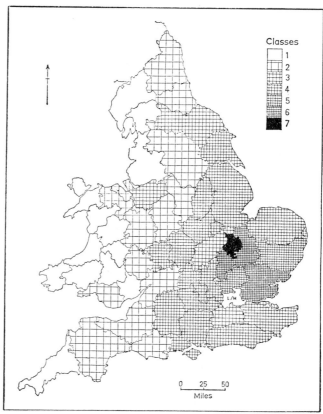

246 When wheat prices fell, cultivation of land with very light or heavy soil was sometimes abandoned. Large areas of heavy soil in south Essex fell out of cultivation and stand out in black on the map of 1894.

247 There were considerable spatial variations in the impact of the Great Depression. This is illustrated by the data on Bankruptcies in the London Gazette *for 1881–3 after Perry.*

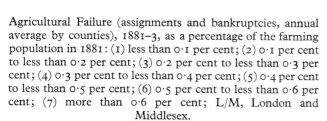

Agricultural Failure (assignments and bankruptcies, annual average by counties), 1881–3, as a percentage of the farming population in 1881: (1) less than 0·1 per cent; (2) 0·1 per cent to less than 0·2 per cent; (3) 0·2 per cent to less than 0·3 per cent; (4) 0·3 per cent to less than 0·4 per cent; (5) 0·4 per cent to less than 0·5 per cent; (6) 0·5 per cent to less than 0·6 per cent; (7) more than 0·6 per cent; L/M, London and Middlesex.

248 *The Old Market, St Ives, Huntingdonshire. This was a period of increasing emphasis on stock farming. Fodder became cheaper as arable land fell out of cultivation and as imported feed became available.*

249 *Farmland was progressively lost to houses, railways and factories but some was preserved for recreation and as water catchments. Letting of shooting to town-dwellers was said to be the salvation of Norfolk agriculture. Partridge shooting on a Norfolk estate in 1881.*

changed situation was at first obscured by a series of bad harvests, and much of the impact was absorbed by landowners through the remission or reduction of rents from the high levels that had prevailed in mid-century. Only gradually was the need for more fundamental adjustments realised.

The fact that the incidence of depression was very uneven throughout the country does not seem to have been fully appreciated. Wheat prices were the first to fall, and for most arable farmers wheat was the principal cash crop and generally the keystone of the farm economy. Many sought to economise by leaving land in temporary grass and by reducing expenditure on maintenance. Those on very light or heavy soils, where the risks were greater and alternatives fewer, were hardest hit, and landowners found it difficult to let farms on such land and took large areas in hand. Some poor land tumbled down to weedy self-sown pasture or went out of cultivation altogether; 'a terrible map, dotted full of black patches' showed the land that had fallen out of cultivation in south Essex, and arable fields in the Breckland were abandoned to heather.

The extent of derelict fields is, however, debatable – some may have been temporarily abandoned in an attempt to avoid payment of rates and tithes. Land undoubtedly did go out of cultivation and, as depressed conditions continued, some parcels of poor land were withdrawn from agricultural use and planted with trees. What is certain is that, as the changed situation became clear and prices continued to fall, arable land was laid down to grass and temporary grass was reclassified as the permanent pasture it had become. In all, over 1,000,000 hectares of arable land were converted to permanent grass between 1870 and 1900. This conversion was probably the most widespread of the changes resulting from falling prices, though it was hindered in eastern areas of light rainfall by difficulties, real or imagined, in establishing permanent grass.

On land that remained arable, adjustments in cropping were made as farmers sought to substitute crops that were less affected by price reductions than wheat or less labour-demanding than fodder roots. Oats tended to replace wheat, especially in western and northern counties, and more potatoes were planted where soils and location made them acceptable cash crops, though attempts to promote the growing of sugar beet were abortive. Where soils and climate were appropriate an interesting development was the extension of market gardening into agriculture, with the introduction of field crops of vegetables such as peas. Orchards and soft fruit also offered opportunities for diversification and the areas under these crops increased, particularly in eastern counties.

Prices of meat and livestock products also fell, but the reductions began later and were less marked; livestock farmers also benefited from imports of cheap feedingstuffs and from low prices for home-grown grain, while English meat retained advantages in quality over imported produce and fresh milk enjoyed complete natural protection. Labour requirements for livestock or grass were generally lower and, with greater areas of grass available, farmers adopted or enlarged livestock enterprises. Numbers of cattle rose by over a quarter and the share of gross farm income derived from livestock and livestock products increased markedly. But there were considerable regional differences. The high cost of folding sheep on arable land encouraged farmers to dispose of such flocks, and there was a general decline in sheep keeping in the eastern lowlands, while numbers remained high in the uplands where there were no alternative enterprises. The rapidly growing towns provided an expanding market for milk and farmers adopted dairy farming where possible, although proximity to a town or a railway station was essential and the absence of suitable buildings or adequate water supplies a serious handicap.

In the traditional dairying areas, such as Cheshire, the spread of dairying was complicated by the impact of rising imports of dairy produce on those farmers who made their milk into farmhouse butter and cheese. Faced with falling prices, they attempted to sell milk wherever possible, a switch that was facilitated by the emergence of wholesale dairymen and by the construction of country depots at railway stations. An increasing volume of such milk found its way to London, and so striking was the milk trade at stations along the line from Maidenhead to Wantage that it was said to be known as the Milky Way.

In the agricultural economy of the whole country there was a marked shift of emphasis from crops to livestock and, since prices did not fall uniformly, depression was most severe in those eastern counties where farmers depended most heavily on cash cropping; those in western counties were less affected and had less need to change their farming systems. Some measure of these regional differences is provided by changes in land values between 1879 and 1894; these fell by 40 per cent in parts of eastern England but by only 7 per cent in the west. There were many local variations within these regional contrasts, reflecting differences in soil, climate and access to markets. One Hertfordshire farmer maintained that a location away from the railway was 'agricultural death' and the gradient of farm rents supports his opinion.

Migrants from other parts of the United Kingdom, notably dairy farmers from Scotland and livestock farmers from southwest England, played an important role in the adoption of new farming systems. They brought new ideas and enterprises that were better suited to the prevailing conditions than those traditionally practised. The Ayrshire dairy farmers who came in large numbers to Essex, in at least one instance complete with dairy herd, showed what was possible with hard work on these difficult soils, while the origins of fruit-growing around Wisbech can be traced to the example of a single migrant from Kent.

The scale of change must not be exaggerated. The agriculture of 1900 was recognisably that of 1870, though England was rather greener, the pattern of cropping more varied and more cattle were to be seen in the fields. Farming had a less prosperous air, although there was some recovery in the late 1890s and severe depression returned only in the 1920s. Nor did all improvement cease; new farm buildings, especially dairies and cottages, were sometimes necessary to attract or retain tenants and farmworkers.

CONCLUSION

Whatever the severity of depression, the basic cause – a policy that allowed the unrestricted import of agricultural produce – was itself a reflection of the changing balance between town and country. However great the harm to the agricultural interest, there can be little doubt that the policy benefited the urban majority. By the turn of the century, agriculture employed little more than a tenth of the labour force and probably provided a smaller share of the national income. As well as being markets for produce, towns were also beginning to affect the countryside in other ways, such as the renting of shootings, the dedication of lowland commons for recreation and the use of uplands as water-gathering grounds. Nor were these changes without agricultural significance, as the claim that the partridge was the salvation of Norfolk farming suggests. More direct was the progressive loss of farmland to houses, railways and factories. It probably exceeded the gains through reclamation of moor, heath and bog, and although it attracted much less attention from contemporaries, it was in many ways the most profound and most permanent change in English agriculture in the nineteenth century.

FURTHER READING

Barnes, F. A. 'The Evolution of the Salient Patterns of Milk Production and Distribution in England and Wales, *Trans Inst Brit Geog*, 25 (1958), 167–95

Bear, W. E. 'Flower and Fruit Farming in England', series of articles in *J Roy Agric Soc England*, 3rd series, 9 and 10 (1898–9)

Caird, J. *English Agriculture in 1850–51* (1852)

Chambers, J. D. and Mingay, G. E. *The Agricultural Revolution 1750–1880* (1966)

Clapham, J. H. *An Economic History of Modern Britain*, 3 vols (reprinted, Cambridge, 1963)

Cobbett, W. *Rural Rides* (Everyman edition, 1912)

Coppock, J. T. 'The Changing Arable in England and Wales 1870–1960', Chap 3, R. H. Best and J. T. Coppock, *The Changing Use of Land in Britain* (1962)

Perry, P. J. *British Farming in the Great Depression* (Newton Abbot, 1974)

Hall, A. D. *A Pilgrimage of British Farming* (1912)

House of Lords, *Select Committee on the Improvement of Lands* (PP 1873)

Gonner, E. C. K. *Common Land and Inclosure* (2nd edn, 1966)

Lawton, R. 'Rural Depopulation in Nineteenth Century England', in R. W. Steel and R. Lawton (eds), *Liverpool Essays in Geography* (Liverpool, 1967), 247–55

Orwin, C. S. and Whetham, E. H. *History of British Agriculture 1846–1914* (2nd edn Newton Abbot, 1971)

Pratt, E. A. *The Transition in Agriculture* (1902)

Royal Agricultural Society of England, *Journal*, Prize Essays, 1845–69

Rider Haggard, H. *Rural England* 2 vols (1902)

Royal Commission on Depressed Conditions of the Agricultural Interest (The Richmond Commission), *Reports and Minutes of Evidence* (PP 1879–82)

Royal Commission on Agricultural Depression, *Reports and Minutes of Evidence* (PP 1894–7)

Saville, J. *Rural Depopulation In England and Wales 1851–1951* (1957)

Smith, W. *An Economic Geography of Great Britain* (2nd edn, 1953)

Thompson, F. M. L. *English Landed Society in the Nineteenth Century* (1963)

Trow-Smith, R. *History of British Livestock Husbandry 1700–1900* (1959)

16 LIVING IN VICTORIAN TOWNS

by DAVID WARD

IN spite of demolition and redevelopment on a rather massive scale, most British cities still display the imprint of nineteenth-century urban growth. Ornate monuments of municipal government, unostentatious warehouses and factories, cavernous railway stations and diverse edifices of religion are for many cities symbolic of a more vigorous youth and a more clearly defined provincial identity. These visual relics represent a rapidly diminishing material record of the extraordinarily compressed urban history of so many provincial industrial cities whose national stature was established during the nineteenth century.

Many of the new centres of manufacturing had been prosperous market towns and had supported flourishing craft industries long before the industrial revolution but the physical legacies of this earlier growth are fragmentary and diminutive. The buildings and precincts erected during the Victorian era, particularly those now stripped of their envelope of congested housing, have become a source of fascination as a positive and distinctive inheritance of a much maligned age; but this does not obscure or redeem the ugliness and discomfort which marked the domestic living conditions of the vast majority of urban residents.

250 Monuments to industry, commerce and the railways dominate the urban skyline by the mid-nineteenth century, though the countryside was still within reach. 'St Pancras Hotel and Station from Pentonville Road – Sunset' by John O'Conner, 1882.

251 Churchyard, St Paul's Square, Birmingham.

Indeed, the wealth of aesthetic scrutiny and the abundance of political judgments which for long interlaced descriptions of nineteenth-century cities tended to conceal our knowledge of the range and variety of life which starved, subsisted and flourished within them.

There is no lack of detailed information upon the conditions of life in Victorian cities but, whereas in the more remote past urban settlements displayed a marked stability in size and appearance over reasonably long periods, each decade of the nineteenth century produced considerable changes within and around the cities. These unprecedented changes occurred under different local political and economic conditions and it was only towards the end of the century that their common inheritance became obvious. The term 'Victorian city' has thus come to describe the cumulative results of rapid urban growth which in some parts of the nation had begun two generations before Queen Victoria came to the throne.

WORKING CLASS HOUSING

One of the most easily recognised and conspicuous features of Victorian cities was their expanding area of densely packed working-class housing which accommodated two-thirds or more of their total populations. Irrespective of variations in local building styles, in civic initiative or in regional prosperity, the vast majority of urban residents lived under conditions which differed only slightly from place to place. There was, nevertheless, a range in the quality of low-rent housing within and between cities. The worst conditions were endured in damp cellars threatened by inundations from saturated sub-soil; these opened on narrow courts which, though devoid of adequate drainage and ventilation, housed the water supply and sanitary facilities of the adjacent houses.

At its best, the housing consisted of short rows of cottages with separate utilities; the rows fronted onto paved and drained streets of reasonable widths. In many cities even these superior cottages were constructed back-to-back in order to maximise the amount of land used for building in relation to that left open for access and ventilation. Substantial single-family houses, originally designed for middle- or high-income residents but in districts which failed to maintain their elevated status, were also converted into multi-family

194

252 Shear Court, Leeds, was created by rear walls of adjacent housing – a common form of back-to-back development.

tenements with only minimal structural adjustments. In most provincial industrial cities, however, this particular source of low rent accommodation was not extensive; only a small proportion of their populations were people of wealth and they rarely built their dwellings in areas suitable for later working-class occupancy.

Engels distinguished three types of dwellings in Manchester in the 1840s. The oldest cottage property was squeezed within the narrow yards of shops and residences of the medieval town or on vacant land already surrounded by substantial new structures which lined the major thoroughfares leading out of the town. Each development had been completed without reference to adjoining buildings and access was usually obtained by means of a narrow passageway or tunnel cut through the original building which fronted on the street. Presumably the original dwellings were converted into tenements or lodging houses if not required for commercial or industrial purposes. Once the older dwellings and surviving open spaces within the built-up area had been developed, cottage property was constructed on the edge of the town and especially around newly established factories. These new cottages

were built in the form of courts of back-to-back dwellings distinguishable from the more centrally located yard property by the greater regularity of their arrangement, the provision of surface drainage channels and, occasionally, paving. The majority of these cottages consisted of two rooms – a kitchen on the ground floor and a bed chamber above – and they rarely occupied more than four metres square. Some possessed small attics which served as extra bedrooms and others had cellars which were rented as additional one-roomed dwellings. The third and best type of housing consisted of rows of larger dwellings with through ventilation; but the rear alleys of these superior structures were frequently lined with back-to-back cottages.

The numbers of workers in different types of dwellings varied from city to city; in particular, the occupancy of cellars was highly localised. In 1845, 20 per cent of the working-class population of Liverpool lived in cellars, in Manchester the proportion was 12 per cent, and in Leeds 3 per cent; but in Birmingham there were no cellar dwellings. Local restrictions on street dimensions, quality and construction of back-to-back cottages were introduced at different dates. Manchester prohibited the construction of back-to-backs in 1848, but in Leeds they were built well into the twentieth century. Although the timing of these legislative restrictions increased local variations in

housing standards, for the most part prescribed housing codes strongly influenced new housing only in the last three decades of the nineteenth century.

The diminutive and inadequately provided cottages of the working class were neither new nor distinctively urban; but their extent and arrangement were novel. In the absence of careful public supervision, extensive areas of cottage property were constructed without adequate ventilation, a supply of pure water, or effective drainage; the accumulations of stagnant water and filth between congested buildings threatened the health of the suffering residents and, by contagion, the entire population.

CAUSES OF CONGESTION

Apart from the failure of local authorities to recognise and assume responsibility for the sanitary needs of their growing populations, the small scale of building enterprise and the use of tiny parcels of land for new construction compounded the housing problem. Most cottage property was built by small entrepreneurs who seldom possessed the resources to complete their modest developments and, although many builders intended to dwell there, the arrangement of buildings was designed to maximise the rental yield of a small holding often at the cost of poor ventilation and improper sanitation. Piecemeal development of small and irregularly shaped holdings at high densities by a host of small builders inhibited the creation of wide through streets and often obstructed natural drainage lines. Many developments terminated abruptly at windowless back walls of adjacent enterprises; and variations and distortions of the basic linear cottage arrangement resulted from trying to fit extra dwellings into the irregular extremities of small holdings. Certainly, the arrangement of buildings exhibited a much closer relationship with the earlier pattern of ownership than it did with relief or natural drainage.

Even if cottage construction had attracted more substantial capitalists, the fragmented and irregular pattern of land ownership within the inner sections of most industrial cities would have made the accumulation of holdings suitable for a larger scale of development costly and difficult. Large estates suitable for residential development were generally pre-empted for middle- and high-priced dwellings and, if necessary, withheld from the land market until the demand of relatively affluent people had assumed remunerative dimensions. This practice reduced the supply of land for even modest developments in some sections of most cities. The most striking example of the relationship between housing congestion and land availability occurred in Nottingham where, until 1845, the authorities refused to petition for the enclosure of the surrounding open fields which confined the growing population to an extremely small area.

Tenure also contributed to the problem of congestion. As a means of reducing capital costs most small builders preferred leases to outright purchases of freehold land for they hoped to reap profits and recover capital from economies of construction and high-density occupancy long before their leases expired. Although the sale of leasehold estates often limited the use and form of subsequent building, many holdings were subdivided and leased to 'jerry builders' who failed to maintain their property. Cities with decidedly limited amounts of leasehold property were not thereby insulated from housing problems. The higher costs of freehold land tended to encourage high-density development in order to support the enlarged capital investment. Small builders were forced to develop extremely modest parcels of land and problems of incomplete obstructed streets and of irregular house alignments were particularly acute.

254 Most of the worst slums of Victorian Britain have now been cleared, together with their small-scale units of ownership. The congested and piecemeal development of small holdings was halted by the introduction of building by-laws. However the old ownership pattern still influenced the position and alignment of streets, modifying the rectilinear ideal of the street improvers. Property boundaries and housing pattern in Armley, Leeds.

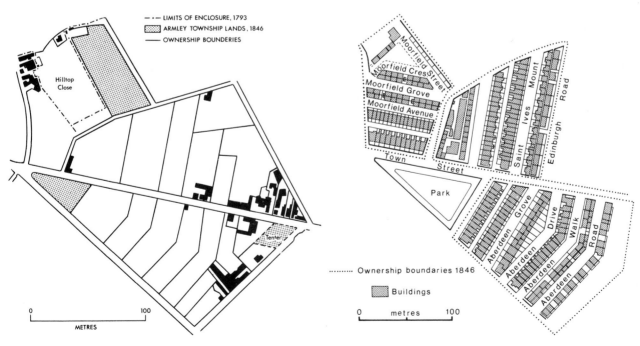

255 *Multi-storey flats and terraced rows in Salford record the different standards and styles of housing of past and present.*

WORK-RESIDENCE RELATIONSHIPS

Inferior and congested housing in nineteenth-century cities is often attributed to the imperative need of Victorian workers to live near their places of work. Although local transport facilities were greatly improved during the last third of the century, most low paid workers who had long and unpredictable hours and uncertain tenure of employment lived within walking distance of their jobs. Since most households relied upon the incomes of several members of the family, the multiplication of individual fares would have discouraged most low-income households from depending upon public transport. For most of the nineteenth century, however, few British cities were extensive enough to prevent a worker from walking to a job almost anywhere within its limits. The high density of working-class housing was a leading cause of the compact dimensions of many populous industrial cities but similar densities prevailed around factories established in relatively open country where land was plentiful and cheap.

Although some factory owners whose premises were far removed from existing settlements provided nearby housing which was usually considerably better than that constructed by speculative builders, most new low-rent accommodation erected near to factories on the edge of existing settlements was developed piecemeal by small builders. Only for a brief period did their isolation protect them from the more severe sanitary problems of centrally located housing. Consequently, it was the construction of low-rent housing in the vicinity of growing sources of industrial employment that determined the residential choices of working-class families rather than a conscious desire to minimise the journey to work at the cost of congested housing.

Inferior housing standards were also graphic records of the low and uncertain incomes of the urban working class. If residential property were to remain competitive as a profitable investment, the rent levels of dwellings which provided the barest needs of comfort and health of the occupants would have been beyond low earners' means. In the absence of public housing, rent subsidies, controls and a substantial rise in incomes, the regulation of house quality and building densities would have discouraged investment in low-rent structures without providing alternative accommodation.

PUBLIC IMPROVEMENTS

How then did Victorians raise housing standards in the second half of the nineteenth century? The most immediate improvements in living conditions were the result of massive public investment in sewers, water supplies, drainage and waste removal. Standards of public cleanliness improved quite dramatically once the relationship between accumulations of filth and contagious diseases had been publicised and accepted; and new restrictions were gradually introduced to control the spacing and alignment of new dwellings and streets. Initially these regulations were applied as local by-laws but many were codified for general application by the Public Health Act 1875. Although their more substantial structure and more spacious arrangement distinguished the new by-law houses from the more crowded and irregular cottage property, the desire to build as many dwellings as possible on small parcels of land continued to influence the alignment of buildings and to create discontinuities in the street pattern.

Mainly because of the expense and legal complexities of demolition and redevelopment, the large stock of

housing built before the introduction of building by-laws remained a serious problem. New compulsory purchase powers were obtained to clear property regarded as a threat to public health, but most improvements were small. Piecemeal demolition was needed before outside conveniences could be provided in areas where entire streets had previously depended upon one or two facilities. The largest clearance schemes were the result of street widening and railway construction. These improvements were celebrated as agents of slum removal but, displaced families frequently experienced great difficulty in obtaining alternative accommodation at rents which they could afford. The railways demolished only dwellings absolutely neces-

256 Factory owners built industrial villages around their isolated factories. This type of housing was superior to contemporary speculative building in quality and arrangement. Cottages at Saltaire, near Shipley.

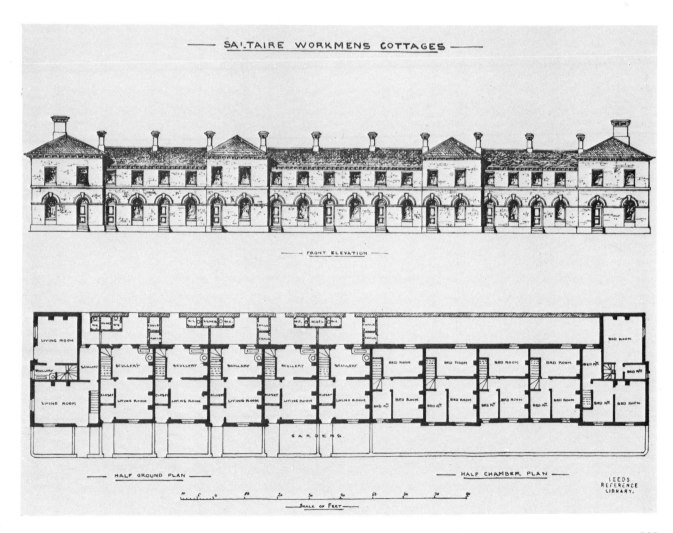

SALTAIRE WORKMENS COTTAGES

FRONT ELEVATION

HALF GROUND PLAN   HALF CHAMBER PLAN

SCALE OF FEET

LEEDS REFERENCE LIBRARY.

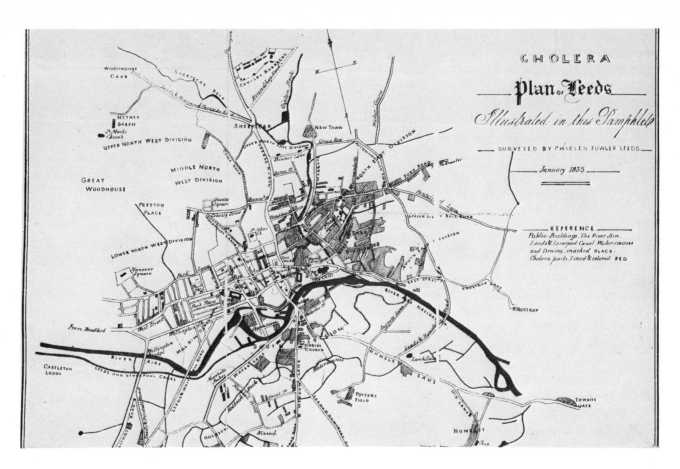

257 The terrible cholera epidemic, resulting from inadequate water supplies, sewers, drainage and water removal, alerted the Victorians to the necessity of raising living standards. The shaded areas in this reproduction of a contemporary map show cholera districts in Leeds, 1835.

sary for their right of way and surviving houses faced additional discomforts of noise and smoke. A limited number of tenements were constructed by municipal authorities and philanthropic trusts but in spite of their low dividends and spartan style, their rents were well above the means of the poor for whom alternative dwellings were very scarce.

RESIDENTIAL SEGREGATION

The problem of re-housing displaced tenants was alleviated, to some degree, by the movement of the more prosperous sections of the working class to by-law housing in the inner suburbs. This process was accelerated by the provision of cheap, regular and rapid tramway services which catered for the middle and lower ranks of society; the longer established railways had served a more exclusive clientele until the passing of legislation requiring the provision of workingmen's trains. The houses vacated by new suburban residents increased the supply of centrally located low-rent housing but the departure of some socially mobile families increased the isolation of the most impoverished households from the rest of the urban population. Urban residents were thus separated by variations in income and status, in contrast with conditions at the beginning of the century when only the most affluent citizens lived in separate and exclusive precincts.

For long the residential quarters of the wealthy were built near to or contiguous with existing limits of towns but with the development of railway services more truly suburban areas emerged in and around peripheral villages. Since there was a strong tendency on the part of wealthy families to settle in districts in the same general direction from the city centre, high-income residential areas usually coalesced to form a wedge of substantial housing with a long established and prestigious central district at its apex. Such wedge-shaped areas tended to retain their exclusive status and affluent residents throughout the nineteenth century, whereas the status of later peripheral additions of more bourgeois people was less long lived. As

258 Parsimonious surveyors cleared railway rights of way through slums with scant regard to adjacent housing. Plan of Riley's Court, Leeds.

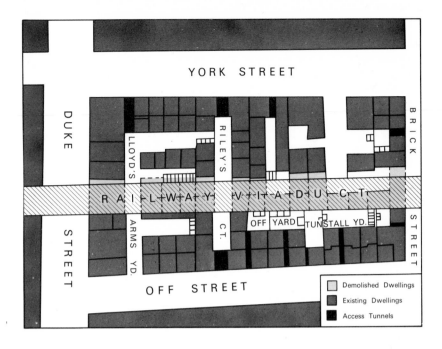

YORK STREET

DUKE STREET

BRICK STREET

LLOYD'S ARMS YD.

RILEY'S CT.

R A I L + W + A + Y + V + I + A + D + U + C + T

OFF YARD

TUNSTALL YD.

OFF STREET

Demolished Dwellings

Existing Dwellings

Access Tunnels

259 Riley's Court, Leeds.

socially mobile families sought newer housing in
more outlying locations, their original housing and
districts were inherited by less prosperous people but
the most affluent quarters were generally insulated
from this process of invasion and succession. In most
provincial industrial cities, however, neither the
emergence of a wedge-like area of affluent residents
nor the outward movement of more bourgeois families
was well established until the middle decades of the
century and many areas continued to house a mixture
of local retailers, artisans, labourers, domestic outworkers and some factory workers. More prosperous
people occupied larger dwellings on the major
sheets; labourers, domestic 'outworkers' and other
low-paid workers lived in cottages on narrow alleys
and rear yards. Certainly, for a generation at least,
new factory owners and managers expressed their

260 'Railways over London' from London *by Gustave
Doré, 1871.*

status by the size and style of their dwellings rather
than by the exclusiveness of their residential locations.

By the middle of the nineteenth century, however,
contemporary observers were complaining of the
polarisation of urban society into Disraeli's 'Two
Nations' expressed on the ground by an affluent
'West End' and an impoverished 'East End'. But the
exclusive precincts of the wealthy were neither large
nor new; and, although concentrations of abjectly
destitute people, especially in Irish quarters, had
recently attained disturbing dimensions, large sections
of mid nineteenth-century British cities continued to
house people of diverse occupations and incomes.
During the first part of the century, many lower-

261 Difficulties of providing minimum-standard housing at rents that workingmen could afford encouraged public authorities to build multi-storey tenements in the hope of trimming costs. Civic tenements, Marsh Lane, Leeds.

middle-income people retained relatively central residences at or near to their places of work and much of the peripheral growth of cities comprised modest housing constructed around newly established sources of employment.

Low and moderate rent property, often interspersed with factories and workshops, accounted for a larger proportion of the physical expansion of provincial industrial cities than did the exclusively residential quarters of the upper middle class. The total populations of the mixed industrial and residential additions far exceeded local employment opportunities and the diverse occupations of their residents suggest that many were employed in other parts of the city. Although some parts of the mid-Victorian city were occupied exclusively by the most affluent and impoverished segments of urban society, the complexity and texture of the intervening areas have remained less well defined.

Sanitary indictments of early Victorian cities emphasised not only well-known and highly localised threats to public health but also impressive local variations in street conditions and house quality. These variations were often obscured by the presentation of mortality data for relatively large sub-districts within the city. But high death rates occurred in any section of the city in which narrow unpaved and undrained streets were almost completely enclosed by congested and ill-provided housing. Frequently, these mortal and morbid conditions flourished immediately behind rows of substantial dwellings which fronted on wide, paved streets; and accidents and miscalculations in piecemeal development resulted in the location of superior houses on poor streets and inferior housing on well maintained thoroughfares.

The local variations in living conditions influenced mortality rates, and in part, determined the interspersal of people of different occupations, incomes and status. The social geography of the early and mid-Victorian city was thus quite different from that at the end of the century. By then more effective commuting facilities enabled the socially mobile residents of the central residential areas to move to the inner suburbs. Under these circumstances, new housing standards had a more limited influence upon the quality of low-rent dwellings than did general improvements in the public environment and modest changes in social mobility.

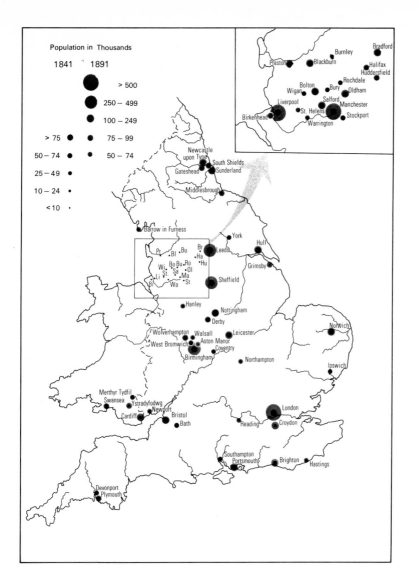

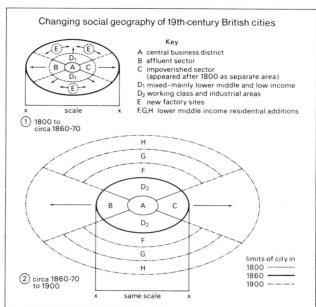

262 *Population growth in the major cities of nineteenth-century England.*

263 *Changing social geography of nineteenth-century British cities.*

FURTHER READING

Ashworth, W. *The Genesis of Modern British Town Planning* (1954)

Booth, C. *Life and Labour of the People in London* (1891–1903)

Briggs, A. *Victorian Cities* (1963)

Chadwick, E. *The Sanitary Condition of the Labouring Population* (1842)

Chapman, S. D. ed *The History of Working-Class Housing: A Symposium* (Newton Abbot 1971)

Checkland, S. G. 'The British Industrial City: The Glasgow Case', *Urban Studies*, 1 (1964), 34–54

Dyos, H. J. *Victorian Suburb: A Study of the Growth of Camberwell* (Leicester, 1961)

Dyos, H. J. 'The Slums of Victorian London', *Victorian Studies*, 11 (1967), 5–40

Dyos, H. J. ed *The Study of Urban History* (1968)

Engels, F. (trans by Henderson, W. O. and Chaloner, W. H.) *The Condition of the Working Class in England* (Oxford, 1958)

Geddes, P. E. *Cities in Evolution* (1949)

Hoggart, R. *The Uses of Literacy* (1957)

Jordan, R. F. *Victorian Architecture* (1966)

Kellett, J. R. *The Impact of Railways on Victorian Cities* (1969)

Laslett, P. *The World We Have Lost* (1965)

Lawton, R. 'The Population of Liverpool in the Mid-Nineteenth Century', *Transactions of the Historic Society of Lancashire and Cheshire*, 107 (1955), 89–120

Mayhew, H. *London Labour and the London Poor* (1851–1862)

Mortimore, M. J. 'Landownership and Urban Growth in Bradford and its Environs in the West Riding Conurbation, 1850–1950', *Transactions of the Institute of British Geographers*, 46 (1969), 105–19

Mumford, L. *The City in History* (1961)

Pfautz, H. W. ed *Charles Booth on the City: Physical Pattern and Social Structure* (1967)

Pollard, S. *A History of Labour in Sheffield* (1959)

Reissman, L. *The Urban Process: Cities in Industrial Societies* (1964)

Robson, B. T. 'An Ecological Analysis of the Evolution of Residential Areas in Sunderland', *Urban Studies*, 3 (1966) 120–42

Rowntree, B. S. *Poverty: A Study of Town Life* (1901)

Turner, R. E. 'The Industrial City—Center of Cultural Change' in C. F. Ware, *The Cultural Approach to History* (1940), 228–42

Vance, J. E., Jr 'Housing the Worker: Determinative and Contingent Ties in Nineteenth Century Birmingham', *Economic Geography*, 43 (1967), 95–127

Ward, D. 'The Pre-Urban Cadaster and the Urban Pattern of Leeds', *Annals of the Association of American Geographers*, 52 (1962), 150–166

Weber, A. F. *The Growth of Cities in the Nineteenth Century* (1899, 1962)

Of many relevant British Parliamentary Papers three in particular are suggested:

Report of Commissioners for Inquiring into the State of Large Towns and Populous Districts (1844)

Report of the Royal Commission on Housing the Working Classes (1884–1885)

Report of the Select Committee on Town Holdings (1887)

Page numbers in italics indicate illustrations